# THE NEW JEWELRY
## CONTEMPORARY MATERIALS & TECHNIQUES

**Carles Codina**

*arts and crafts series*

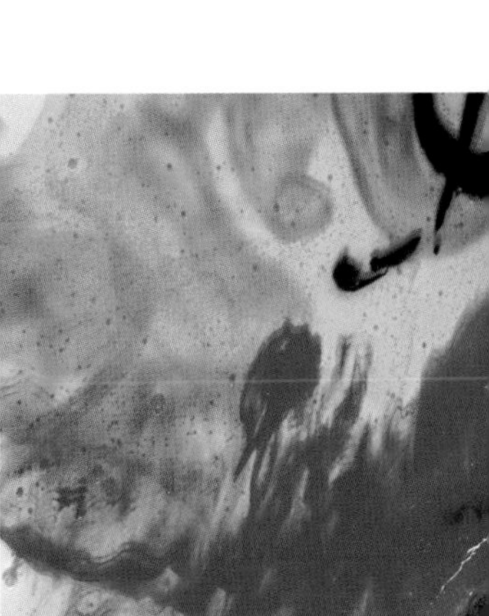

# THE NEW JEWELRY

## CONTEMPORARY MATERIALS & TECHNIQUES

A Division of Sterling Publishing Co., Inc.
New York

Library of Congress Cataloging-in-Publication Data

Codina, Carles.
New jewelry : a modern concept of jewelry & costume jewelry / Carles Codina.
p. cm.
Includes bibliographical references and index.
ISBN 1-57990-734-2 (hardcover)
1. Jewelry making. 2. Nature craft. 3. Found objects (Art) 4. Costume jewelry. I. Title.
TT212.C625 2005
745.594'2--dc22
2005016029

First Edition

Published by Lark Books, A Division of
Sterling Publishing Co., Inc.
387 Park Avenue South, New York, N.Y. 10016



Distributed in Canada by Sterling Publishing,
c/o Canadian Manda Group, 165 Dufferin Street
Toronto, Ontario, Canada M6K 3H6

Distributed in the U.K. by Guild of Master Craftsman Publications Ltd., Castle Place, 166 High Street, Lewes, East Sussex, England BN7 1XU
Tel: (+ 44) 1273 477374, Fax: (+ 44) 1273 478606, e-mail: pubs@thegmcgroup.com, Web: www.gmcpublications.com

Distributed in Australia by Capricorn Link (Australia) Pty Ltd.,
P.O. Box 704, Windsor, NSW 2756 Australia



If you have questions or comments about this book, please contact:
Lark Books
67 Broadway
Asheville, NC 28801
(828) 253-0467

Manufactured in China



ISBN 1-57990-734-2

Project and Production
Parramón Publishing, Inc.

Editorial Director:
María Fernanda Canal

Editor:
Tomás Ubach

Assistant Editor and Image Archivist:
María Carmen Ramos

Text:
Carles Codina,
with collaboration by Monica Gaspar in "Bijouterie: Strategies for Appearance"

Project Execution:
Alex Antich, Susana Aparicio Ortiz, Barbaformosa, Walter Chen, Carles Codina i Armengol, Pilar Cotter, Carlos Pastor, Josep Carles Pérez, Marion Roethig, Sonia Ruiz de Arkaute, and Miquel Robinat

Collection Design:
Josep Guasch

Photography:
Nos & Soto, and Alex Antich (in "Creating an Object Digitally")

Illustrations:
Jaume Farrés

Layout:
Estudi Guasch, Inc.

Production Director:
Rafael Marfil

Production:
Manel Sanchez

Translated from Spanish by:
Eric A. Bye, M.A.

First Edition: September 2004

Ronda de Sant Pere, 5, 4th Floor
08010 Barcelona, Spain
Subsidiary of Norma Publish Group

www.parramon.com

Printed in Spain





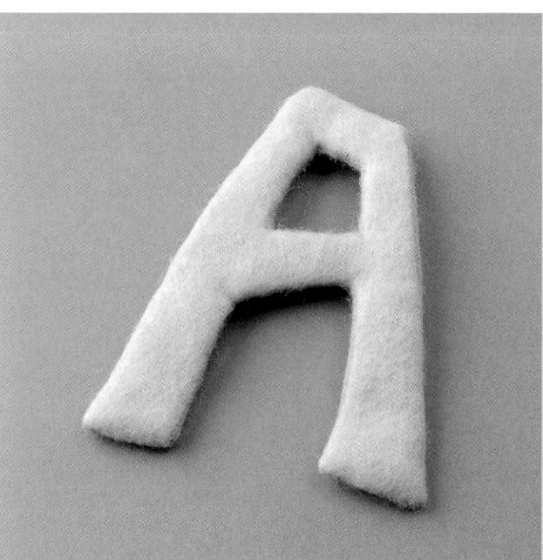

# Table of

# Contents



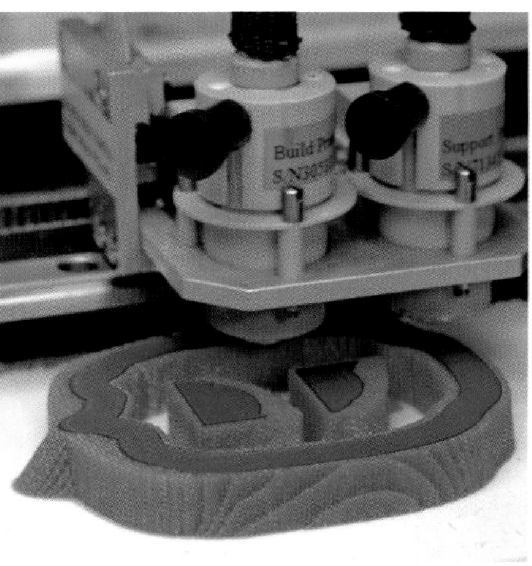




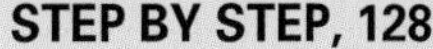

# Introduction

This book explores the use of alternative materials for jewelry making—what I describe as a new kind of "bijouterie" or costume jewelry. You won't find jewelry here in which gold or silver is the main attraction. Instead, you'll see how a piece of paper, some clay or wood, or common items like metal and rubber bands can be transformed into distinctive, creative jewelry.

The book offers a broad range of techniques for working with these unconventional materials. My goal is to offer easy and accessible approaches to jewelry making for the small-scale artisan, creative designer, student, and those who I like to refer to as "makers of objects."

I have placed great emphasis on both formulating and selecting a series of projects to stimulate creativity using unusual materials. I also describe new resources and interesting technical applications. My ultimate aim is to establish a new relationship between design, in its broadest sense, and the small-scale fabricator of objects.

Because of the value of the materials used, such as gold and silver, the complexity of the techniques involved, and the professional secrecy that they have historically entailed, it can be challenging for jewelry making to be accessible to everyone. Consequently, I have stayed away from complex projects and expensive materials like gold and silver in order to prove that it is possible to make jewelry without being a jeweler, and to make very artistic projects with very few resources.

I'm not so much interested in the concept of costume jewelry or jewelry, as I am in the concept of what's accessible. The costume jewelry we all recognize—which attempts to imitate jewelry, the costume jewelry of fashion and *glamour* offered at a competitive price and in large quantities—is the type of costume jewelry in which I personally have never felt any interest.

I am more interested in the processes that are based on certain concepts and values that often are more akin to contemporary art than to the requirements of the marketplace. Thus, I believe that making creative objects should involve a certain amount of reflection and a close personal relationship with the materials, and that it should also involve a slow, precise method of working that will produce a consumer item that is more durable, more stylized, and much more personal.

This evaluation of the qualities of a material, understanding them, and then treating them as an object is a very personal reality, oftentimes divorced from such factors as fashion, industry, and the glamour of certain aesthetic systems. Thus, a simple piece of trash, a piece of wood, a seed, a little clay, and some bits of bamboo from a worn-out item, can become the primary focus of highly stylized "new jewelry," as opposed to mass produced items with perceived commercial viability.

**Carles Codina i Armengol**

**Carles Codina i Armengol** (born Mollet del Vallès, 1961) is a professional jeweler who has combined creative work in his studio with teaching as a jewelry instructor in the Escola Massana in Barcelona for more than 18 years. His work has been displayed in Europe and in America. He is also the author of *The Complete Book of Jewelry Making,* published in 1999, and *Goldsmithing and Silver Work,* published in 2001, both by Lark Books.

# The Value of Commonplace Objects

Conceptual art, from which contemporary artistic jewelry inherits its values, has shaken up conventional thinking that believes the only valid jewelry is jewelry that is a solid, durable piece made utilizing sophisticated technical ability and skill—in short, that the idea or the artistic value behind the specific object is of little or no value compared to traditional production using precious metals and gems.

Something is changing, at least on the surface, in the already-scattered framework of contemporary makers of objects. The ornamental objects that attract our attention most are often the ones that have been made with scant means, using commonplace or discarded materials. There is a growing attraction in choosing and sifting through items discarded as useless or out of style and using them to create new works.

Creating ornamental objects using these mediums in the contemporary context is an endeavor in which technology plays a very important part. The great sophistication of the existing mediums and resources means precisely that many artistic jewelers and new do-it-yourselfers can choose an alternative: to work with few mediums, thereby converting the objects into something anthropologically close to both the person and to daily life. With this attitude, the maker of objects aspires to the domination of the individual over technology. In essence, it is the sense of experiencing renewed surprise, of refreshing an acquaintance with old materials, and the reinterpretation of unusual objects that make it possible to create different and innovative jewelry.

Among the various attitudes concerning the value of everyday objects, there is a renewed interest in them on many levels: the process and the creation, the transformation of the object, the incorporation of new elements and techniques, and learning from the materials themselves. This desire to dignify the undignified makes it possible to view the objects in a different way. As a result, there is a rising interest in the artistic trade of jewelry making, not as a mere formal repetition of the past, but rather as a process that dignifies the object itself and respects the idea behind it.

▲ Necklace made from many interlaced elastic bands 1 to 1½ inches (2.5 to 3.8 cm) long; work by Itxaso Mezzacasa

▲ Brooch by Xavier Ines Monclús, *Brutality,* 2003. Several metals were used in the construction of this piece, including silver and bronze, and it also includes parts and materials from old toys.

▼ *Umadau.* Brooch made of ivory palm with a luminous LED inside; created by Nicolás Estrada

◀ Brooches made by Susanne Schneider from sewn sterile dressings

▲ Ring made from a plastic advertising doll. It was pierced with a drill and polished. Made by Kepa Karmona

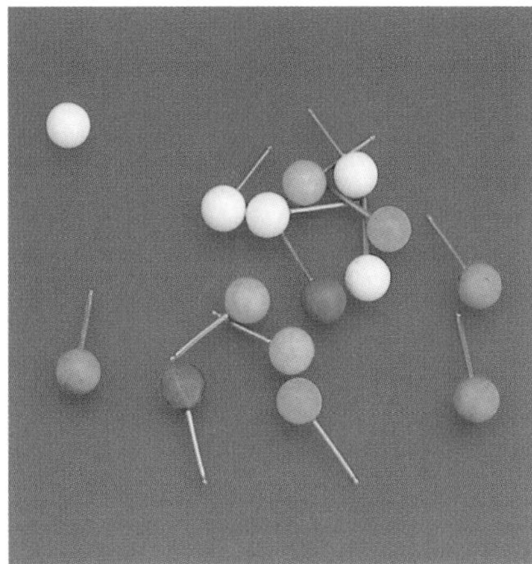

▲ Earrings made by Marc Monzó from various plastic pellets commonly used in compressed air pistols; he added a gold post to them.

▲ Brooch made from various found materials: the remains of a doll, a thimble, and a piece of a toy bracelet. Work by Estefanía de Llobet

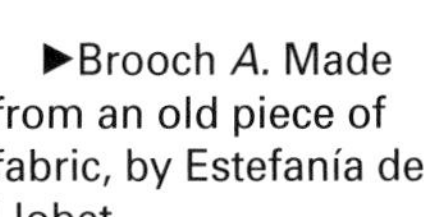

►Brooch *A*. Made from an old piece of fabric, by Estefanía de Llobet

▼ The only material used in making this necklace was lots of rubber bands 1 to 1½ inches (2.5 to 3.8 cm) long. The technique is different from the one used with the necklace shown previously; in this creation, Itxaso Mezzacasa has twisted the rubber bands back on themselves to create a totally different necklace.

▼ *The Better to See You With,* 2002. Brooch made of silver, gold, printed paper, textiles, and various materials and applications of polyester resins, made by Silvia Walz

# Costume Jewelry: Strategies for Appearance

## Dreams Made Possible

The term *fantasy jewel* was coined in 1873, when the first trade union for costume jewelry was formed in Paris. The trade union grouped together those jewelers that made jewelry fashioned from non-precious materials and those that produced so-called imitation jewelry. Thanks to the mechanization of a large part of jewelry making, it became possible to create low-cost adornments that would adapt easily to changing fashions, and which found ready acceptance among the middle classes. In order to distinguish genuine from imitation adornments, the term *"joaillerie"*—jewelry—was given to describe pieces made solely using precious gems.

This separation, which implied a type of socio-economic discrimination, has had a major impact on our present notion of jewelry. To a certain extent, the "high" jewelry using precious stones has remained faithful to conservative aesthetic repertories, whereas costume jewelry, despite its mass production, has enjoyed greater room to experiment with materials and the aesthetic sensibilities of each era. However, as explained later in this book, in the middle of the 20th century, enterprising jewelers were to put those terminology boundaries to the test.

From a contemporary viewpoint, in which any material can have aesthetic potential, the genealogy of costume jewelry is fascinating. For centuries it has embodied the genius of its artisans in making their clients dream. For example, a layer of yellow paint was all it took to suggest gold in the most modest funeral rites of ancient Egypt; false pearls were made of powdered glass and egg white in the 14th century; in Paris in the mid-18th century, Georges Frédéric Strass turned lead crystal, with its stunning reflections, into a fashion hit.

That being said, the intention of this book is to emphasize the technical and aesthetic qualities of these and other products, all of which have met the need for self-adornment in every period of time.

▼ Necklace with natural shapes designed by Chanel (1883-1971) in the 1940s. It is made of blown glass mounted on gold plate. Barbara Berger collection.

# Phony is Chic: From Deprivation to Exuberance

At the beginning of the 20th century, costume jewelry entered the framework of haute couture, a flourishing industry that favored the inclusion of the latest technological novelties into the production of *"designer jewelry"* (bijoux de couture). Accessories were designed by the same fashion designer, and the artisans were anonymous. It wasn't until the 1950s, when the identity of the costume jewelry designer became established, that his name appeared on jewelry pieces.

Coco Chanel (1883-1971), an icon of elegance, developed a line of adornments inspired from antiquity, such as large Byzantine crosses and long strings of false pearls with a Hindu flair that created an impressive, luxurious effect against her sober suits. Chanel entrusted these pieces to the Gripoix company, a dynasty begun at the end of the 19th century by Augustine Gripoix. For the next four generations with women at the forefront, the company produced jewels for suppliers of theater *accessories* and for costume balls such as the ones organized by the fashion designer Paul Poiret.

Chanel was to change the direction of this company by having it produce jewelry not for dazzling in masked balls, but rather to be worn in the streets, giving the adornments a value of modernity and boldness. Her major contribution was *vrais bijoux en toc* (true second-rate jewelry), the exuberance of which contrasted with the austerity of the clothing, an ironic commentary on the adaptation to the difficult times between the wars.

Chanel's lifelong rival, Italian born Elsa Schiaparelli (1890-1973), entered the fashion scene around 1925. One of the most famous designers and manufacturers of costume jewelry, Roger Scemama, began his career by working for her. Schiaparelli had great artistic sensitivity, and she quickly established a connection with the vanguard movements, highlighting her collaborations with Salvador Dalí and Meret Oppenheim to design printed dresses and costume jewelry buttons. She understood costume jewelry as "travel jewelry" which was created in unprecedented designs, such as the telephone earrings by Dalí and the necklace of aspirin tablets imagined by the poet Louis Aragon.

After the trauma of WWI, society needed amusement and escape. The roaring twenties were the era of the Charleston, jazz, and the aesthetic of Art Deco. This movement, which grew out of the 1925 Paris exposition of decorative arts, can be defined as the confluence of the domestication of cubist art, the colorist impact of Russian ballet, and the forcefulness of African art.

Art Deco encompassed a period of imagination and experimentation in which jewelry shared the cold beauty of machines and augmented its palette of materials with lacquer and crystal, while costume jewelry adopted new industrial materials such as bakelite, a synonym of multi-colored ornaments and a true fetish material for future collectors.

▲ Brooch in the shape of a rose, designed by the Nettie Rosenstein Accessories Company of New York, ca. 1950. Made of paste on gold plate. Barbara Berger collection

The economic depression caused by the stock market crash of 1929 only increased the production of costume jewelry in the face of a plunge in the production of luxury products. The United States began to move to the forefront with its production of *fabulous fakes*, which on the one hand faithfully imitated pieces of European high jewelry, and on the other produced figurative pieces loaded with humor, with large bows, and exuberant, cascading shapes known as *cocktail jewelry*.

Phony became chic, and it remained so to the point that women would buy real jewelry because it looked like imitation. One example of the aesthetic of the phony is the jewelry designed by Salvador Dalí in the 1930s and 1940s. These rich pieces of extreme exuberance both fascinate and unsettle us because of the delirious wastefulness of the gold and precious gems used in their creation.

▼ Wide bracelet of glass and semiprecious stones by Elsa Schiaparelli (1890-1973), who was very well known for designing dresses decorated with gemstones.

## The Apotheosis of Appearance

Although costume jewelry originated in France, the United States became its second home after WWII. While European companies were making just a few hundred items or limited series of their designs, in the U.S. it was possible to produce thousands of pieces of a single model.

One of the most representative companies of the time reflective of the economic prosperity and attainment of the "American dream" was Joseff of Hollywood, Inc., which was founded in California in 1938. With great commercial foresight, the company specialized in producing costume jewelry for the grand productions of Hollywood in matte gilded metal that didn't reflect the spotlights and thus avoided undesirable reflections.

Miriam Haskell was another of the main American costume jewelry companies; it has been a pioneer in the field since 1924 and has a select clientele among the international *jet set*. Its gallant style, which recalls the rococo, was based on flowers and large clusters of multicolored beads.

The 1950s marked the golden age of costume jewelry in the United States. Roger Scemama, Miriam Haskell, Coro, Trifari, Eisenber and Sons, and Bonaz, among others, were some of the most prominent companies. Metal rationing after WWII fostered exhaustive research into different types of plastics. Lightweight, inexpensive, and in a full range of colors and finishes, they offered infinite possibilities for costume jewelry and were capable of accommodating almost instantly any fashion—such as the *tutti-frutti* jewelry inspired by the amusing fruit turbans worn by singer and dancer Carmen Miranda.

◄ Xavier Ines Monclús, Contemporary Jewelry, 2003. Silver, gold, and plasticized paper

► David Watkins and Wendy Ramshaw, *Something Special Paper Jewelry,* 1967, "Optik Art Jewelry" series. Victoria and Albert Museum, London. Photo: Bob Cramp

# Jewelry and Do-it-yourself: An Intimate Dimension to Art

In the mid-1960s, frivolity and *glamour* became stale concepts that the new generation associated with an excessively well-off society. Now youth demanded a commitment to the authentic and the natural. The youth of that generation proposed that imagination could change the world. Creativity became democratized: artists shared the creation of works of art with their spectators, industrial designers produced furniture that people could put together themselves, and fashion offered convertible dresses—all this heralded the start of the do-it-yourself era.

Within the context of jewelry, in 1964 the British jewelers Wendy Ramshaw and David Watkins introduced a series of cutout jewels known as *Something Special.* These two creators, along with other important figures in Germany (Hermann Junger and Gerd Rothmann), Holland (Gijs Bakker and Emmy van Leersum), Spain (Anna Font and Joaquim Capdevila), and the United States (William Harper and Robert Ebendorf), were pioneers in what's known as the new jewelry. This international tendency considered all types of materials to express the jeweler's personality, which claimed the artist's freedom as its own. As a result, adornment was transformed into a stimulating field for sculptural and conceptual experimentation.

Contemporary jewelry challenges the traditional separation between "high" and "low" jewelry or bijouterie, suggesting a provocative fusion between the two and moving ahead one step by situating these new objects in the realm of art. This tendency preserves an age-old tradition of jewelry and a will to create unique pieces through impeccable craftsmanship. From costume jewelry it enjoys using a broad variety of materials, both artificial and natural, plus its immediacy in production and its subsequent status as adornment that's accessible to everyone.

In the 1980s this tendency radicalized its assumptions to yield postmodern ornaments of theatrical dimensions. Its proponents sought the greatest spontaneity, coiling up nylon filaments (Caroline Broadhead, United Kingdom), cutting out light materials such as paper (Nel Linsen, Netherlands), and wood (Marjorie Schick, U.S.A.), or assembling PVC and steel cables (Ramon Puig Cuyás, Spain). These attitudes attempted to demonstrate that one could make jewelry practically without being a jeweler.

Presently the tendencies in art and design seem to be leaning once again in this do-it-yourself direction. More and more, those with a flair for the creative want to learn step-by-step procedures that can be practiced in a home setting, and which give creativity a more intimate dimension while still remaining intense and imaginative.

The American artist Tom Friedman, with his sculptures of chewed gum, the Dutch designer Jürgen Bey, with his humorous manipulations of old furniture, and the Catalan jeweler Xavier Ines Monclús, with his use of such humble materials as an ice cream stick, are part of this movement. All of them clearly opt for self-sufficient production methods that are often appropriate to arts and crafts. They seek a certain slowness in the processes, a *tempo* that's alien to the dizzying pace of life, and the purchase of objects that favor reflection and a more intimate relationship with the things that truly are important to us.

That's precisely how the projects in this book are regarded: within the context generated by these types of artists, designers, or simply "makers of objects," as Carles Codina refers to them in his introduction. Ingenuity, imagination, and immediacy define the potential framework for making adornments that are appropriate to this philosophy of accessibility.

**Mònica Gaspar**

▲ Silver and glass complements for the runway by Giménez Zuazo, winter 1999-2000, designed by Estela Guitart

► Felieke van der Leest, *Hare O'Harix and his Six Carrots,* 2000. Combination of silver jewelry techniques, incorporating a plastic found object and crocheting

In this chapter you will learn to make jewelry and ornamental objects from modest resources. The essential technical procedures that are explained will allow you to work with many different types of materials including paper, wood, plastic, and glass, as well as polymer modeling clay and Precious Metal Clay. These everyday materials and basic techniques are readily available to anyone with artistic leanings. They are inexpensive, easy to find, and can be used to produce great results without the use of sophisticated tools. For most of the projects you need use only your hands or a few simple household tools; in others, you will need some basic workshop tools such as a saw or a serviceable torch and a few other tools that will allow you to create a broad range of items.

# Techniques with Unconventional Materials

# Paper

Because of its low price, variety of types, and range of colors, paper is one of the most readily available materials in the creative realm. This section shows some of the great creative possibilities of paper and explains the way in which pulp is worked—a technically simple task that requires no great outlay of money or technological knowledge, and that makes it possible to fashion a tremendous variety of interesting items. A second feature of paper is its ability to be folded—specifically papyroflexia, which makes it possible to produce lots of interesting results. These two very different ways of working paper constitute a contemporary vision of jewelry, one in which the real importance of the work process can be seen.

▲ The process of making paper by hand has remained essentially the same throughout time. Materials such as rag fiber, ground wood pulp, cotton, and wood cellulose are used in its composition.

## The History of Paper

Prior to what we now recognize as paper, other materials were used for writing. Papyrus, for example, was commonly used. It was made using cellular layers from the pith of this plant arranged in a longitudinal pattern over others in a transverse direction. This arrangement was soaked in water, pressed, and then dried. Although it was possible to write on papyrus, like rice paper, it was not a true paper. In reality, it was a usage and a manipulation of a plant to give it a sheet-like appearance.

The development of paper is one of the greatest advances of humankind. Its origins were in ancient China, where people wrote on lumpy fabric made from the remains of silk buds, a material closer to cloth than to what we now consider paper, but on which it was possible to write.

Tsai-lun, who was then responsible for taking care of craft objects in the eastern Han court of the Chinese emperor Ho Ti, developed the first paper using fibers from rags, fishing nets, wood bark, and hemp. This fact was confirmed by the 1957 discovery of an imperial tomb from the Han dynasty, in a place called Pa-Chiau in the province of Shen-Si. Some laminated fibers were found in this tomb; when they were analyzed, it was determined that they were hemp.

Up to the year A.D. 500, paper production was confined to China; it was introduced to Japan in A.D. 610, to Central Asia around A.D. 750, and to Egypt around A.D. 800. The production process of papermaking has undergone constant modification, one of the most important ones being contributed by the Arabs in the 8th century. They used recycled rags as the main ingredient in making paper and were also responsible for introducing paper to Europe.

With the invention of printing, more and more tests were reproduced, and that provided a major impulse to paper manufacturing. Paper's basic ingredient was rags through the 16th and 17th centuries, but alternative solutions were being sought in order to reduce costs and bypass the resulting scarcity of rags. The first efficient papermaking machine was invented in 1808.

While the small-scale production of paper has remained essentially the same, the materials used in making it are different. For example, wood cellulose, cotton, and ground wood pulp, both natural and chemical, are frequently used, as well as different mixtures of rag pulp and fiber. The turning point for

▼ Using these preprinted sheets of paper patterns and by first adhering them onto card stock then cutting, folding, and gluing as directed, it is possible to construct two interesting cutout rings. Work of Estefanía de Llobet

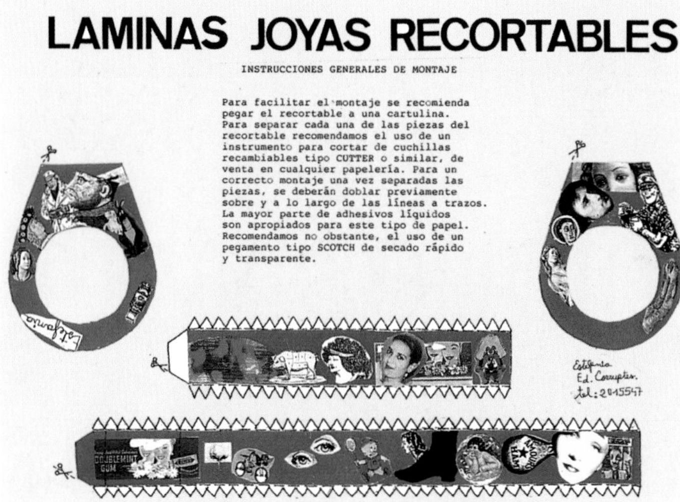


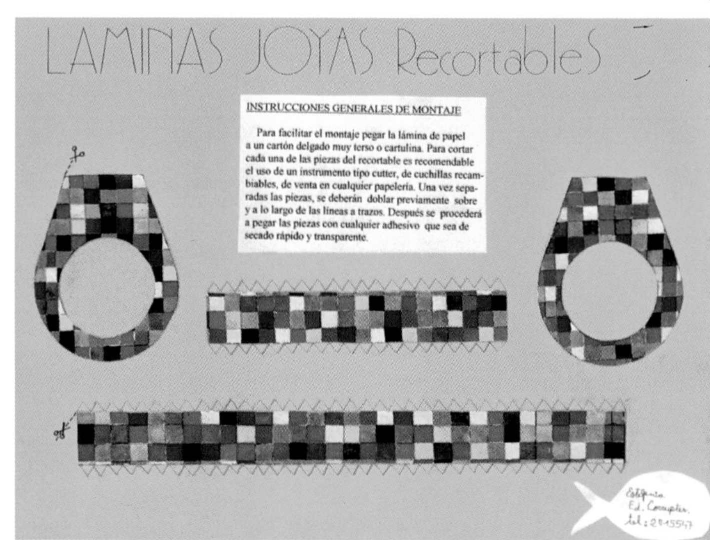

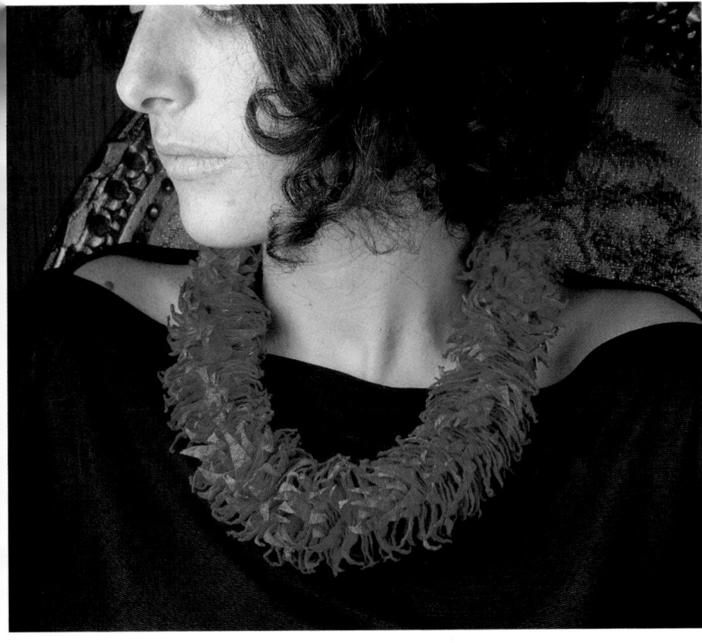

▲ Necklace made of silk paper hand folded by Ana Agopian, 2003

▲ Paper bracelets made by Luis O. Acosta, 2003. Photo by Felix Kalkman

making paper less costly came in the 1840s when a new process for grinding wood into pulp and the first chemical process for producing it were introduced.

## Paper Pulp

The manual process for making paper pulp has not changed over the years. Although today different materials are used in making paper, it is still essentially the product of interlacing cellulose fibers. Raw material is cut up in water to form a mass of fibers in suspension; in a second step the mass of interlaced fibers is spread onto a porous surface to let the water filter out.

During the process, the fiber is reused by moistening it in water and then mixing it with various products to strengthen it once the water evaporates. This transforms the mass into a very tough and durable material with which various shapes and objects can be made.

It is possible to buy already-prepared paper pulp at craft supply stores. It can also be made by cutting up paper in a meat grinder; ground-up toilet paper and newspaper can also be used.

▲ Wood and papier mâché brooches made by Sonia Ruis de Arkaute, 1988

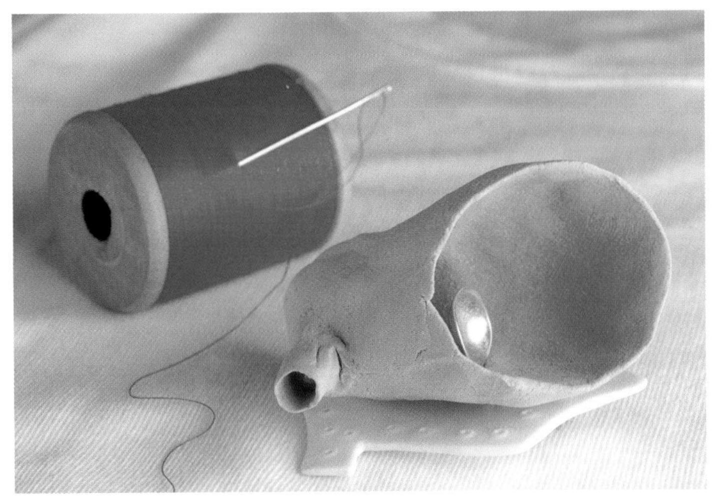

◀ Brooch made of ceramic and cut-up pieces of paper made by Gemma Draper, 2002

# Preparing Paper Pulp

For this project, a papier-mâché pulp prepared in advance, which is readily available in local stores, is used. Paper pulp can also be prepared by cutting up paper in a meat grinder. The paper pulp is easy to work and offers limitless creative possibilities. At first it is a very fragile material, so it has to be mixed with white carpenter's glue. To reinforce it, make inner structures of wood or metal covered with paper pulp so that the final object will be rigid and durable.

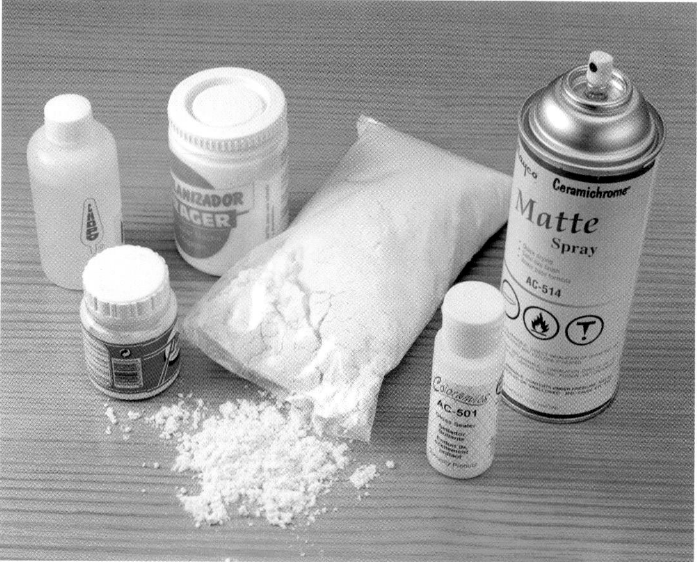


◀ **1.** To make paper pulp, in addition to cut-up paper you will need a little petroleum jelly, white glue, and water. Once the piece is done, you can spray it with varnish to protect it.

▶ **2.** The ground paper is piled up on a smooth surface, then a small hollow on the top of the pile is formed by hand. After adding a small amount of petroleum jelly, lots of water, and white glue, gently knead the mixture.

▼ **3.** Add more water and firmly knead the mass on a smooth surface. It's a good idea to keep a container of water at hand and rewet your fingers in order to keep the pulp from sticking to them.

▼ **4.** Work the mass until you get a fine, homogeneous mixture.

▶ **5.** Paper pulp can be colored by adding the desired color and kneading the pulp again. In this instance, liquid watercolors are used to provide the color.

▼ **6.** For this piece, Sonia Ruiz de Arkaute used paper pulp tinted with blue liquid watercolor. This made it possible to create a light blue color.

▼ **7.** Sonia Ruiz de Arkaute, *In the Shower,* 2002. Brooch made of tinted paper pulp over wood

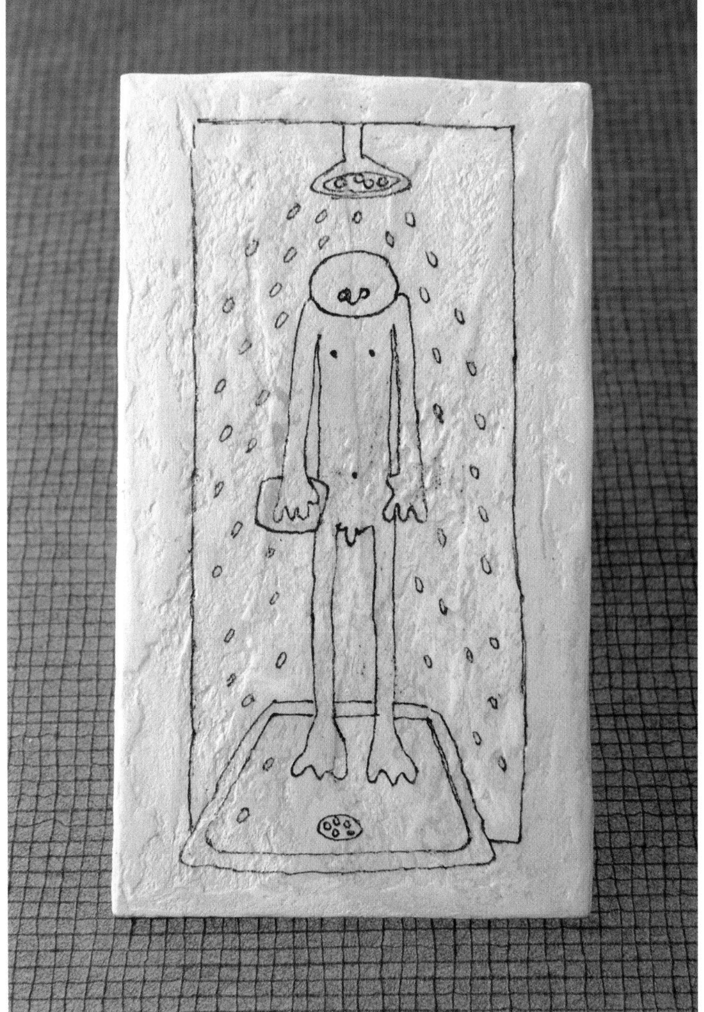

# Paper Brooches, by Sonia Ruiz de Arkaute

For this project, Sonia Ruiz de Arkaute has chosen papier-mâché pulp and is applying it onto an inner plywood structure. This is a work done directly with the hands using children's drawings whose expressive lines show the artist's feelings and her particular way of viewing the world.

▶ **1.** The initial idea comes from drawings done on paper. Here Sonia Ruiz de Arkaute's sketch will later will be transferred onto tracing paper.

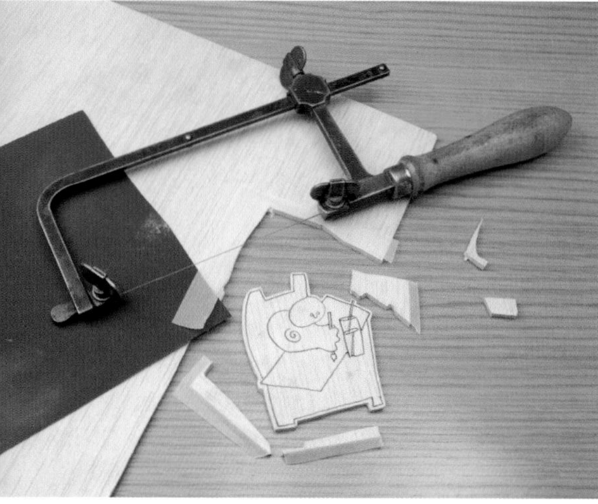

◀ **2.** The tracing paper is glued onto the sheet of plywood. Once it's dry, it is cut out with a jeweler's saw around the outside perimeter of the drawing. Then the tracing paper is removed.

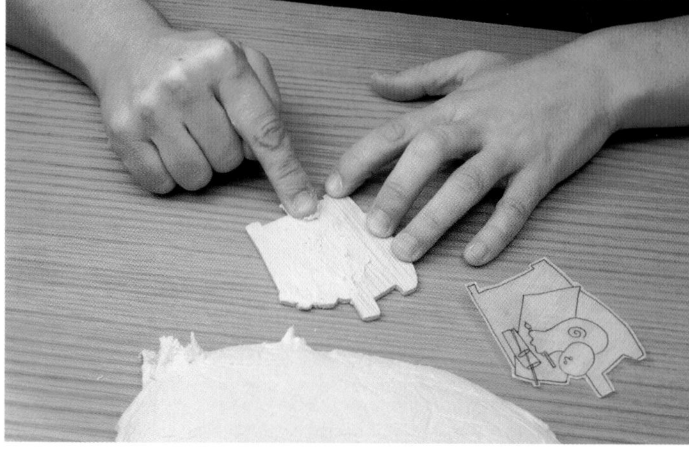

▶ **3.** Pieces of previously prepared papier-mâché pulp are applied with the fingers to create a layer that completely covers the surface of the wood.

◀ **4.** The edges are always delicate areas, so it's a good idea to use some tool—a spatula, for example—to fill this part of the piece.

▲ **5.** Once the papier-mâché pulp on the surface is dry, it is sanded. A hair dryer can be used to speed up this process, if desired.

◀ **6.** Using a black marker, the initial drawing is redrawn on the paper surface.

▲ **7.** The paper can be turned virtually any color. Here, Sonia Ruiz de Arkaute uses a water colorable pencil, which is applied smoothly and in irregular lines.

▲ **8.** Next, watercolor is applied directly on the outer areas of the piece.

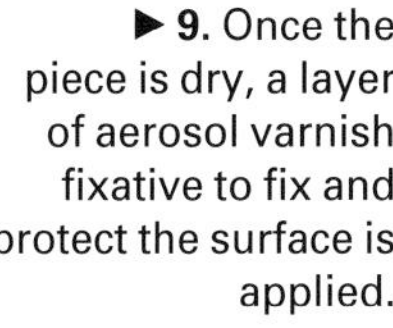

► **9.** Once the piece is dry, a layer of aerosol varnish fixative to fix and protect the surface is applied.

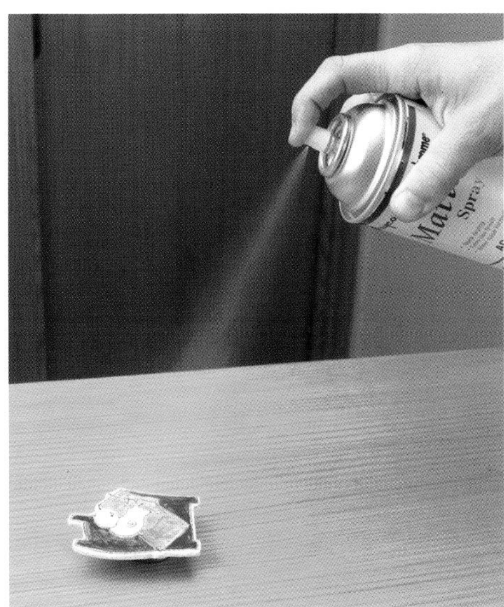

▼ **10.** *Loar Drawing,* 2002. This is the final product, after gluing the clasp on the back; by Sonia Ruiz de Arkaute.

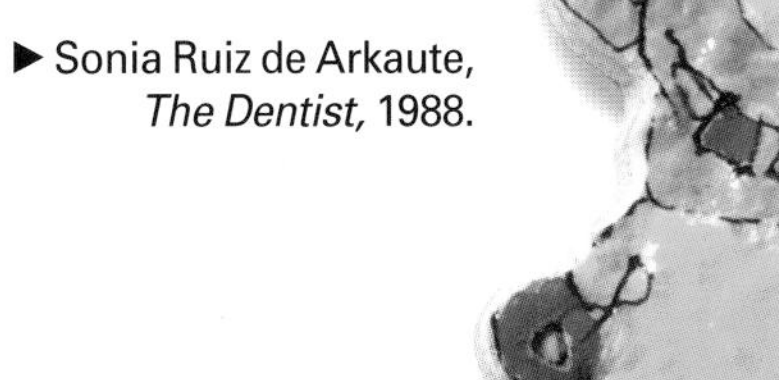

► Sonia Ruiz de Arkaute, *The Dentist,* 1988.

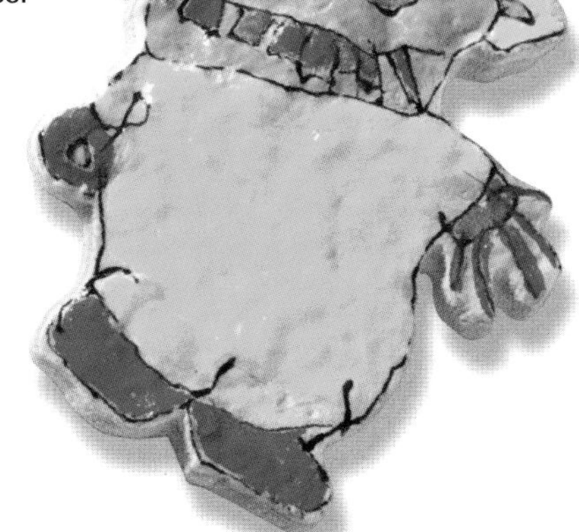

▼ Sonia Ruiz de Arkaute, *W.C.,* 2002.

## Folded Paper Bracelet, by Walter Chen

Papyroflexia is a very ancient means of artistic expression that is clearly rooted in Chinese culture. As Walter Chen demonstrates, paper folding is an art that requires great discipline and attention to detail, along with cadence and rhythm during the process. It's a manual process that produces amazing results from nothing more than a sheet of paper.

The very process also is important. Beginning with making the paper folding tools by hand, cutting them out of bamboo cane, making the seal out of stone, conducting different initial tests before making the project, and ending with the final presentation, paper folding is a project that must be understood in its whole and not just as an end result.

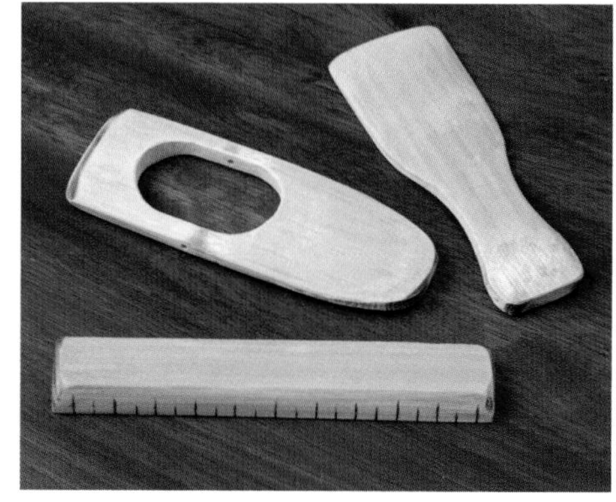

▲ Walter Chen made the tools by hand; that process is as important as the product made from the paper.

▲ **1.** To begin, a piece of paper is selected that is neither very stiff nor very limp, since it must not break or weaken as it is folded. Choose a fairly rigid paper so that the fold lines can be clearly marked and so that the paper retains the rigidity necessary to preserve the texture of the object. Here Walter Chen uses parchment paper in an equivalent weight of about 48 (180 g/m2).

▲ **2.** Before beginning any work with paper, it's a good idea to do a couple of test runs using any disposable paper. Take note of the construction, the procedure, and the measurements. This saves time and gives a fairly accurate idea of the final result.

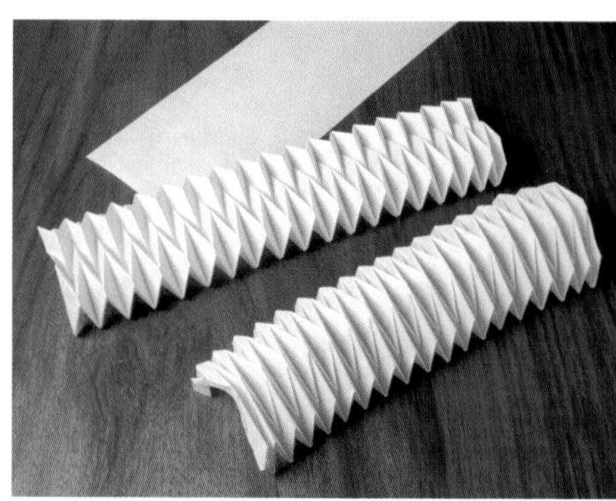

▲ **3.** Once you have acquired a certain amount of practice and done a few sample pieces, attempt a definitive piece using a piece of parchment paper. Experiment using different widths, lengthening certain parts, and so forth, and discard any unsatisfactory results.

▲ Folded paper fan made by Pu Hsin Yu

◀ **4.** It's a good idea to determine and adjust the length of the strip of paper that must be cut out, so that the bracelet will be reversible once it's folded and closed.

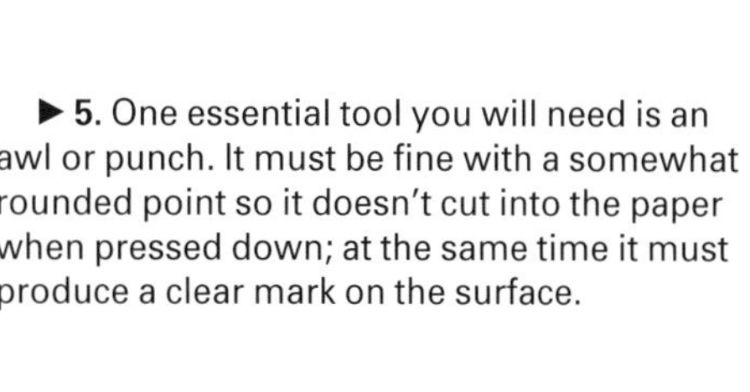

▶ **5.** One essential tool you will need is an awl or punch. It must be fine with a somewhat rounded point so it doesn't cut into the paper when pressed down; at the same time it must produce a clear mark on the surface.

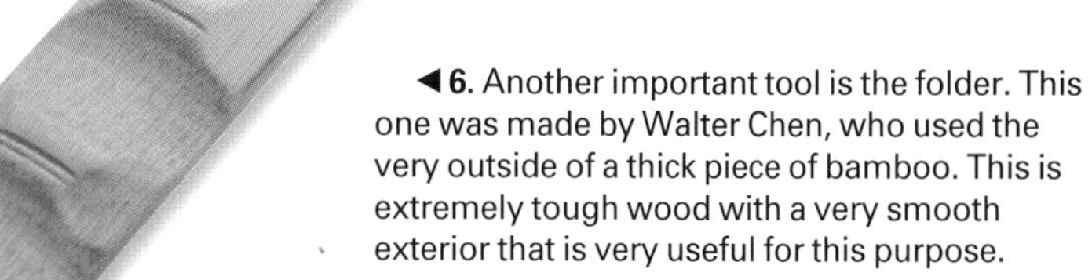

◀ **6.** Another important tool is the folder. This one was made by Walter Chen, who used the very outside of a thick piece of bamboo. This is extremely tough wood with a very smooth exterior that is very useful for this purpose.

▲ **7.** Other tools that will be needed are a hobby knife, a graduated rule with a metal edge for cutting, a fine-point pencil, an eraser, and a stiff brush for removing the eraser rubbings.

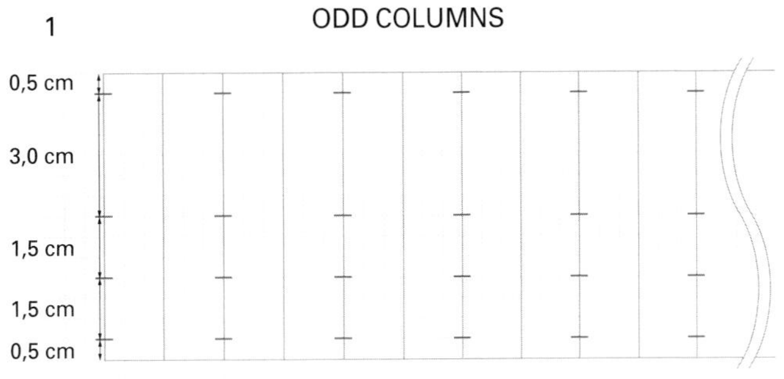


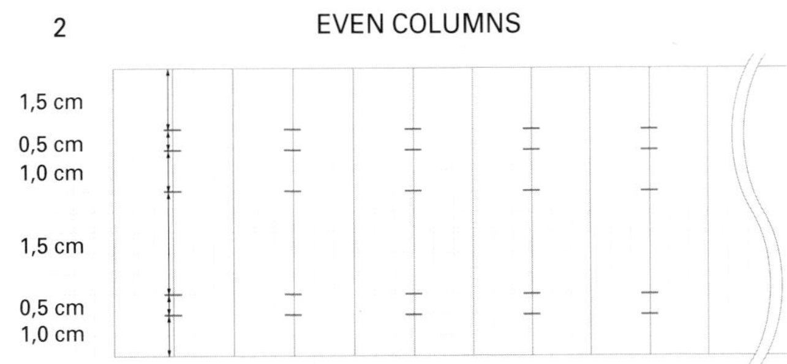


3 (1+2)

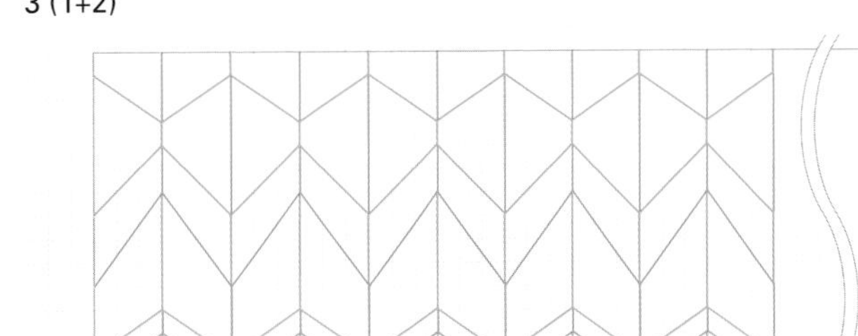

— Peak

— Valley

◀ **8.** Using graph paper, sketch out the steps to be followed for laying out the work.

▲ **9.** Walter Chen starts by cutting a strip 2 ¾ inches (7 cm) wide and 25 inches (63.5 cm) long. That length will make it possible to reverse the bracelet after it is connected at the ends.

◀ **10.** Next, a pencil is used to mark vertical columns about 9⁄16 inches (1.4 cm) apart. The width can be increased; that way, more volume is created.

▲ **11.** The fine-point pencil is used to mark off the columns, taking care not to press down excessively.

▲ **12.** According to design number one, the pencil is used to mark certain points in the odd column (red dashes in the layout sketch).

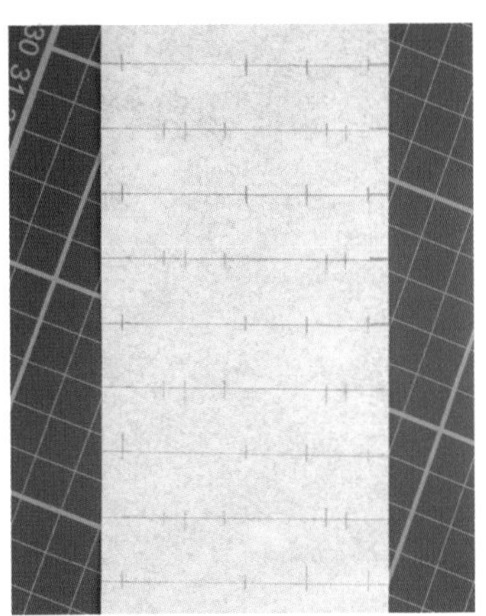

▲ **13.** Now the points are marked off on the even columns (likewise in red) in accordance with design number two.

▲ **14.** The next step involves joining the various points with the pencil as in layout sketch number three, which is the sum of the two previous ones.

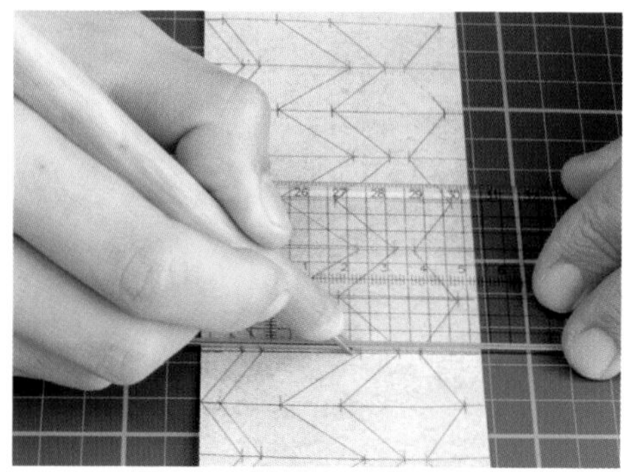

▲ **15.** Once the design is sketched out in pencil on the paper, use the awl to go over all the lines previously laid out. It's important for the underlying surface to be neither very hard nor very soft. Here we have used a special cutting surface.

▲ **16.** An eraser is used to remove all the lines drawn in pencil.

▲ **17.** The grooves must be clearly delineated on the paper; a groove that's too deep would tear the paper in folding; one that's too shallow would produce an unclear crease.

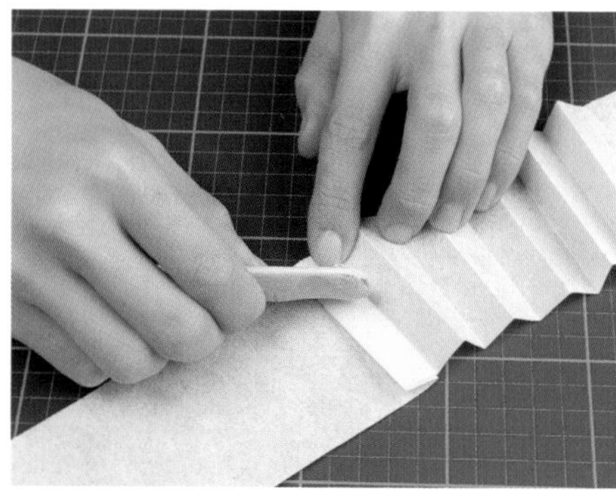

▲ **18.** The bamboo folder is used to alternately fold all the vertical columns as shown in the photo to create a shape with accordion pleats. The grooves are pressed down to define them very clearly.

▲ **19.** The thumb and index finger are used to bend the ends toward the inside.

▲ **20.** Using the same fingers but now pressing with the left hand from beneath, all the "hill" folds are raised as shown in the photo.

▶ **21.** Once all the "hill" folds are raised, the folded structure is compressed to accentuate the entire pattern of folds.

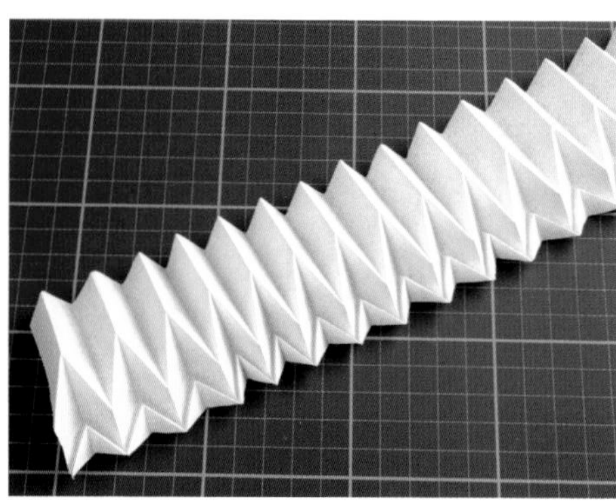

▲ **22.** Here is the result of the first phase. The strip of paper is folded perfectly.

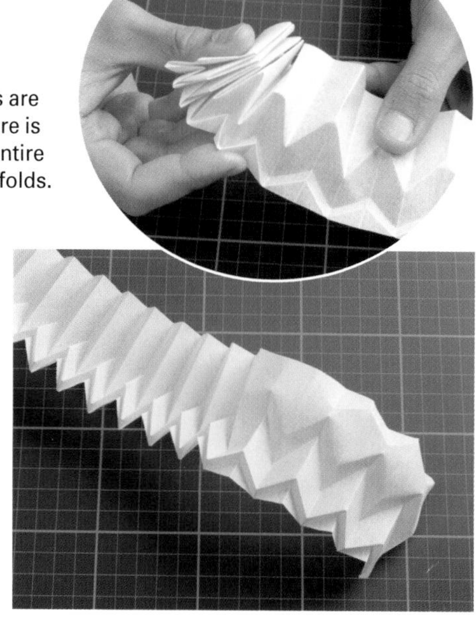

▲ **23.** Next, the paper is stretched out to give the fingers more room to work in folding and pressing the other side, following the instructions from the layout.

▲ **24.**Now each line is pinched alternately to sink a new plane toward the interior.

▶ **25.** As before, the paper is again compressed by squeezing with the fingers. Once the strip is stretched out again, the bracelet is finished. The ends need to fit together perfectly.

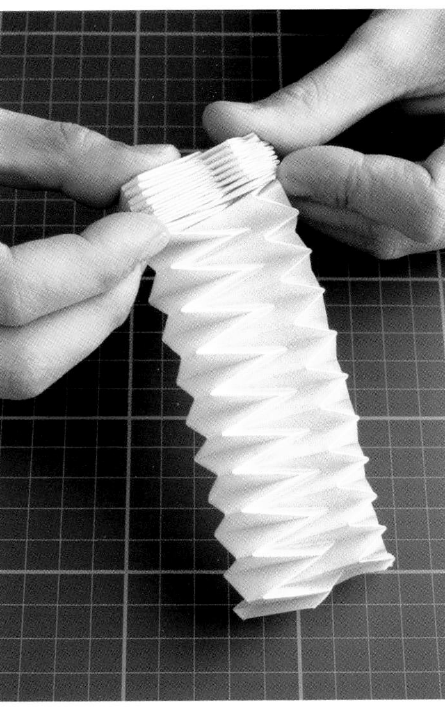

▶ **26.** To join the ends, Walter Chen uses a reversible and neutral polyvinyl acetate adhesive that is normally used in restoration work. When this product dries, it turns into a strong, flexible adhesive film that's soluble in water.

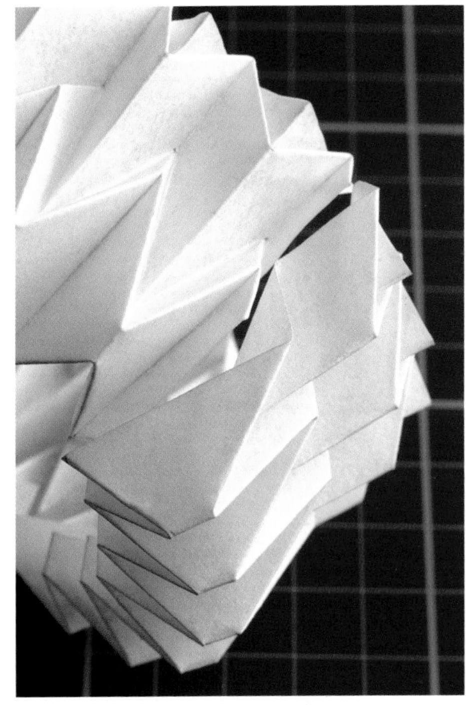

▼ **27.** A 1/32-inch (1 mm) metal drill bit is used to manually drill small holes in the ends of each side of the bracelet.

▼ **28.** A silicone thread is passed through the holes; this will allow complete reversibility of the bracelet by preserving the elasticity of the folded paper.

▼ **29.** A small silver tube is passed over one end of the thread. The ends of the thread are knotted as shown in the photo, and then the knot is slipped into the little tube.

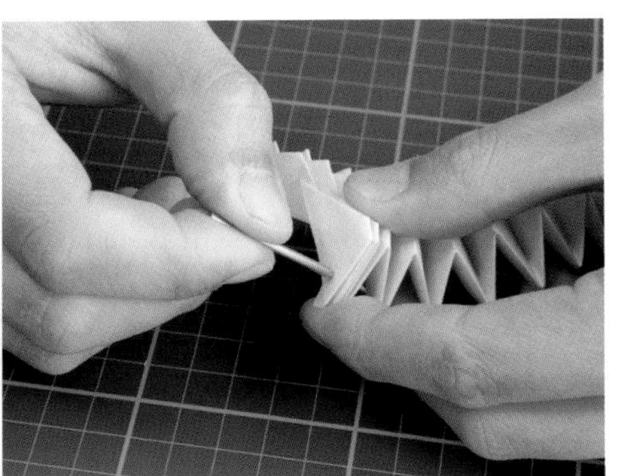

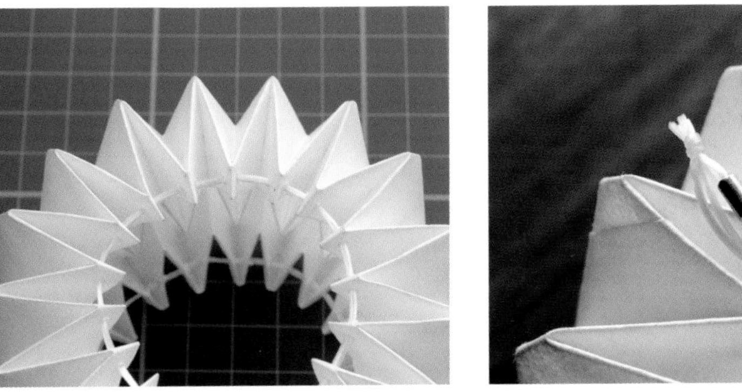

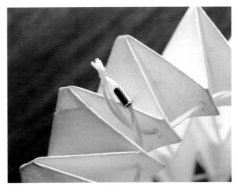

▲ **30.** If the dimensions of the bracelet are right, the silicone thread will make it completely reversible.

▲ **31.** Finally, the personal stamp of the artist, Walter Chen, is applied; the die is fashioned in stone.

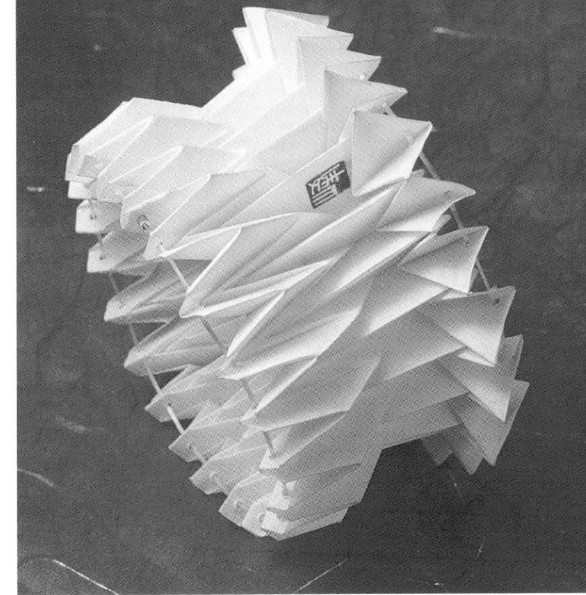

▶ **32.** Paper bracelet by Walter Chen, 2003

# Ceramic Objects

Clay is the basic material used for all ceramic work. This mineral substance is an aluminum oxide silicate composed of silica, aluminum oxide, and water, and it comes from the decay of feldspathic rocks through the action of water. One of its characteristics is that it hardens permanently when fired in a kiln, a discovery dating back to at least 6000 B.C.

There are different types of clays with different consistencies and properties. In general, clay is a mineral substance that possesses good plasticity when moist and is easy to shape. This plasticity is regulated by the quantity of water absorbed and by the wedging (kneading) it must undergo before being used to shape any object.

Most clays are not adequate by themselves for use as a proper ceramic paste; they first need to be mixed with stiffeners to keep the pieces from cracking or warping during drying, or from developing defects during firing. Such stiffeners include quartz, feldspar, calcium carbonate, dolomite, grog (ground fire brick), and talc. Stiffeners also reduce shrinkage in the clay during drying and act as fluxes, reducing the vitrification temperature. Different ceramic pastes are created by varying the proportions and combinations of these materials.

▲ Everyday ornaments, 2004, by Pilar Cotter

In this section, the use of two ceramic materials, stoneware clay and Egyptian paste, will be demonstrated.

## Objects Made of Stoneware Clay, by Pilar Cotter

Stoneware clay is an impermeable and very tough material once it is fired, and it also vitrifies and is opaque. It has a high firing temperature that varies between 2192° and 2372°F (1200° and 1300°C), after which the result is a ceramic in shades of marble, gray, beige, or brown.

The characteristics of a ceramic are determined by the composition of the clay and the way it is prepared. Other factors play an important role, such as the firing temperature, which must be correct for each type of clay, the heat reached in the firing kiln, and the enamels applied to the clay.

There is one type of clay that is appropriate for **modeling** and a different one for **slipcasting.** Here are the components used in each paste, expressed in percentages:

It may be appropriate to add deflocculant to the slipcasting puree to reduce the quantity of water in the resulting liquid and make it flow more readily and conform properly to the inside of the mold, thus producing a more precise shape. That way the mold absorbs less water, which reduces the turnout time between pieces, and the mold lasts longer. There are numerous companies that sell preprepared clays for modeling or slipcasting.

| STONEWARE PASTE FOR MODELING | |
|---|---|
| Clay | 60 |
| Kaolin | 10 |
| Feldspar | 15 |
| Quartz | 15 |

| STONEWARE SLIP FOR SLIPCASTING | |
|---|---|
| Clay | 42 |
| Kaolin | 16 |
| Quartz | 19 |
| Feldspar | 19 |
| Fine grog | 4 |

► Brooch of oxidized silver, Egyptian paste, and several glass beads, by Barbaformosa and Carles Codina i Armengol

## Preparing the Paste

In preparing a paste for slipcasting, it's a good idea to add a deflocculant, that is, to separate the particles of clay from one another and keep them in suspension. That way the casting material is very fluid and shrinkage is reduced. To that end, the following formula is used:

**FOR 2 POUNDS, 3 OUNCES (1 KG) OF PASTE:**

⅓ ounce (9 g) of sodium carbonate
⅔ ounce (18 g) of sodium silicate
16 ounces (480 mL) water

The sodium carbonate is dissolved in a mortar with hot water, then placed into a container along with the sodium silicate. It is stirred, and then the clay is added slowly while continuing to stir until the result is a homogeneous mash.

Take another plastic container, weigh it to find out the tare, and fill with water until it weighs two pounds, three ounces (1 kg). Make the water level then pour it out. This same container is filled up to the marked line with the paste previously liquefied in a blender; that yields a weight of approximately 60 to 61¾ ounces (1.7 to 1.75 kg). If it weighs more, add a little more water to the paste and weigh it again. If it weighs less, add a little more base paste to the mash and weigh the container again until you have the quantity indicated.

The success of the casting paste lies in its density. Once that's adjusted properly it's used just as it is, as long as it has the desired thickness. If it's important that the slip be more liquid because you need to put it into a container with a small opening, you may add a little more silicate, but never more than half the amount put in initially, since an excess would thicken the paste too much.

If you can't deflocculate the paste it may be because of the clay used, since not all are capable of being deflocculated. In that case it's a good idea to change the base clay.

If slipcasting molds are being used without first defocculating the paste, after a few castings some irregularities will appear on the surface of the pieces, along with some small holes,because of the excess water.

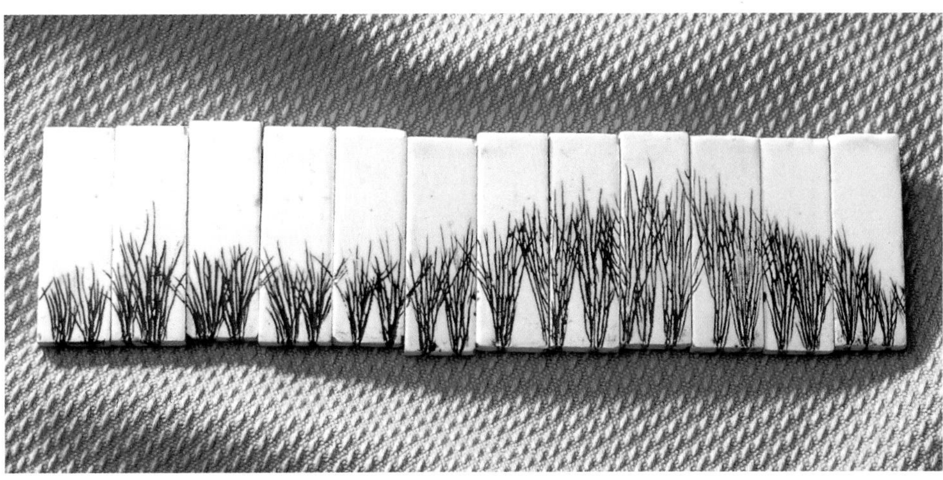

► Pilar Cotter, *The Walk,* 2003

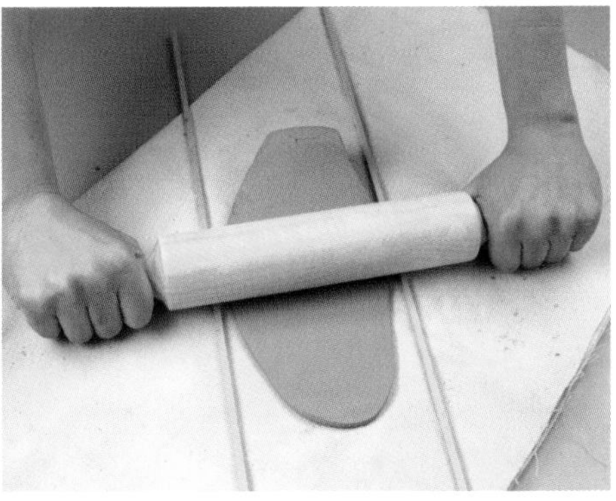

▲ **1.** The clay body is rolled out on a porous surface between a pair of wooden strips to even out its thickness.

▼ **2.** The model is placed into the clay in such a way that it is covered by two halves so it can later be taken apart easily. The wooden end of a paintbrush is used to make the four marks referred to as keys; their function is to fit between the two halves of the mold once it is completed.

## A Brooch Made by Duplicating a Single Model

Pilar Cotter demonstrates how to make plaster molds using a rigid model or any item that may be of interest. In this instance, a ceramic model has been made in advance; the purpose of the project is to reproduce a series of items from stoneware paste. Any type of fine-grained clay with a plastic texture for making the walls of the molds can be used, including normal red clay.

## Plaster Molds

Molds are an age-old resource very closely connected to the evolution of ceramics. The material most commonly used in making them is gypsum; its use dates back to the days of ancient Egypt, where it was used in molds for sculptures. Gypsum also was used in ancient Greece and Rome.

In this instance, plaster will be used, which is a very fine gypsum produced through calcination. After making a slipcasting mold, liquid clay, also known as slip, will be poured into it. When the slip is poured into the mold, the plaster absorbs part of the water contained in the slip mixture, and the outer area that is in closest contact with the plaster wall hardens. If you pour out the slip that has not hardened after a certain time, the result is a hollow object.

To begin, the clay is rolled out on a cloth using a roller and two strips of wood; that way a thick, uniform layer of clay that will be used in making the mold is produced. Any of the common red clays will work well.

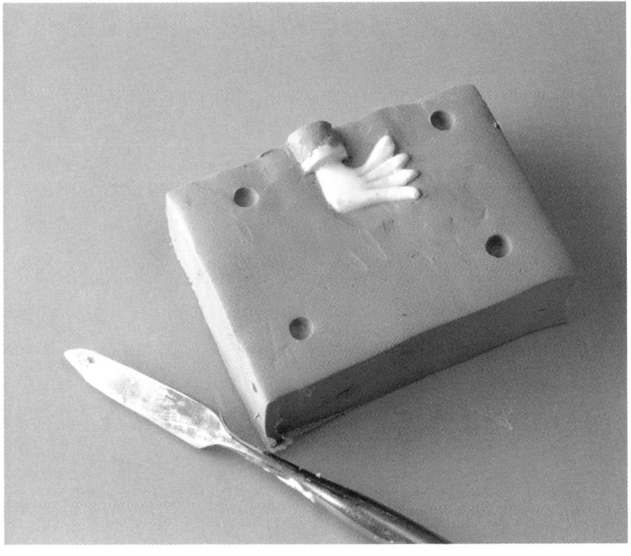

◄ **3.** The walls of the mold are made using the same clay built up to a certain height. The model has to be perfectly centered inside the mold without covering up the keys.

## Preparing the Plaster

To prepare the plaster, first pour some water into a container. Next, sprinkle the plaster over the water in such a way that it is completely sifted when it contacts the water; that prevents the formation of annoying lumps in the mixture. The proportion is flexible, but there is a limit at which the water becomes saturated with plaster and loses its consistency.

Hand mix for several minutes until the plaster is a yogurt-like texture. Set the mixture aside for roughly three minutes; before it starts to thicken, pour it into the mold. The secret consists in pouring the plaster when it's on the verge of setting up. If poured too soon, the plaster is deposited on the base of the mold and the water on the surface, and then the cast will not be uniform or achieve the desired hardness.

► **1.** Prepare a fine plaster and carefully pour it into the mold, making sure that it completely fills all the spaces. The model to be reproduced can be of any material that stands up to moisture: fired ceramic, plastic, metal, and so forth.

► **2.** Once the plaster has set up properly, the clay walls are taken apart, the plaster containing the model is taken out, and the second half of the mold is made.

► **3.** The walls are once again made of clay and attached to the previous mold. The surface of the hardened plaster and the model are lightly coated with water and bleach to keep the other part of the mold from sticking to it. Fill the mold with plaster; complete drying takes a couple of days at room temperature.

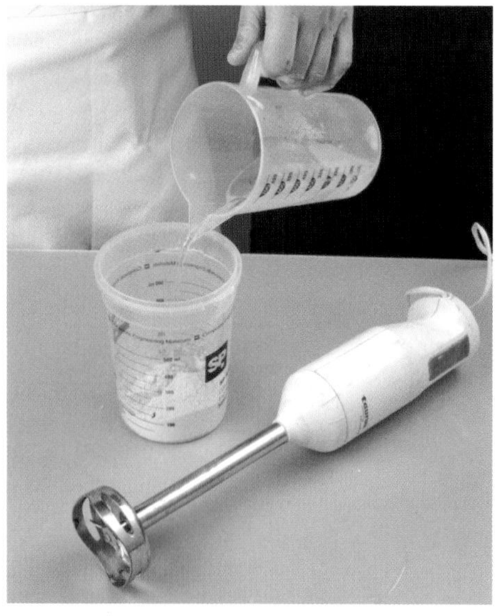

▲ **4.** Once the mold is thoroughly dry, prepare the clay slip so it has a texture similar to that of baby food.

▲ **5.** Inject the mixture into the mold with a large-capacity syringe. This process is known as slipcasting. The mold has to be completely dry so that it absorbs the water from the slip. If it is slightly damp, the sides can be sprinkled lightly with talcum powder.

▲ **6.** The pieces of the mold are separated and allowed to dry. If the clay was previously deflocculated and the mold is perfectly dry, the pieces will come out of the mold quickly and easily, since they are small.

## Firing and Enameling

The process of firing clay is known as bisquing; it involves a preliminary firing that hardens the piece before applying the enamel. This really entails a double firing. The first one, the bisquing, is achieved by progressively increasing the temperature of the kiln, producing a heat curve that cures the piece properly. The temperature is slowly increased to 392°F (200°C) over three hours, with an increase of 302°F (150°C) per hour until reaching 1868°F (1020°C). Once there, that temperature is held for about 15 minutes, and then it is decreased little by little to room temperature.

Once the pieces have cooled off, an enamel for ceramics from a specialty supplier is prepared according to the manufacturer's instructions and applied over the entire surface of the object; then a second firing is done at 2282°F (1250°C). Once that temperature is reached, it is held for about 15 minutes. The kiln is then allowed to cool to room temperature.

It is important to adjust the procedure and firing temperature to the properties of each clay to prevent breakage in firing. The modeled pieces have to air dry for several days in advance, and once they are completely dry, they are put into a kiln and fired. If put into the kiln wet they might explode during the firing.

▼ **2.** After the bisquing, the enamel is prepared according to the manufacturer's instructions, and the various pieces are submerged in the liquid before putting them into the kiln for the second time. The layer of enamel must be fine and even; otherwise, it would run during the firing, and the piece would be stuck to the plate.

► **1.** Once all the pieces have been cast, gone over, and dried appropriately, they are subjected to bisquing before being enameled.

► **3.** Some pin-type bases and backers are prepared; these are available from craft supply stores.

► **4.** Pilar Cotter, *Flying time*, 2004

## A Ring Made Using Clay Impressions, by Pilar Cotter

In the past, ceramic was typically decorated in one of two ways: either by pressing with the fingers or some other object while the clay was still soft, or by using an awl when the clay was leather hard or dry. The malleability of clay and its other properties make it possible to decorate it both before and after drying; it is also possible to sand or burnish the surface with a hard rock, a piece of cane, and the outside of a metal spoon. Once the clay is fired, it takes on the hardness appropriate to the ceramic material to which it corresponds.

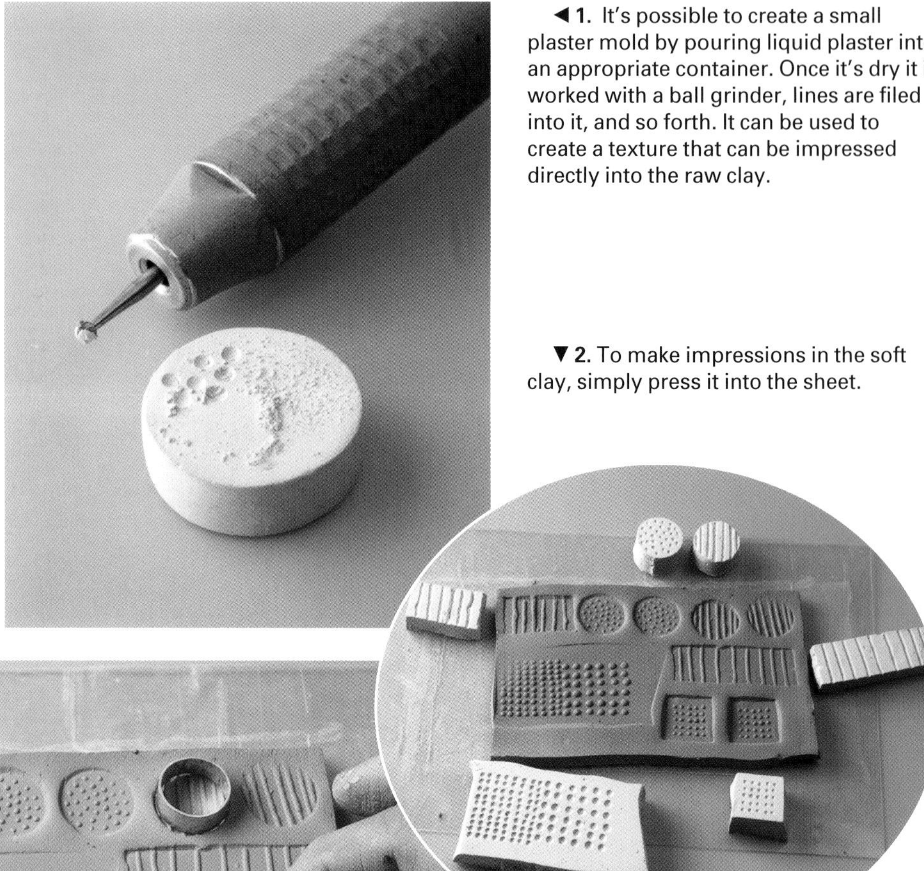

◀ **1.** It's possible to create a small plaster mold by pouring liquid plaster into an appropriate container. Once it's dry it is worked with a ball grinder, lines are filed into it, and so forth. It can be used to create a texture that can be impressed directly into the raw clay.

▼ **2.** To make impressions in the soft clay, simply press it into the sheet.

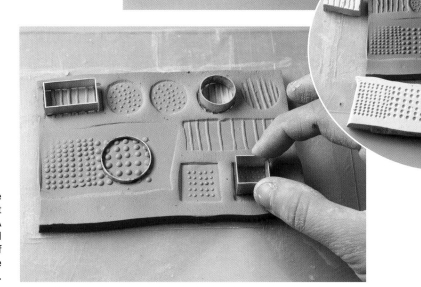

▶ **3.** Metal cutters are used to cut different shapes on the clay. A small angle or 45° bevel is added to the edge of the cutters to improve the cut.

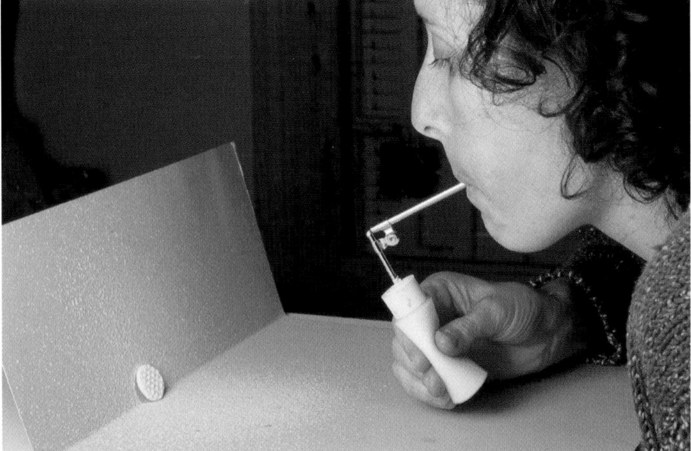

▲ **4.** In working with a simple piece, it is possible to bypass the bisquing process and use a single firing and apply the enamel directly onto the raw clay, but be aware that it won't have the same durability as a piece that has been bisqued. Next, the piece is enameled by applying the enamel with a blowpipe. This produces a thin, even layer of enamel that will give the pieces their final color once they are fired.

▲ **5.** Silver and ceramic rings made by Pilar Cotter

# Egyptian Pastes, by Barbaformosa

The use of Egyptian pastes is one of the most ancient types of ceramic varnish known. They were developed in Egypt around the year 5000 B.C., yet even today some items in vibrant turquoise, the typical color of this technique, can still be admired in Egyptian art museums. This is a paste with a high content of soluble sodium salts that is incorporated into the clay and comes to the surface during the slow drying process, eventually turning into ceramic enamel.

Egyptian pastes are really a ceramic paste that is appropriate for use in jewelry today, just as it was in ancient Egypt. The pastes make it possible to create a surface enamel without having to apply it. With a single firing, this ceramic converts into a vitreous, tough material that takes on a great variety of shades and colors and can also produce varied and interesting effects. It is an ideal material for making beads or applying to pieces of jewelry.

## Composition

Egyptian pastes are always prepared using an initial base paste. Several compositions can be made, and the proportions can be varied until the best formula is found that creates pastes with a greater or lesser degree of plasticity. The basic composition commonly includes feldspar, silica, chalk, kaolin, clay or fine sand, sodium carbonate, and sodium bicarbonate. Various amounts of oxides or commercial colors are added to the base to create the different colorations.

### Matte Base Paste

This paste has a high degree of plasticity. It can be used to make more complex, elaborate projects, and can even be used for throwing small objects on a potter's wheel. The matte quality exhibited after glazing is modified by adding from one to two percent more sodium to turn it glossy.

| | |
|---|---|
| Sodium feldspar | 40% |
| Silica | 21% |
| Sodium carbonate | 6, 5% |
| Sodium bicarbonate | 6, 5% |
| Chalk | 5, 5% |
| Kaolin | 15, 5% |
| White clay | 5% |

Once the base paste is prepared it can be colored with oxides that will produce the following colors, and which are characteristic of Egyptian clays.

**Turquoise**
Copper oxide from 1 to 5%
**Blue**
Cobalt oxide from 0.5 to 2%
**Purple**
Manganese oxide from 2 to 5%
**Green**
Chromium oxide from 1 to 5%

Using colorings, it is possible to produce other shades such as yellow, pink, orange, ochre, red, purple, and black. The proportions vary between 5 and 15%.

▲ Rings made from Egyptian paste, silver, and aluminum, 2004. Created by Barbaformosa and Carles Codina i Armengol

▲ Rings made of silver and Egyptian paste, 2004. Work by Barbaformosa and Carles Codina i Armengol.

### Glossy Base Paste

This paste is not very plastic, and is a poor choice for very complex works or projects made on a wheel. However, once fired it produces deep, glossy glazes with lots of cracks, plus an excellent white hue. The proportions are the following:

| | |
|---|---|
| Sodium feldspar | 47% |
| Silica | 33% |
| Sodium carbonate | 7% |
| Sorium bicarbonate | 7% |
| Chalk | 6% |

◀ The varying proportions of oxides and colorants provide a range of intense colors.

## Preparation and Work

In order to prepare these ceramic pastes, it's important to mix the most problematical products first and then add the less demanding ones in the proportions indicated. It's recommended that distilled water or rainwater be used in order to achieve the best results.

First the water is measured, using 1.0 to 1.2 fluid ounces (30 to 36 mL) of distilled water for every 3.5 ounces (100 g) of clay. Next the sodium carbonate and bicarbonate are weighed and mixed with the greater part of the measured water, making sure that there are no lumps. Then the oxide is poured in and mixed, followed by the rest of the components.

Once the dough is prepared, it is dried on a nonporous surface until the excess water evaporates. It must never be allowed to dry on a porous surface, since the sodium is soluble and it would be lost along with the water. Weigh the paste and use it when it reaches the ideal state of hardness. To store, wrap in plastic to keep in the moisture.

Egyptian pastes generally are not very plastic and cannot be used for some projects, so it's a good idea to make simple pieces like beads or small objects.

▲ **1.** It's important to measure the water precisely. For 3.5 ounces (100 g) of clay, from 1.0 to 1.2 fluid ounces (30 to 36 mL) of distilled water is poured into a measuring cup. The sodium carbonate and bicarbonate are also weighed.

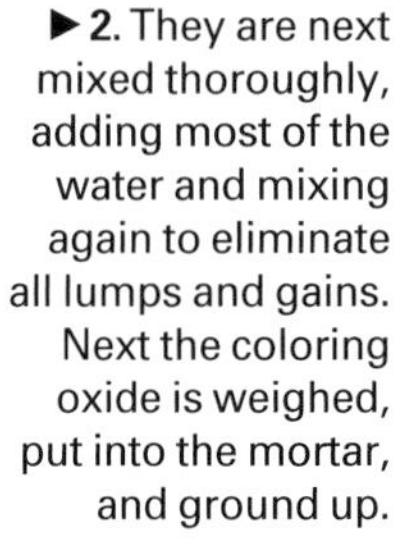

► **2.** They are next mixed thoroughly, adding most of the water and mixing again to eliminate all lumps and gains. Next the coloring oxide is weighed, put into the mortar, and ground up.

◄ **3.** Then the other materials are added.

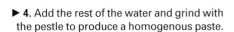

► **4.** Add the rest of the water and grind with the pestle to produce a homogenous paste.

► ► **5.** Finally, the container is emptied onto a nonporous surface such as a fine sheet of plastic, using a spatula to get out as much of the paste as possible.

▲ **6.** After drying for several hours, it is kneaded well by hand to a uniform texture.

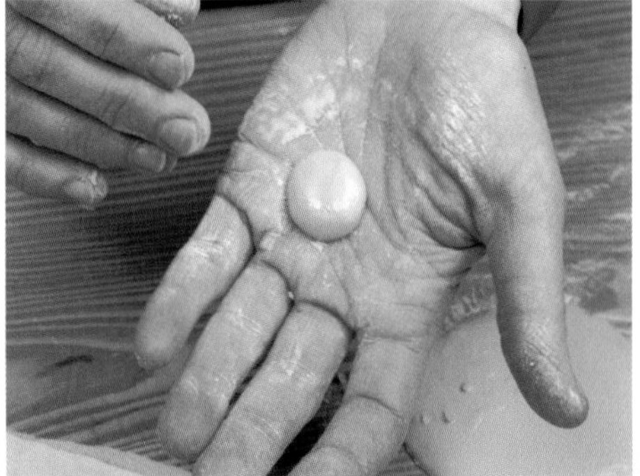

▲ **7.** Form a ball from a piece of clay.

▲ **8.** A hole is made in the middle of each with a rod.

◀ **9.** During the drying process the sodium comes to the surface and leaves a sort of fuzz. Once the object is completely covered with sodium the piece is fired.

◀ **10.** The properly prepared paste can be manipulated in different ways. It can be turned on a potter's wheel to make objects such as the ones shown here.

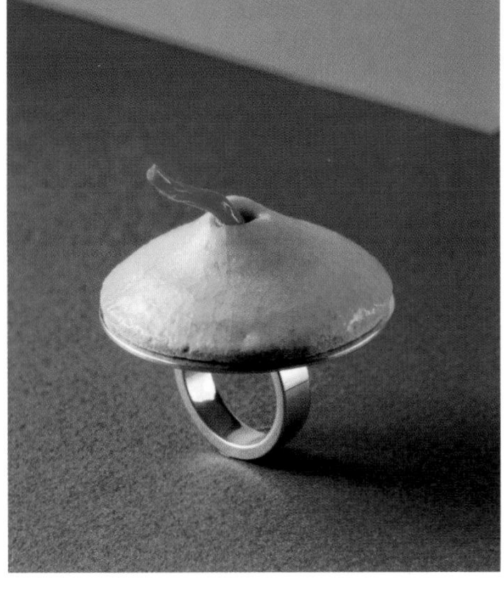

▶ **11.** Silver, turned Egyptian paste, and coral ring made jointly by Barbaformosa and Carles Codina i Armengol.

## Drying and Firing

As with all ceramics, once the shaping is done, the piece must dry thoroughly before it can be fired in the kiln. The drying process commonly lasts between three days and two weeks, depending on the ambient temperature, the size of the piece, and its thickness. Throughout the drying stage the sodium comes to the surface and leaves a type of fuzz that will, in the course of firing, turn into ceramic enamel. It's important not to disturb the layer of sodium on the surface after drying; otherwise, the piece will be flawed after the firing.

In order for the sodium to rise to the surface properly, the kiln must reach 1724°F (940°C) through a gradual temperature increase over, at a minimum, a six-hour period. Thus the kiln is programmed to increase to 392°F (200°C) in two hours, and from that point on, the temperature increases 302°F (150°C) every hour up to 1724°F (940°C). Once that temperature is reached, it's recommended to hold it for 10 minutes or longer, depending on the kiln being used. The enameled surface ends up being tougher than the clay itself.

◀ Pieces that have been fired in the kiln. Note the tiny pieces of ceramic at the base of each object in order to prevent the piece from sticking to the plate during firing. Another way to place the pieces into the kiln is to smooth the base of each one with sandpaper before firing.

▼ Turning rings made of silver, gold, Egyptian paste, coral, and precious gems, 2004. Work by Barbaformosa and Carles Codina i Armengol

▼ Turning rings made of aluminum, silver, gold, and Egyptian paste, 2004. Work by Barbaformosa and Carles Codina i Armengol

# PMC

Precious Metal Clay, or PMC, is a fairly new material to the market. It was developed and patented by the Mitsubishi Materials Company in Japan in the early 1990s. This is a very interesting product that is currently being used to create small objects in gold, silver, and platinum; it also serves as a complement in other creations when used with various materials.

PMC is a quick and easy material to work with, making it possible to create jewelry and a variety of items in precious metals. That's because PMC is dough-like and initially is very malleable, similar to ceramic clay. No special tools are required for working with it, and even those with no knowledge of jewelry or metal techniques can get started and explore different methods involved in creating items from precious metals.

## Composition

PMC is made up of three components. The first is the pure metal: gold, silver, or platinum. The metal is ground into very fine particles to create a floury texture. Then this metallic powder is mixed with a second component, organic binder, the formula for which is the exclusive property of the manufacturer. The third component, which constitutes about 10 to 20 percent of PMC, is water.

The pulverized metal and the binder added to the mixture are chemically stable; thus they will scarcely be altered in use. However, it's a different situation with the water, which evaporates easily when the PMC is being worked. So, it's important to know how to preserve this material, how to restore it if the piece becomes too dry, and how to prepare it properly in advance. It is also important to know the characteristics of the material as it is worked.

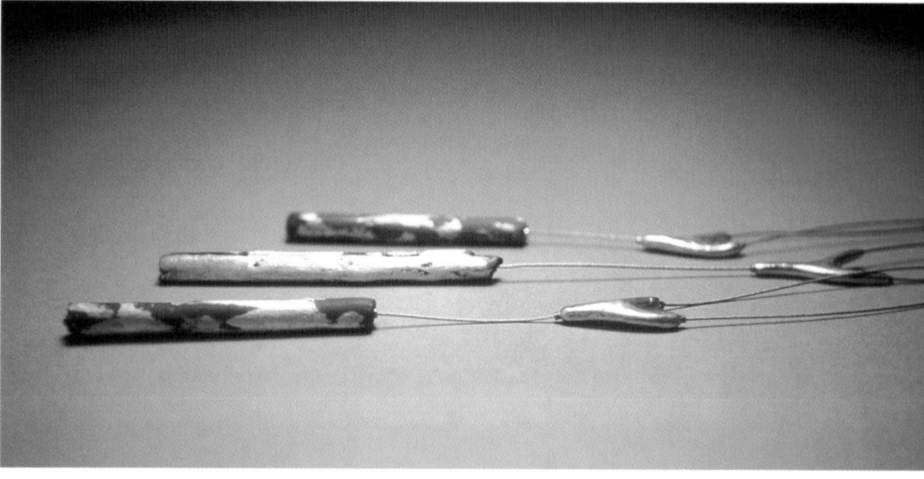

▲ Detail of a necklace. Tube of clay with superheated PMC on the surface, by Marina Gouromihou

▼ Earrings made from PMC and steel, by Brigitte Adolph

▼ Brooch made of PMC, enamel, and gold, by Brigitte Adolph

▼ PMC and steel ring, by Brigitte Adolph

◄ PMC and sand rings, by Marina Gouromihou

## Types of PMC

This chapter discusses how to work with normal or standard PMC, although recently PMC plus or PMC+ has appeared on the market. The newer PMC functions the same way as the standard and looks the same, but there is more metal and less binder in its composition. Because the metal particles are finer than those in standard PMC, a denser PMC is produced that causes less shrinkage than normal PMC.

Experience indicates that it doesn't reproduce imprints or engraving as faithfully as the regular PMC; however, the reduced work time and shrinkage in drying make PMC+ ideal for making pieces that require greater rigidity, such as the setting of a ring or other fine structures. The advantage of PMC+, however, is the reduced work time needed from shaping to final firing, as well as the ability to work with different firing times and temperatures.

Another version, PMC3, is more dense than PMC+ and allows curing at even lower temperatures. You can work even more quickly with PMC3. Both are available in the form of a dough that can be modeled, in fine sheets, and in a slightly more liquid dough that allows use in small syringes. It is even possible to make PMC wire, join pieces, and create surface texture.

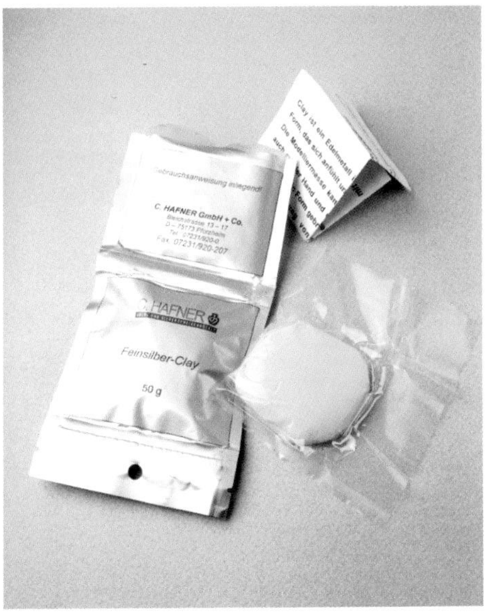


◀ A 1¾-ounce (50 g) packet of standard PMC.

▼ Store PMC that has been tightly wrapped in plastic in a sealed container.

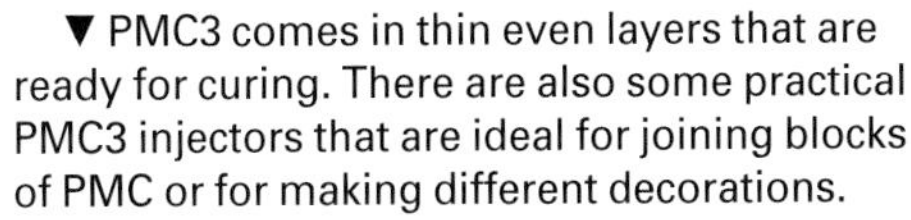
▼ PMC3 comes in thin even layers that are ready for curing. There are also some practical PMC3 injectors that are ideal for joining blocks of PMC or for making different decorations.

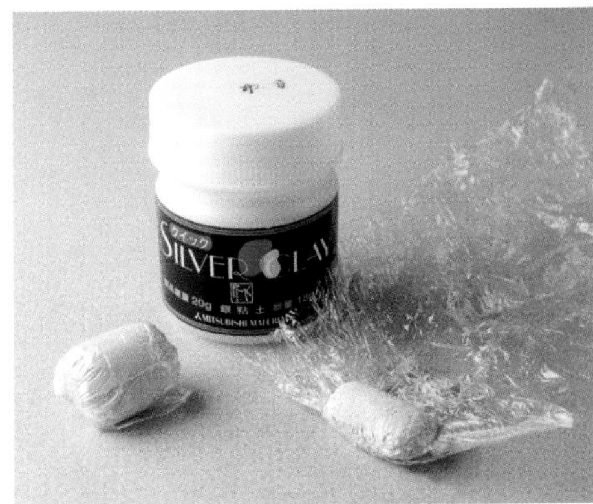


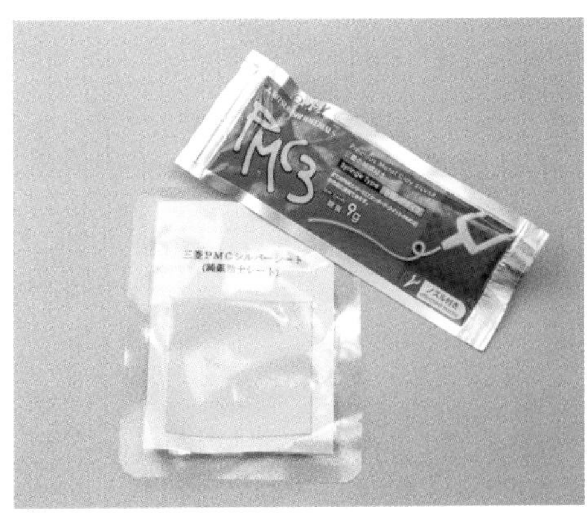


## Preservation and Mixing

When opening a package of PMC, it appears wrapped in a thin layer of plastic. It's advisable to store the PMC in that way to avoid water loss through evaporation. Because water loss changes the consistency and malleability of PMC, it's important to avoid this problem as much as possible. Use just the right amount of PMC to start the project, and keep the rest in the sealed envelope, wrapped in a sheet of plastic.

To be worked correctly, PMC needs the right consistency and texture. These are determined by the amount of water it contains, since the two other components, the metal and the binder, are stable products. It must be neither too soft nor too hard. If it contains too much water, it turns into a paste that's sticky to the touch and it sticks to the tools, making it impossible to work with. On the other hand, if it's too dry, it splits and cracks when it's handled.

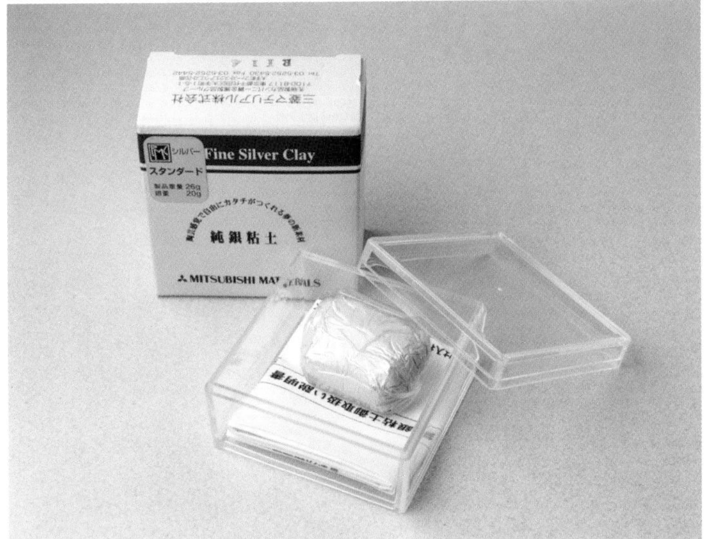


◀ PMC comes in small plastic boxes or in hermetically sealed packets. If unopened, PMC will last a year under normal conditions; but once the container is opened, the PMC must quickly be wrapped in a sheet of fine plastic.

◀ PMC of the proper consistency. The ideal consistency provides malleability without cracking at the edges and without sticking to the fingers; it should clearly show the fingerprints that result from squeezing it.

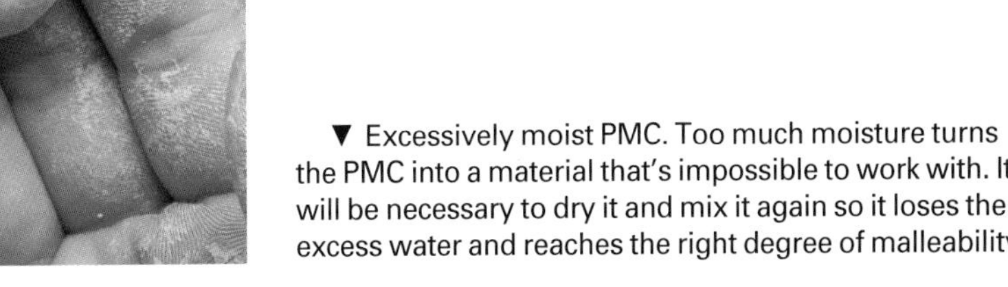
▼ Excessively moist PMC. Too much moisture turns the PMC into a material that's impossible to work with. It will be necessary to dry it and mix it again so it loses the excess water and reaches the right degree of malleability.

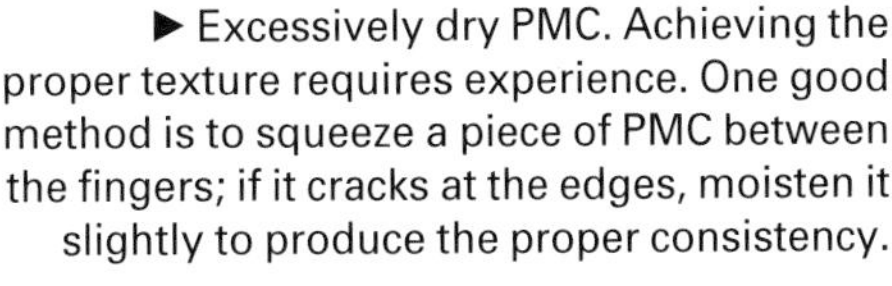
▶ Excessively dry PMC. Achieving the proper texture requires experience. One good method is to squeeze a piece of PMC between the fingers; if it cracks at the edges, moisten it slightly to produce the proper consistency.

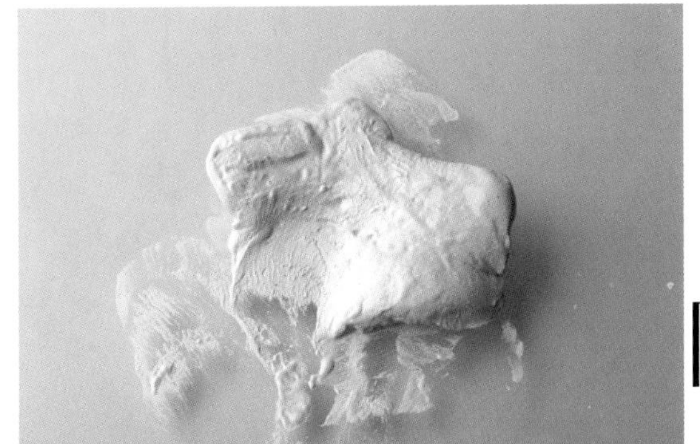

## Rehydrating

PMC often dries out, so it's useful to learn how to moisten it and return it to the precise point at which it can be used for modeling. As a general rule, all it takes is adding a few drops of water to moisten it, kneading it gently, and setting it aside for a couple of minutes. At other times, though, the PMC may be completely dry. If this happens, it will be necessary to cut it into small slices and grind it up into powder with, for example, a kitchen cheese grater or similar implement. Submerge the dry PMC in water until it dissolves; remove the excess water and knead once again to produce the correct consistency.

Another way to recover the PMC is to grind the dry material in a mortar and turn it into dust, then add a small amount of distilled water. After a few minutes the material dissolves and is free of lumps. Remove excess water by pouring it off, then knead the PMC again. To keep the PMC rehydrated, slightly moisten fingertips and knead the material again.

## Tools

PMC is easy to work, and requires few tools. The best surfaces for working on are a smooth piece of glass or an equally smooth sheet of plastic. This material is not toxic to the touch, but does cause certain reactions on metal surfaces, so it's advisable to avoid these surfaces. Likewise, do not wrap PMC in aluminum foil.

Any tool can be used to cut PMC—hobby knives, sticks, and paintbrush handles, for example. If necessary, moisten fingertips or the surface with a little olive oil to make the modeling a little easier.

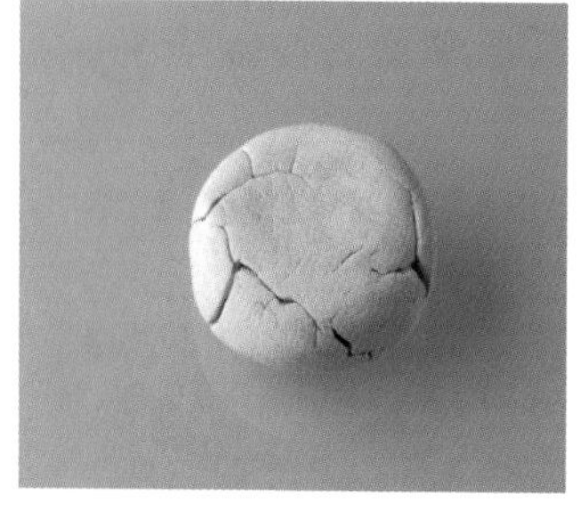

▲ PMC that has become too hard or dry can't be manipulated properly; cracks appear and it can't be worked. However, with a little practice it's easy to achieve the right texture.

◀ To soften a dry lump, poke holes in it with a rod, apply some water from a sprayer, and set aside for a few minutes. Knead again inside the plastic to help the water penetrate, set aside, and it will be usable again.

◀ If the lump is hard as a rock, grate or cut it into pieces with a scalpel, submerge in water and knead with a wooden palette until it dissolves.

## Joining Pieces with PMC

Projects made from PMC (sheets, decorations, threads, and others) often have to be joined together. Sometimes, applying simple pressure while the PMC is still uncured works. To facilitate the bond, apply a little water to the joint with a small brush, allow it to soak a few seconds, and then press the two parts together. Another option that's much better than the first one is to use syringes of PMC. These are ideal for joining pieces in their raw state. The syringes are filled with PMC, which is applied to the joint before pressing the pieces together, as if using a glue. These syringes are also used for filling the joints and covering up small hollows or surface imperfections; once the PMC is dry, it's easy to remove any excess with sandpaper.

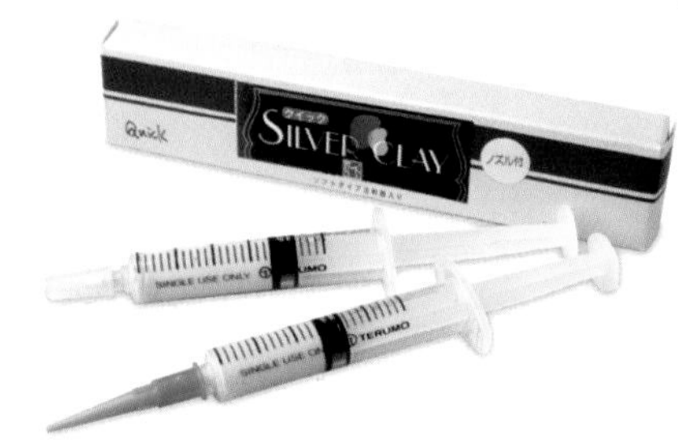


▲ **1.** Syringes for PMC come with several needles of different diameters for making threads of different thicknesses for joining or decorating PMC surfaces.

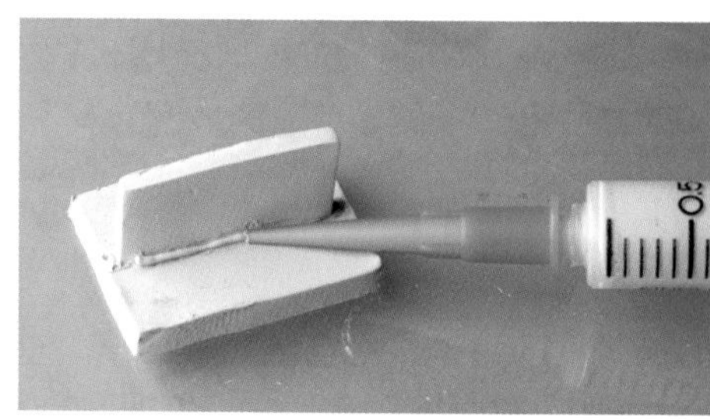

▲ **2.** The PMC is put down in an even bead, and then the paste is pressed with a spatula to make it stick to the plates.

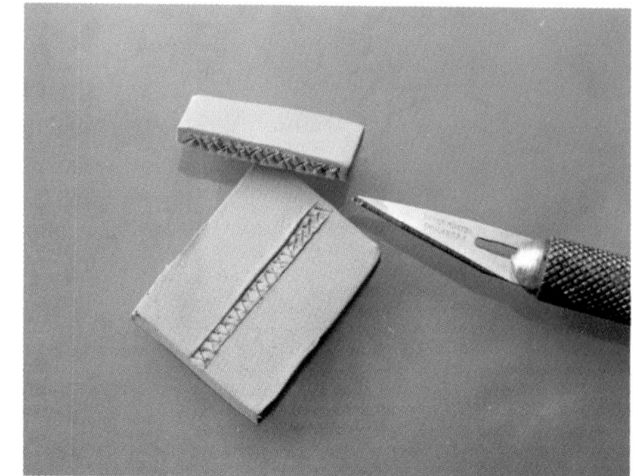

▶ **3.** To join two surfaces using PMC slip, it's helpful to make a couple of preliminary cuts on both surfaces to make it easier for the slip to penetrate and assure a strong bond.

▲ **4.** The PMC slip is applied with a spatula; after a few seconds the two surfaces can be pressed together.

### Joining Pieces with Putty

It is possible to make putty from fresh or dry PMC. If it is completely dry, the PMC is grated or ground up in a mortar; then the resulting dust is submerged in water. A spatula is used to continuously press the mixture to assure the complete dissolution of the powder and the elimination of lumps. Continue kneading until the slip has the consistency of baby food, then store it in a sealed jar.

PMC putty is very useful for joining PMC correctly and covering up cracks. It is also possible to create interesting surface textures by applying it directly onto raw sheets of PMC.

▲ **5.** To give the joint a good finish, apply slip along the length and allow it to dry.

▲ **6.** Once the slip is dry, even out the surface with a spatula or a bit of sandpaper. regular.

## Drying

Drying is a necessary process before firing the PMC. As with ceramics, too much moisture when the PMC piece is introduced into the kiln causes irreversible damage to the material, so the water must be removed before firing any object.

Once the piece is made, it is allowed to dry in a dry place. This process may last several hours or even days, depending on the surrounding temperature and the size of the piece. The drying can be accelerated by directing hot air onto the piece with a hair dryer. The air needs to circulate over the entire object, so a support in the shape of a grate can be very useful.

Some projects can be made using dry PMC, such as engraving, or other creative designs made from such tools as drill bits and spatulas, working directly on the surface of the PMC.

FIRING CHART

| | Standard | PMC | PMC3 |
|---|---|---|---|
| **Shrinkage** | 30% | 10-15% | 10-15% |
| **Temperature** | 1652°F / 900°C (2 hrs.) | 1652°F / 900°C 10 min.<br>1562°F / 850°C 20 min.<br>1472°F / 800°C 30 min. | 1292°F / 700°C 10 min.<br>1202°F / 650°C 20 min.<br>1112°F / 600°C 30 min. |
| **Format Block** | | blocks, fine sheets, and syringes | blocks, fine sheets, and syringes |

► The PMC is put into the kiln on an appropriate refractory support capable of withstanding the high temperatures.

► After firing, a piece may experience shrinkage exceeding 30 percent of its original size. Some pieces, especially thin ones, warp when they dry, but sometimes this is corrected in the firing. The photo shows the difference between the dry piece and the fired piece.

## Firing

Once the PMC is dry it is fired in the kiln. By subjecting it to a high temperature, vestiges of water and binder are removed, and the microparticles of metal that it contains melt.

The water and binder constitute about 30 percent of the original PMC. This implies that once the standard PMC has been fired, the piece will be reduced to 70 percent of its original size, and to 88 percent for PMC+ and PMC3. This shrinkage, which in theory could be an inconvenience, is actually an advantage when engraving or stamping, as it increases the resolution and detail in certain works.

The firing temperature varies according to the PMC used. If working with standard silver PMC, the oven is programmed to 1652°F (900°C); if working with gold, the temperature is raised to 1832°F (1000°C).

An electric kiln of the type commonly used for enamel or microfusion, plus a refractory support to hold the pieces inside the kiln, is used for firing. PMC+ and PMC3 use shorter firing times and can be fired at a different temperature by proportionally increasing the time inside the kiln. In any case, excess firing will not alter the result, but will cause the PMC to turn out weak and fragile.

## Finishing

Once the pieces are fired they have a high purity of the metal content, yielding results up to .999 percent pure. The density of the metal produced is less than that of laminated or forged metal, and slightly lower than that of metal produced by wax casting; thus it should not be used to make items that are likely to be damaged or subjected to heavy pressure, such as clasps, posts, or weak parts.

The metal produced is worked like any precious metal; it can be soldered, filed, sanded, oxidized, and polished. It can even be enameled and treated in galvanic baths.

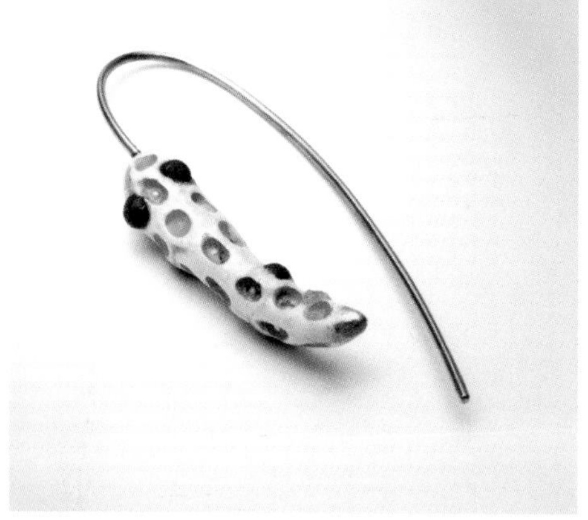

▲ Enameled PMC pendant, by Brigitte Adolph

▲ PMC and Egyptian paste ring, by Marina Gouromihou

## PMC Earrings

Earrings can be made using PMC by simply pressing the material with the fingers onto an old mold engraved in steel. After firing, the earrings will be finished properly, and the surfaces will be oxidized before mounting the design in a gold setting with glass beads.

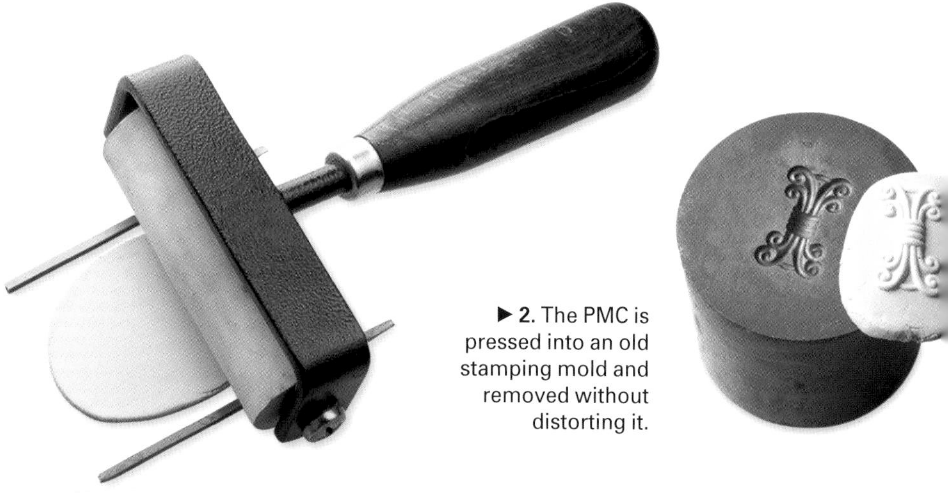

▶ **1.** Once the standard PMC reaches the ideal consistency, a thick sheet using two brass rods and a roller is rolled out. The result is a smooth, even sheet of material.

▶ **2.** The PMC is pressed into an old stamping mold and removed without distorting it.

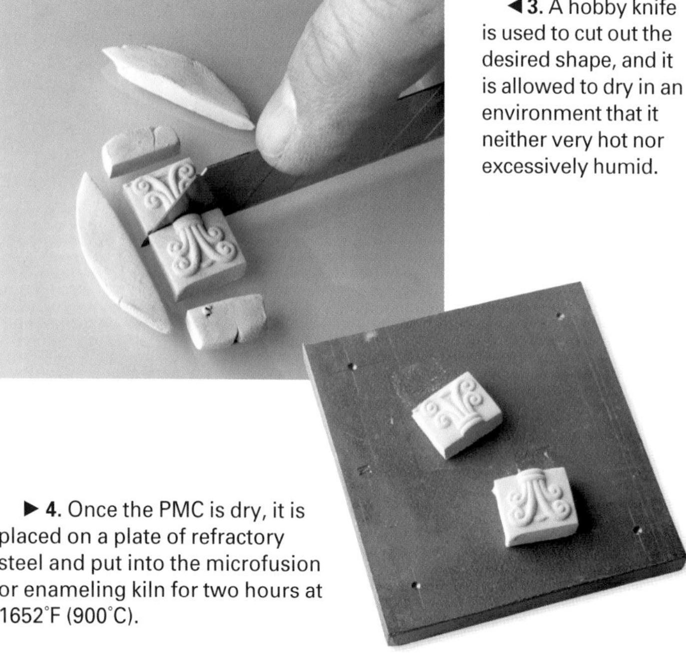

◀ **3.** A hobby knife is used to cut out the desired shape, and it is allowed to dry in an environment that it neither very hot nor excessively humid.

▶ **4.** Once the PMC is dry, it is placed on a plate of refractory steel and put into the microfusion or enameling kiln for two hours at 1652°F (900°C).

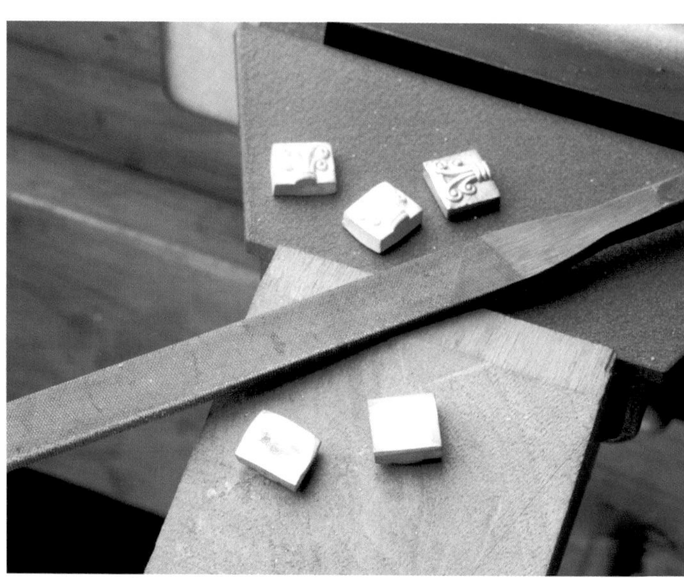

▲ **5.** After firing, the pieces are smoothed with a metal file. The shape is squared up again and the undersides of the two PMC pieces are filed smooth.

▲ 6. The surface is smoothed with sandpaper. The hard-to-get-at places are finished using various accessories for a rotary tool, or by rubbing them vigorously with a bronze brush.

▲ 7. The PMC is encased in a gold framework that turns them into earrings.

◄ 8. A set of glass beads is chosen to finish off the earrings; the artist also made the beads.

▲ 9. In dealing with fine silver, the PMC can be oxidized by immersion in silver oxide and take on the characteristic black color of oxidized silver.

► 10. PMC and gold earrings made by Carles Codina i Armengol

# Wood

This material is one of the oldest used by humans to make tools, provide fuel, and to build homes, ships, and countless other objects that have made it possible for humanity to prosper. This is true of all cultures since the dawn of civilization and, subsequently, carpentry is one of the most highly esteemed and ancient of trades.

Techniques such as veneering, marquetry, and parqueting date from time immemorial, and they were revived energetically in the 17th century by German and Flemish artisans when they used exotic woods to frame more sumptuous materials such as marble and tortoise shell. The use of precious and exotic woods, plus the use of new production techniques, extended throughout Europe, especially in France and Great Britain, where they were used particularly in the construction of luxurious furnishings throughout the 18th century.

▲ Softwoods tend to be resinous, while hardwoods are stronger, with a long and regular grain; they are appropriate choices for projects like the one presented here. The wood must be very dry before working with it. For that reason—and to avoid splitting and rot as well—both logs and planks must to be kept in a dry environment and protected from air currents, abrupt temperature changes, and wood-eating insects.

▲ Different types of hardwood such as boxwood, rosewood, olive, African padoek, ebony, and others can be used to make jewelry. Give thought to the color and the quality of the wood before selecting it.

► Necklace made of ebony, by Hanna Vanneste, 2003

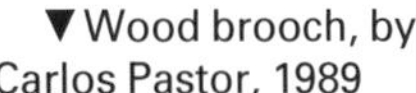

▼Wood brooch, by Carlos Pastor, 1989

► Different sheets of wood in formats that are easy to obtain from a carpenter or from specialty shops such as a supply house for musical instrument makers.

## The Characteristics of Wood

If in addition to the physical properties of wood—such as its rigidity and durability—its natural beauty, variety of colors, and textures it offers are factored in, it becomes a very appropriate material with which to design floors, furniture, and decorative objects.

There are many types of wood that can be used to make a very wide variety of items; however, for parqueting projects like the ones shown in this chapter, it's best to choose strong woods in contrasting colors.

The greater the density of a wood, the stronger and stiffer it generally is. Its strength also depends on how dry it is and the direction in which it was cut with respect to the grain. It is important to select wood that has been dried properly, since dry wood lasts longer than green, is lighter in weight, and undergoes no changes that may damage the work.

Wood is classified as hard or soft based on its origin. In general, wood that comes from deciduous trees is referred to as hardwood and wood from conifers is soft, regardless of its true hardness. The hardwoods which traditionally are used in quality cabinetmaking, have a long, fine, continuous grain, which produces a tighter, smooth texture that facilitates a satiny and shiny polish. Soft woods tend to be more porous, don't produce as fine a finish, and tend to splinter when being worked.

◀ Wood can be protected and attractively finished using waxes and varnishes.

▼ Various waxes and oils, bleaches, natural or synthetic lacquers, sealers, tints for wood, varnishes and other products improve and complete the cabinet maker's work. Among the most traditional finishes is gum lacquer. Although applying it in successive layers with a swab is tedious, it produces superlative results on medium and large projects.

## Working with Wood

Cabinet makers are accustomed to working with high quality woods. This is a trade that focuses mainly on making furniture using very diverse techniques such as joinery and parqueting, among others. A self-respecting cabinet maker must have a thorough knowledge of the qualities and characteristics of each type of wood.

It is necessary to observe the structure of the wood before beginning to cut or drill it. Because of its structure, wood has a series of growth rings. When a log is cut crosswise, these rings can be seen arranged around the center, although in some cases they may appear to be coiled around it. To keep the wood from losing strength, it must always be cut along the grain, avoiding knots, although for small-format projects these warnings can be ignored.

The knots found in wood are small areas of the log where the base of a branch was formed during the tree's growth. The knots are interruptions in the wood grain that create unique qualities and patterns. Some cabinet makers seek out woods with a high concentration of knots.

After cutting, wood must be smoothed by using a range of sandpaper grits—from coarse to fine—and then rubbing with steel wool to remove any scratches or surface lines. Finally, it must be treated with various products designed to improve its characteristics, protect it from attack by wood-eating insects or other organisms, and highlight its beauty by smoothing out possible imperfections.

▼ Other glues used in medium and small projects are the two-part epoxies, instant glues made from cyanoacrylate, and heat-sensitive silicones.

▶ White carpenter's glue is commonly used for gluing wood. It is spread out evenly using a brush or applicator, and the surfaces to be joined are allowed to dry under pressure for a couple of hours.

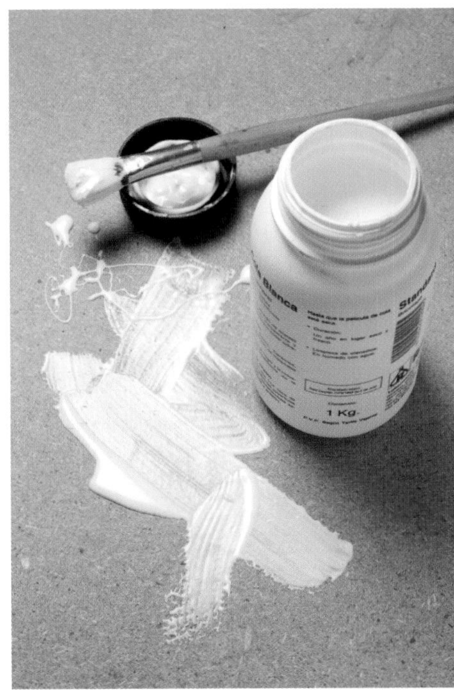

## Wooden Bracelets by Carlos Pastor

The technique presented here is based on parqueting as practiced by the finest cabinet makers, and which formerly was used to make many items, especially floors, but also furniture and decorative objects. One characteristic of parqueting is the repetition of the same design using a series of long pieces that are arranged in a pattern alternating from one side to the other, and are then cut crosswise or on a diagonal once they have been joined properly. That way a board structure is produced that has an alternating pattern of different types and colors of wood. Carlos Pastor uses this technique in many of his pieces, and in this section he adapts it to a personal series of bracelets.

There are many kinds of woods of different densities and hardness that can be used in jewelry making projects, such as mahogany, a dense, strong tropical wood; walnut, which is frequently used for tools and furniture because of its hardness and strength; and oak, likewise a very durable and strong wood. In the following project, Carlos Pastor has chosen elm and rosewood to use in making several bracelets.

**Elm** *(Ulmus sp.)*: This tree is very widespread in the northern hemisphere, and there are several varieties. Its wood displays a pronounced design because of the growth rings; the texture is coarse, and the grain is irregular. It is light brown, sometimes reddish in color. This wood dries quickly, is easy to work, and very strong, especially when submerged in water. Formerly it was used for structural elements that were to be submerged in water, such as fishing boats and barges, and in the construction of piers. Today this wood is used for making furniture and parqueted floors, as well as bowling pins and butchers blocks because of its resistance to splitting.

**Rosewood** *(Dalbergia sp.)*: This is a small tree that currently comes from India and Brazil. The heartwood of the trunk is a dark, reddish brown with a very noticeable grain. It is used for making furniture, knife handles, and parts of musical instruments, as well as high-quality veneers.para realizar diversas pulseras.

▲ Several sections of wood before being cut with an electric saw. These woods are also available in board form, which makes them easier to cut.

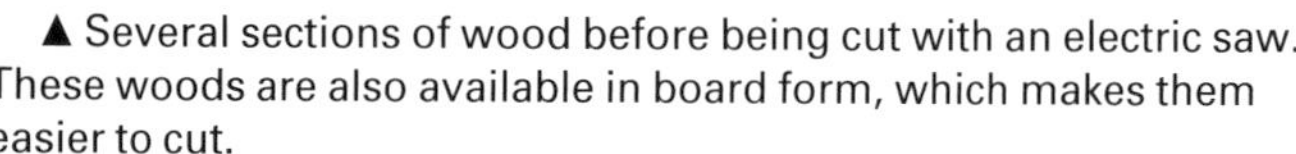

◀ For this exercise, Carlos Pastor has chosen two highly contrasting sheets of elm and rosewood each ½ inch (1.3 cm) thick. He has avoided knots as much as possible and tried to find surfaces and strongly contrasting colors with a regular and uniform grain.

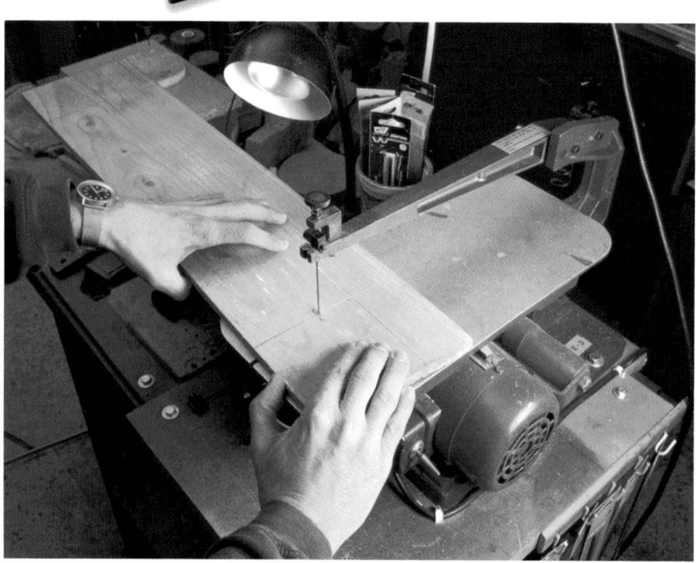

▲ **1.** Using an electric jigsaw, two 4-inch squares are cut out from each of the selected woods.

▲ **2.** Once they are cut out, they are squared up using coarse sandpaper. Two square templates are also made from paper, on which the desired cutouts are drawn.

▲ **3.** The two pieces of wood are joined together using masking tape in such a way that the wood grain follows the same direction; that way they will be easy to separate.

▲ **5.** Block A is cut on the electric jigsaw, following the wavy lines of the original design.

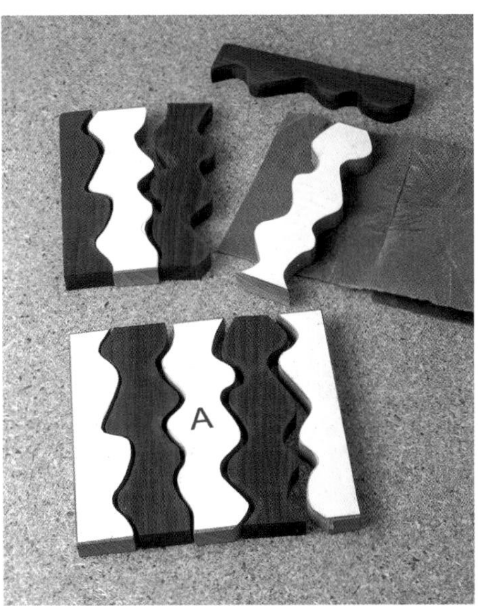

▲ **6.** When the cutting is done, the two blocks are separated and the edges of the different cuts are gone over and smoothed so that the pieces fit together perfectly. Then the wavy strips are fitted together in alternating colors; since they were cut at the same time, they should fit perfectly.

▲ **4.** The first pattern ("A") is attached to the top of the block of wood using white glue. The pattern serves as a guide for cutting a series of wavy strips that will constitute the design of the piece.

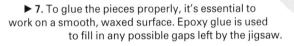

► **7.** To glue the pieces properly, it's essential to work on a smooth, waxed surface. Epoxy glue is used to fill in any possible gaps left by the jigsaw.

▲ **8.** All the pieces are coated with glue and fitted together, pressing them forcefully into place with a small strip of wood. Wear gloves to prevent glue from getting on your skin.

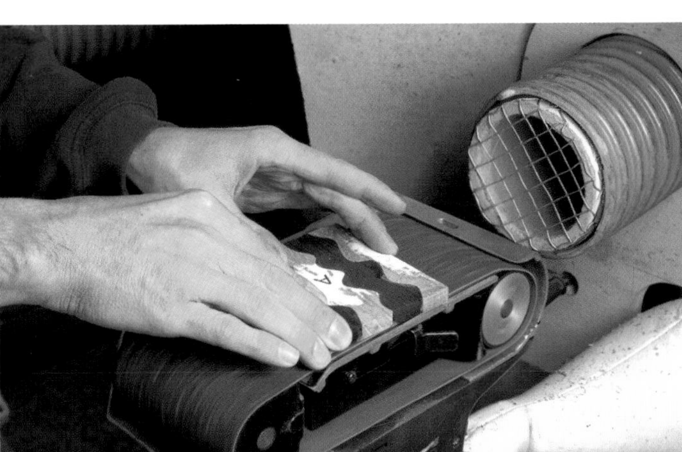

▲ **9.** Once the glue is thoroughly dry, the plates are sanded and squared up on an electric sander. Using the right tools greatly reduces the time required for many steps; it's preferable to use a belt sander rather than a radial one, as shown here.

◄ **10.** The two new sheets are once again taped together with masking tape, and the second design ("B") is glued crosswise on the top.

▲ **11.** Next, the jigsaw is used to cut out the shape indicated on the new pattern, this time in a crosswise direction.

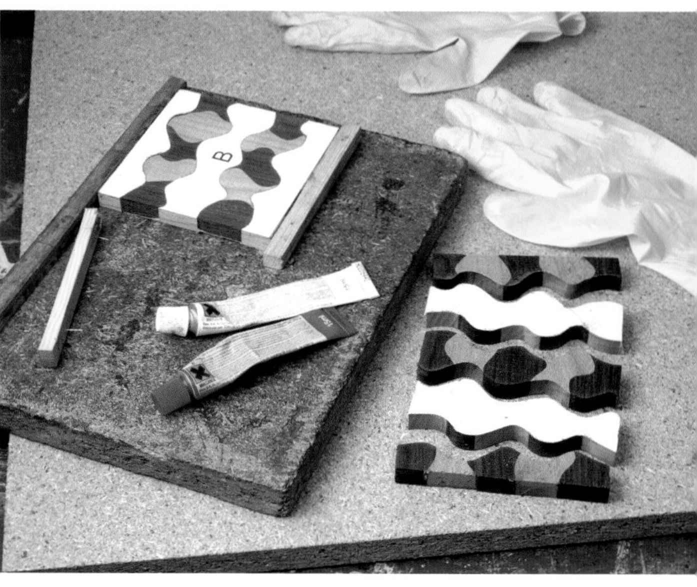

▲ **12.** Once again, the two strips of alternating colors are fitted together, and the two shapes are glued together by clamping them firmly.

▼ **13.** Once the glue is dry, the assembled block is smoothed on the electric sander just as before.

◀ **14.** Here is the result of the two sheets ready to be worked. This technique can be used to create a multitude of effects by varying the number of types of wood used, their arrangement in planes, and the shape and type of cut.

▶ **15.** Now, the inner and outer shapes of the bracelet are marked off. For that purpose it's a good idea to make a template in advance from methacrylate or stiff plastic.

▲ **16.** In order to use as much of the laminate as possible, it is marked in different shapes that later will be used for several pieces.

▲ **17.** First, a strip is cut from the outer perimeter. Then a hole is drilled and all the pieces are cut out from the interior of the sheet.

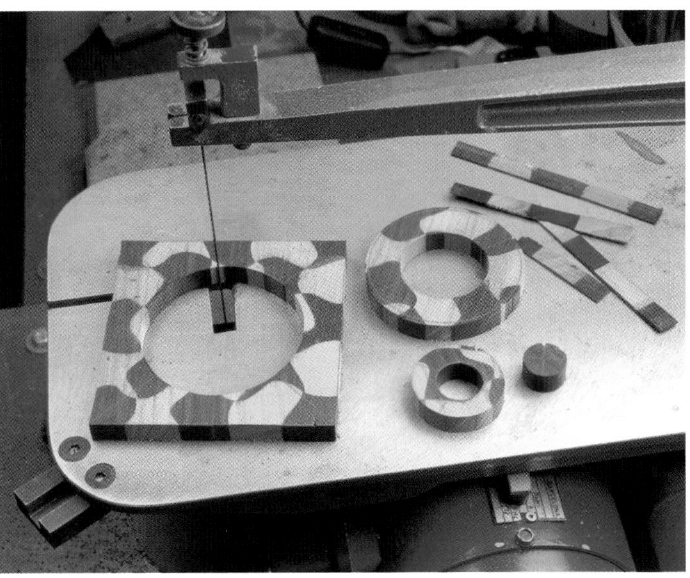

▲ **18.** The thickness of the saw blade used in the cut must correspond to the thickness of the wood to insure a precise cut.

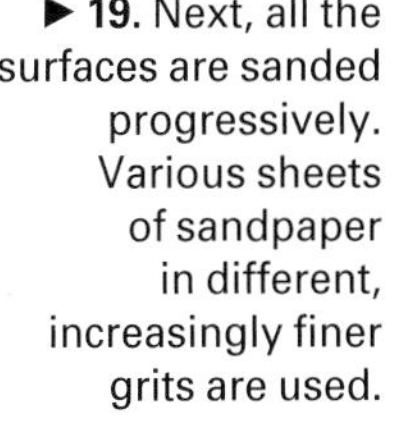

► **19.** Next, all the surfaces are sanded progressively. Various sheets of sandpaper in different, increasingly finer grits are used.

▲ **20.** All the flat parts, including the outline, are smoothed using progressively finer sandpaper down to a wet paper grit of about 400.

▲ **21.** Once the inside is cut out, the edges and the entire surface are sanded using various pieces of sandpaper in increasingly fine grits.

► **22.** Here are the results from the inside. The cutouts can be used for making various pieces such as pendants and rings.

▶ **23.** After using the last piece of fine wet paper, the various faces of the piece are polished and shined using a buffing wheel and a piece of felt or sheepskin, plus a polishing paste specifically for wood.

▼ **24.** The finished piece by Carlos Pastor

◀▲ Bracelets made by Carlos Pastor

## Ivory Palm Seeds

The ivory palm is a member of the Palmacea family, which grows in much of Colombia, Ecuador, Peru, and Venezuela. It is shaped like a palm tree and can grow to a height of 18 to 27 feet (6 to 9 m). The fruits contain numerous seeds or nuts which, when ripened, are gathered and dried for four to eight weeks. The seeds become very hard and take on a consistency similar to that of ivory; thus they are referred to as plant ivory, although chemically they are pure cellulose. The seeds come in a wide variety of sizes, although the usual size is slightly larger than a walnut; colors vary between bluish white and toasted ivory.

Plant ivory is nothing new; it has been used by ivory carvers for more than 200 years to make such things as parts of games, dice, buttons, handles for walking sticks, and pipes. It was once a very commonly used material, but when synthetic fibers came onto the market, plant ivory nearly vanished from sight. However, because of the prohibition of commerce in ivory due to the endangered status of elephants and other animals, the market in plant ivory has recovered. In some South American countries there is even a growing craft industry based on the nut from the ivory palm.

▲ The ivory palm nut was first named by the Indians who live on the banks of the Magdalena River in Colombia. There are different names in Spanish for the nut on the coast and in Peru. This palm generally grows in moist areas of the coastal region, but it also grows in areas near the Andes.

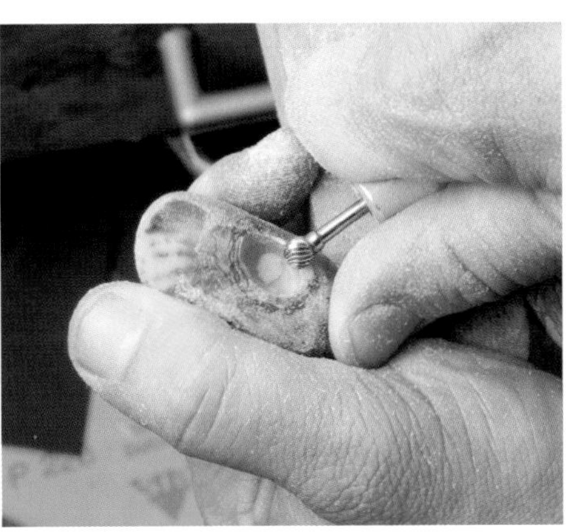

▲ Plant ivory is hard, has a cellular structure, a hollow center, and a grain similar to that of elephant ivory, although it is slightly softer in consistency. It is easily worked using cutting tools and a small rotary tool.

► Many natural seeds and fruits are suitable for working. These containers were made by Nicolás Estrada from two seeds; they are used as cases for his pieces.

▲ The *Secret of Tapunami*, 2003. A delightful piece made from an ivory palm nut. A tiny LED (luminescent diode) gives it a luminous transparency. The light emitted through the top is reflected by a small silver reflector. Work by Nicolás Estrada

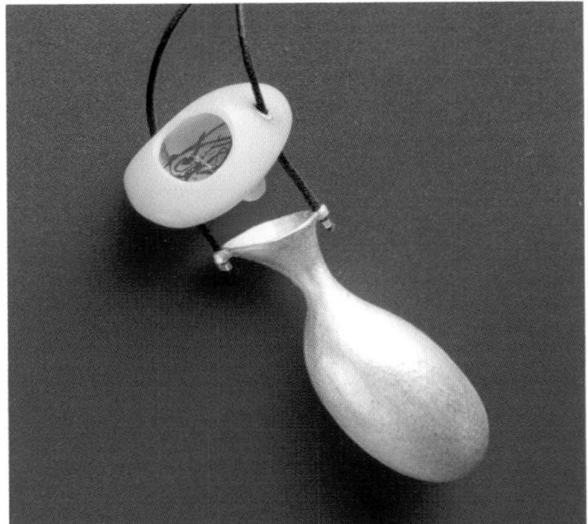

◄ *Path*, 2003. In addition to an ivory palm nut, this piece was made from repoussé silver and saffron, by Walter Chen.

► *Lost City*, 2003. Pendant made from an ivory palm seed with interior lighting. It was made using small LEDs to create a subtle inner light to this ivory palm nut. Work by Nicolás Estrada

▼ *Ferment*, 2003. Pendant made from ivory palm nut, repoussé silver, gold, and meteorite; by Walter Chen

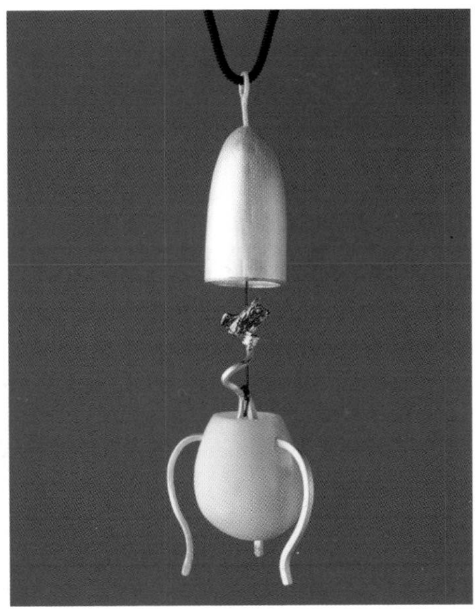

# Glass Beads, by Susana Aparicio Ortiz

In this section you will learn how to make glass beads on a small scale. At the hands of Susana Aparicio Ortiz, you will become familiar with the history of beads and learn an ancient glass technique for making them.

## Glass and Other Beads

Since the coming together of humankind to form the first social societies, people have felt the need to display their rank and position toward each other. They have done so with necklaces, bracelets, earrings, and crowns. The small beads used in these jewelry pieces were made from various materials that were selected not only for their magical and symbolic attributions, but also as a clear sign of social identification. They also made an excellent currency for exchange.

Beads were used in the Paleolithic Age as amulets. Depending on the material from which they were made, they were assumed to have magical characteristics. Such use has remained in vogue through the ages; and in many traditional societies today, beads serve as both objects of interchange as well as a clear sign of distinction.

▲ Beads are made from many types of materials, including ivory, wood, coral, precious gems, ceramic, mollusk shells, and seeds. Many people continue to make glass beads using primitive techniques, and in some places the beads are a medium of exchange. The photo shows a necklace made of ivory teeth from the Fiji Islands.

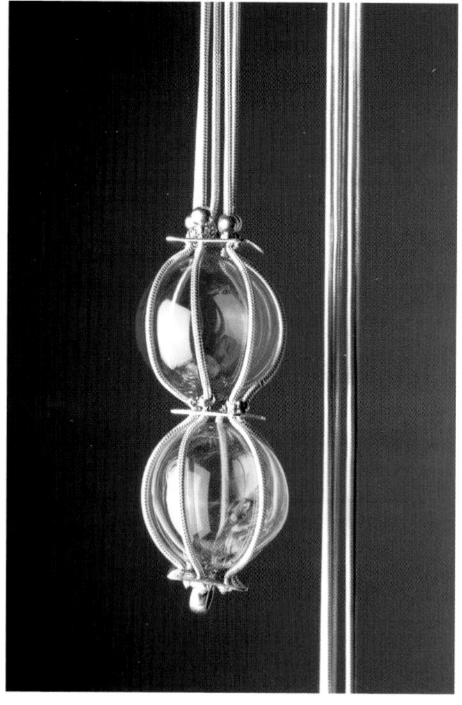

▲ *The Birdcage,* 2003. Blown glass beads by Susana Aparicio Ortiz

▲ *Fruit,* 2003. Glass bead made using the Murano technique by Susana Aparicio Ortiz

## The Origins of Glass Beads

Glass beads are most likely the first objects humans made from glass, as evidenced by numerous archeological relics found from a great number of cultures. Based on pieces made in Egypt that are covered with thin layers of glaze, it is known that sodium-ceramic glass was made as early as 900 B.C. It is difficult to determine precisely when the production of glass objects began, but small objects made of vitreous paste, dating from 700 B.C., have likewise been found in Egypt.

It is believed that glass beads were introduced to Egypt by Asian artisans. The first industries to produce glass beads were established in Syria and Mesopotamia around 4000 B.C.; later production increased to extend throughout the Mediterranean basin, and some noteworthy pieces from the pre-Roman times have been found in Etruscan and Phoenician sites.

Beginning in 900 B.C., when the Hellenistic Age was in full swing, the most important production center for manufactured glass was established in Egypt. In the first century B.C., blown glass was discovered along the Phoenician coast. Later on, during the Roman period, this valued material experienced a great expansion and diffusion.

Still later, between the 17th and 18th centuries, Venice distinguished itself through its enormous production of high quality, handmade beads of different shapes and effects; the spread of glass across several continents was the result of fruitful Venetian commerce. Today, bead production is widespread, most notably in China, the United States, Mexico, Italy, and the Czech Republic, specifically in the area of Bohemia.

► A necklace made from vitreous paste from Ibiza, fifth to fourth centuries B.C. National Archeological Museum, Madrid

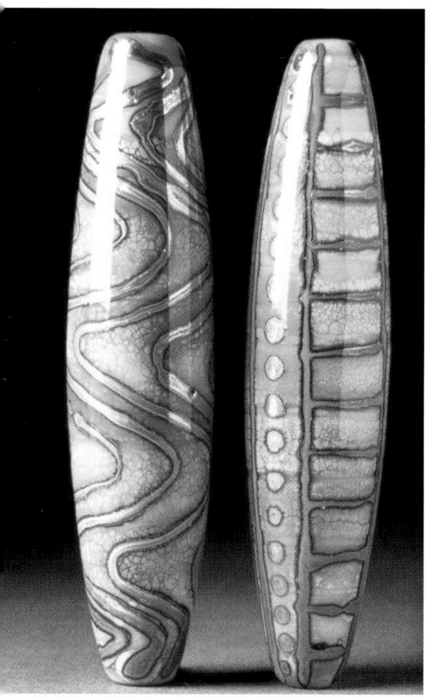

▲ Glass bead made using the *twister* technique by Frédéric Marey, 2002

► Glass bead 1.75 inches x 1.6 inches (45 x 42 mm) by Kristina Logan. Photo by Paul Avis

◄ Glass bead made by Kristina Logan. Photo by Paul Avis

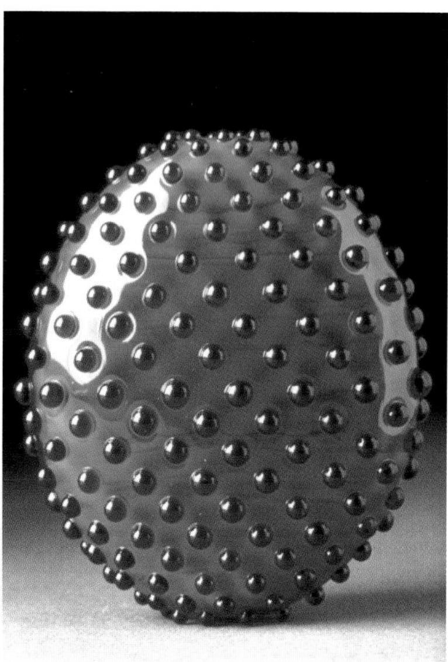

## Glass and its Composition

Glass is a material that is found in nature. It may be volcanic in origin, such as the esteemed obsidian; meteoric, such as tektites; or environmental, such as the fulgurites that are formed when sand melts as the result of a lightning strike.

Humans have succeeded in imitating nature by creating a way to make glass. Glass is made by subjecting pure silica mixed with oxides, salts, and fluxes to a fusion process at a temperature that varies between 2192° and 2552°F (1200° and 1400°C). Depending on the materials with which it is melted, glass takes on certain colors and shades and acquires specific physical properties. These shades of color result from its fusion with different proportions of the raw materials that make it up, such as lead, calcium carbonate, magnesium, and sodium or potassium carbonate. One common composition is made up of kaolin and some fluxes such as borax, to which various salts and oxides are added to give it color.

Glass does not conduct electricity, and it is also a poor heat conductor. It is very rigid in its cold state, but can be cut using interesting techniques that make it possible to create delicate artistic objects. In its melted state, glass takes on other physical properties that make it a material that's easy to mold, and can be used to make countless shapes, such as the necklace beads shown in this chapter, which were made by Susana Aparicio Ortiz.

Making glass beads begins with different round glass rods in diameters between about 7/64 and 5/16 inch (3 and 8 mm). These rods are made primarily from silica and boron (borosilicate glass), or else from sodium and calcium (sodium-calcium glass). This composition allows working the rod in the flame for a long time; once the bead is annealed—that is, heated and then cooled—it becomes very hard, turning into a strong, durable material.

▲ Beads can be made in an infinite variety of shapes and colors. Generally, they are strung to form necklaces or bracelets, but they can also be sewn to clothing or be kept in a collection. Necklace made by Andrea Borst, 2001

# Temperature and the Coefficient of Expansion of Glass

Before tackling a project involving glass, it's important to take a detailed look at its melting temperature and its coefficient of expansion. There are some glasses that melt at low temperatures, around 932°F (500°C), and others that melt at much higher temperatures, around 2192°F (1200°C). Most begin to melt around 1112°F (600° C), at which point the glass begins to lose its initial structure. The glass changes from a solid state to a malleable one, then begins to look like thick honey, then solidifies once again after being manipulated and allowed to cool down.

During this melting process, expansion occurs. Then, during cooling, there is a contraction of the material. This process is governed by a value known as the coefficient of expansion or COE. Depending on this coefficient, if two types of glass with different coefficients of expansion are mixed together, they will contract at different rates during the cooling process; this sets up tensions that cause the piece to break once the cooling process is over.

So, it is extremely important that the types of glass used in making a bead possess the same coefficient of expansion; that way, they can be mixed in a melting process with no danger to the piece.

There are many manufacturers of glass rods that produce beads with different physical properties. The project shown here utilizes Moretti glass, for which the working temperature is around 1733°F (945°C), and which has a coefficient of expansion of 104.

► Glass that is annealed improperly or mixed with a type of glass with a different coefficient of expansion breaks as a result of the longitudinal tensions that originate on its surface from a simple scratch or pressure, or even a minor thermal shock.

◄ Glass rods for making glass jewelry were created in the 15th century in Murano and are still made there today. Moretti rods, produced by Vicenzo Moretti in the 19th century, are the most commonly used throughout the world today.

▲ It's possible to produce many colors and shades of glass. This bracelet, made by Maria Albertina Abbate Garcia, is a standout because of the color quality of the glass and the uniformity of the beads.

## Work Space and Positioning

Making glass beads requires a minimum of equipment and a few precautions. The beads are made directly in a heat source with a working temperature of 2192°F (1200°C) by continually holding the bead on the end of a long stainless-steel rod or mandrel. The process requires holding the same work position and looking at the flame for an extended period of time. So, it's essential to use goggles with special protective filters, since when glass is worked hot the output of infrared and ultraviolet rays can cause serious eye damage.

It is also important to place the tools and the glass in positions where they can be reached quickly. The heat source has to be in a position that makes it as easy as possible to work on the bead. Similarly, the arrangement of the body and the arms must facilitate working comfortably and allow for a steady hand while rotating the bead.

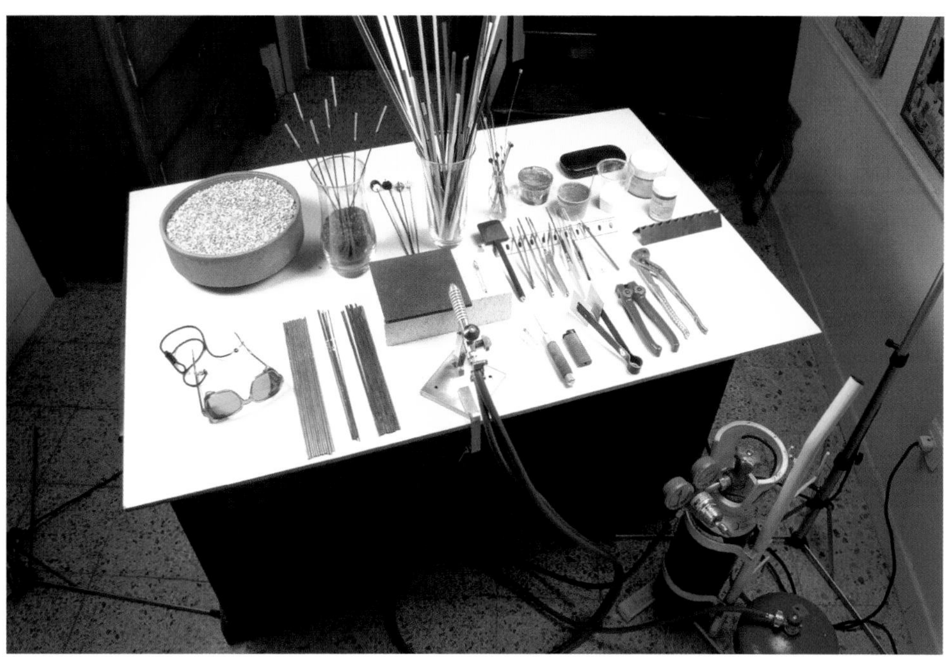

▲ Arrangement of tools and materials: Glass as a material and the process carried out require a space that's free of dust and of all materials that could stick to the melted glass and cause imperfections and tensions that would spoil the final result.

## How to Cut a Rod

One of the first steps to learn is how to cut a glass rod. This is often done to make it easier to manipulate the beads while working on them, since the rod is applied melted at the end onto the bead, which is likewise melted and supported on the mandrel.

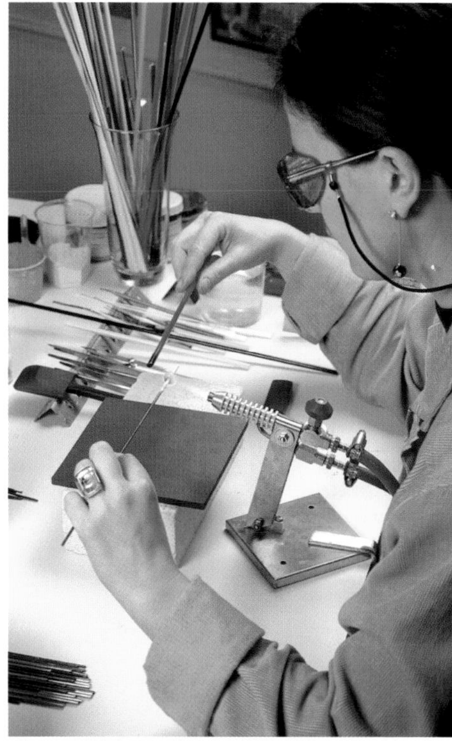

► During the bead making process, one hand keeps the mandrel in constant rotation while the other applies the melted end of the glass rod to the mandrel. Note, too, that protective goggles must be worn.

▲ There are many different types of glass rods.

▼ Rod cutters facilitate making a sure, precise cut in the rod. This tool is equipped with two diamond discs that etch a fine line around the rod at a point where it subsequently is snapped off.

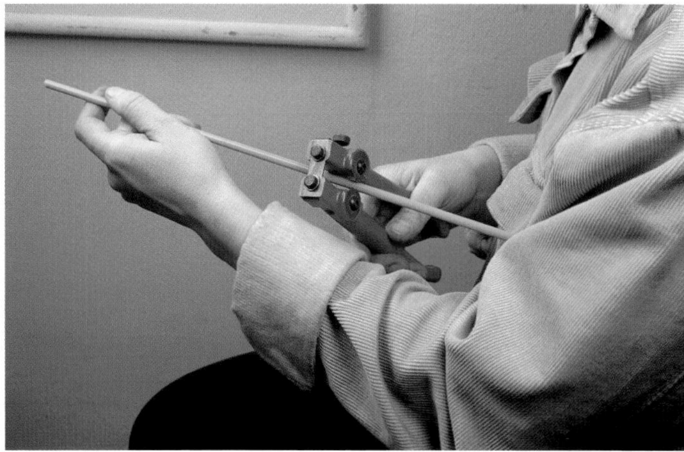

► It's essential to grasp the rod in such a way that it snaps at the point previously scored, without producing undesirable cuts. Rotate the rod cutter around the rod, then snap off at the desired point.

## Tools

Beads are made by melting glass rods, so it's essential to use a torch or burner that mixes propane or butane with oxygen, as that will provide the best pressure and heat source for this work. The appropriate maximum temperature is about 2192°F (1200°C). This torch has numerous gas outlets, which is essential for working with glass, and makes it possible to regulate the pressure precisely to reach the right temperature for making any kind of glass bead without burning the colors.

Since the melted glass can't be applied directly onto the steel rod, as it would stick to the rod, it is necessary to apply a mixture to the mandrel that will allow for easy removal of the bead once it cools. This mixture is known as releasing agent. It is made of 40 percent kaolin and 60 percent aluminum oxide. When mixed with water; these components produce a creamy texture. Once the releasing agent is ready, it is applied to the end of the mandrel; one mandrel is prepared for each bead to be made.

It's essential to have an appropriate work surface or slab for working and shaping the bead. The slab must be flat and made of a nonflammable material such as stainless steel, iron, or graphite. Graphite is preferable because it is rustproof, absorbs almost no heat, and prevents thermal shocks that could break the beads when they come into contact with it.

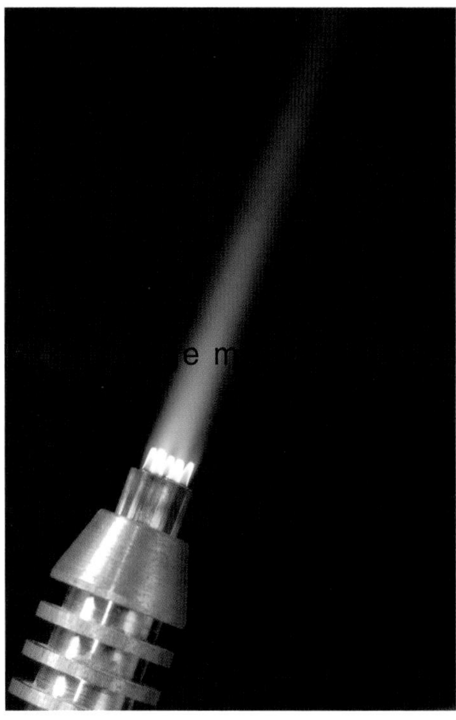

▲ Once the flame is lit, it is backed off by reducing the oxygen pressure so that the gas and oxygen mixture comes out uniformly and smoothly.

▲ A fine layer of releasing agent is applied to the end of the mandrel on which the bead is to be made. Such products are available at craft supply stores.

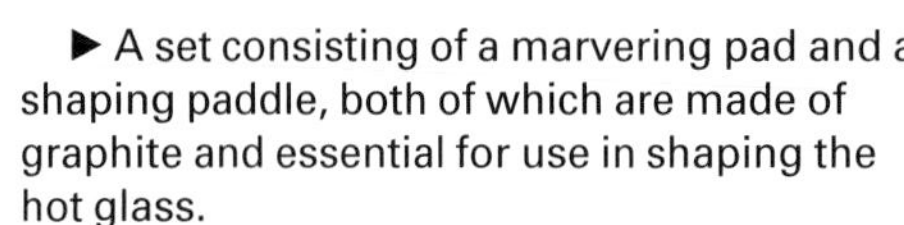

► A set consisting of a marvering pad and a shaping paddle, both of which are made of graphite and essential for use in shaping the hot glass.

◄ When working with melted glass and an oxy-propane torch, it's absolutely necessary to use protective goggles containing didymium, a material that filters out and neutralizes ultraviolet and infrared rays.

▲ A punch can be used to create many of the effects applied to beads. Punches are made of various materials, but steel is the best choice.

► This steel tweezer is used to squash a bead that starts out round.

## Making Stringers from a Glass Rod

The most common diameter of glass rod is about 3⁄16 to 1⁄4 inch (5 to 6 mm), which may be too thick when it comes to applying color to the inside or the surface of a bead. The first step thus involves stretching rods to produce fine glass threads.

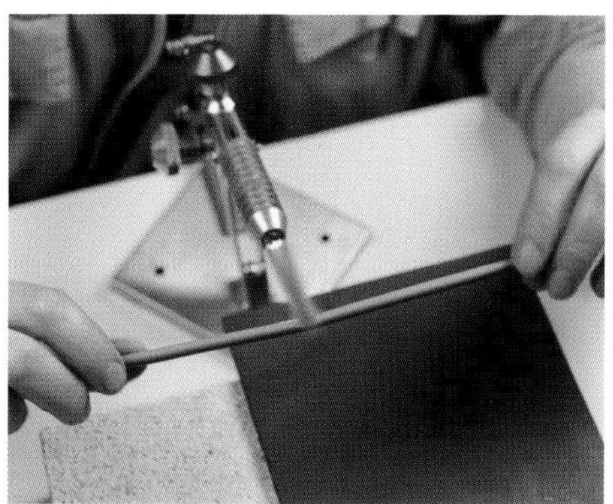

▲ **1.** A rod is heated in the center while being constantly rotated.

▲ **2.** As the glass begins to melt, the rod is kept in constant rotation in the flame; the melted part is pressed inward from both ends, which causes the melted part to swell and form a ball.

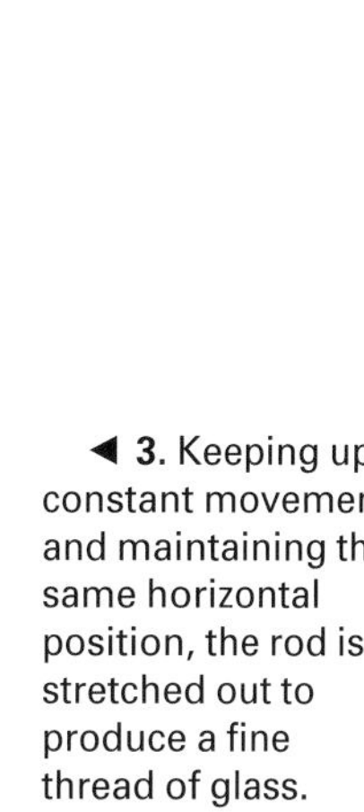

◀ **3.** Keeping up constant movement and maintaining the same horizontal position, the rod is stretched out to produce a fine thread of glass.

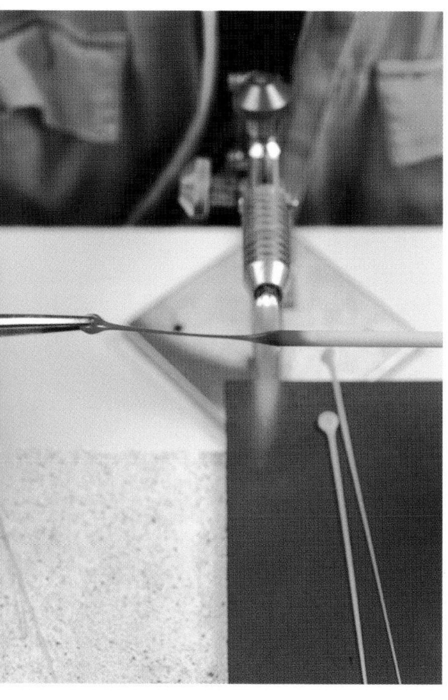

▲ **4.** Another way of producing even finer stringers involves melting the end of a rod, pinching this area with steel tweezers, and quickly pulling the end outward.

▲ **5.** Once the stringer is stretched, it is cut off by once again applying pinpoint heat at the end.

▲ **6.** Various colored stringers of different diameters ready for use.

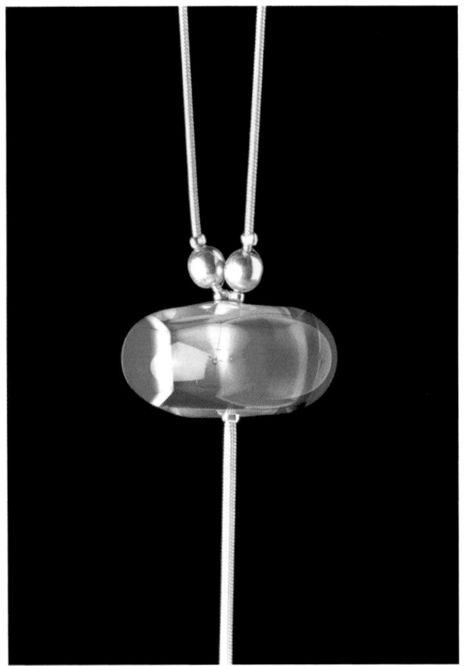

▲ A piece made in layers by Susana Aparicio Ortiz, 2001

▲ Various effects created in glass by the combing technique. Beads made by Susana Aparicio Ortiz, 2002

▲ Bead made by applying threads and working in layers, by Susana Aparicio Ortiz, 2001

## Making Your First Bead

Now that the various components used in making a bead and material and tool preparations have been explained, it's time to tackle making a simple bead. In this instance, Susana Aparicio Ortiz shows how to do it by emphasizing several essential aspects of bead making, including applying the glass to make the initial pearl, the addition of new colors, handling the bead, and the cooling or annealing process, without which the final product could be spoiled.

▲ Beads made by applying rods and then mashing with squashing pliers; work by Susana Aparicio Ortiz

## The Process

When glass melts, it tends, like metal, to occupy the smallest structural space in a regular spherical shape. This property makes it possible to form beads by applying the melted glass onto steel mandrels in continual rotation around their axis.

To begin, the end of the glass rod is heated, then applied to the mandrel previously tempered in the same flame, keeping the glass rod and the mandrel in alignment so their temperatures can be maintained and regulated.

In applying the melted glass to the mandrel and supporting the rod in different ways, it's essential to keep the hands in the proper position. First, the end of the glass rod is heated evenly; the hand that holds the rod must keep it in constant rotation away from the body, and the fingers have to keep up a constant motion of centrifugal rotation.

Once the end of the rod is melted and has formed a little ball, the glass is applied to the mandrel. This involves a change in how the rod is supported. Now the hand holds it as if it was an artist's brush, and it is brought up to the mandrel at a right angle. That way, the mandrel, which is kept in constant rotation, can pick up the melted glass on the end c the rod. While this operation is carried ou the rod remains motionless on the mandrel.

▲ **1.** Slowly, and using a circular motion, he steel rod coated with releasing agent s heated until it turns a light color. This procedure is essential in eliminating moisture, which could cause the releasing agent to ome off, or produce bubbles or tensions n the glass bead. The glass rod to be used is eld behind and lined up with the heat of the ame. It must be annealed slowly.

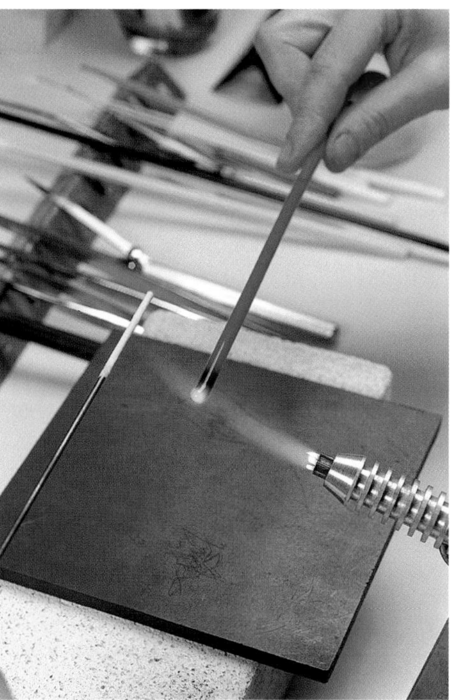

▲ **2.** Now the glass is positioned in front of the flame so that the end begins to melt. When it's subjected to high heat, glass, like metal, tends to take on the most compact structural shape, which is a sphere. With constant centrifugal rotation and the proper temperature control, it's possible to maintain and enlarge this sphere.

▲ **3.** The instant at which the glass is transferred to the rod is extremely important. Now the mandrel and the rod are kept in constant rotation and at the proper temperature. Note the change in the position of the hand that holds the rod once the sphere has formed, just before transferring it to the mandrel.

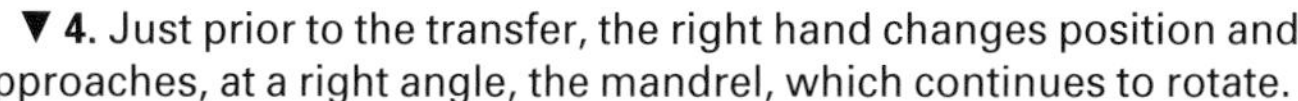

▼ **4.** Just prior to the transfer, the right hand changes position and pproaches, at a right angle, the mandrel, which continues to rotate.

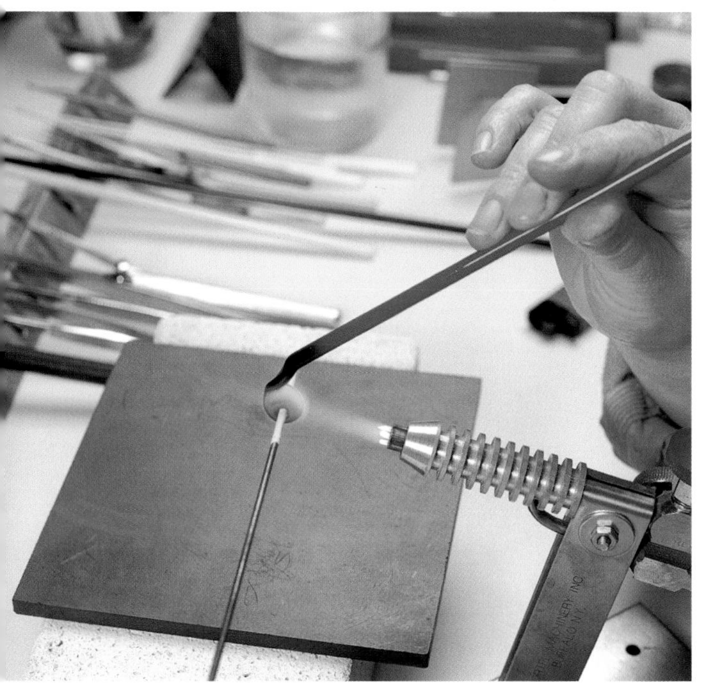

▲ **5.** Once the bead has taken on a spherical shape, and while it is still glowing, this is the time to give it shape by lengthening it, distorting it, or applying color with one of the techniques that will be explained in a later chapter.

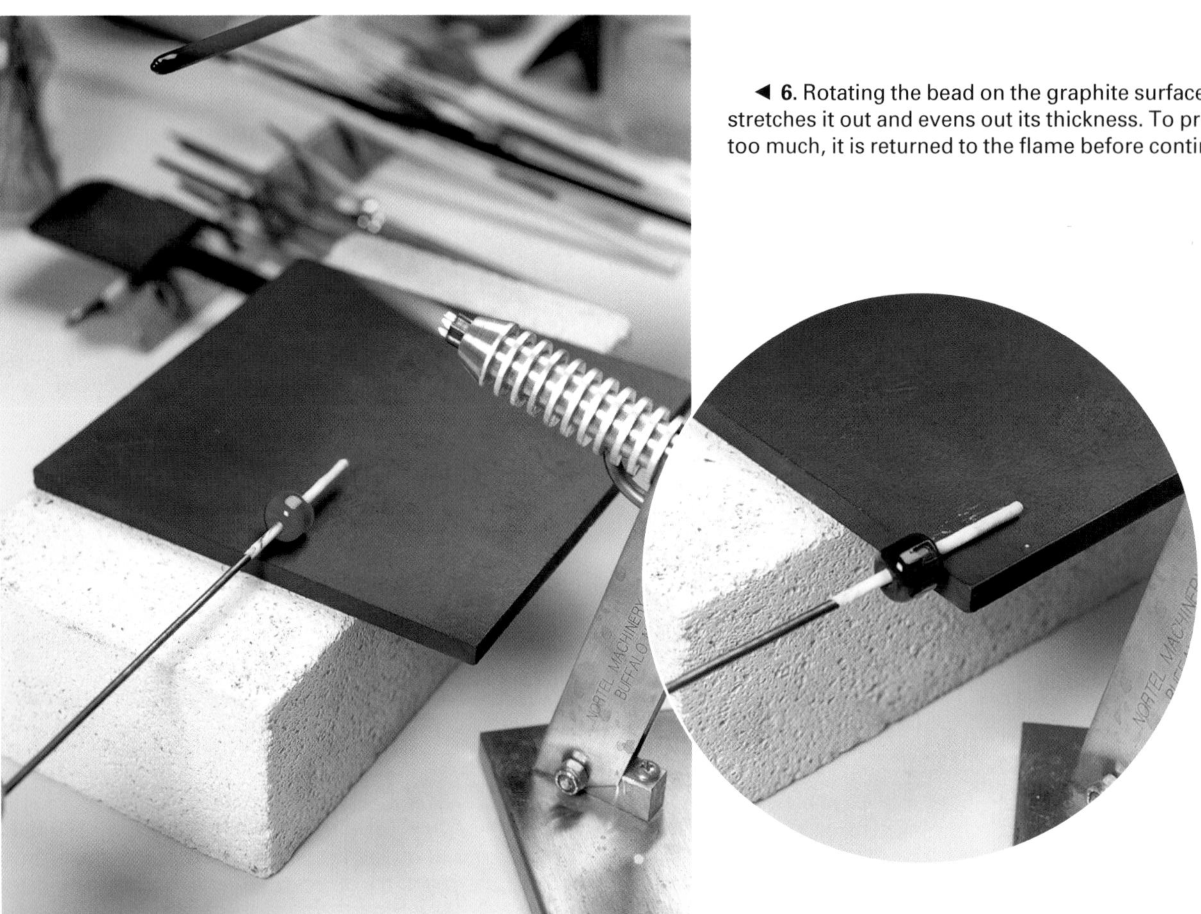

◀ **6.** Rotating the bead on the graphite surface of the marvering pad stretches it out and evens out its thickness. To prevent it from cooling too much, it is returned to the flame before continuing to shape it.

◀ **7.** The edges of the marvering pad can be used to square up the end of the bead.

▼ **8.** The graphite shaping paddle makes it possible to work the details with greater precision; this tool is ideal for flattening and shaping.

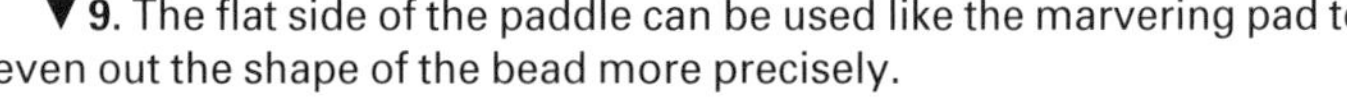

▼ **9.** The flat side of the paddle can be used like the marvering pad to even out the shape of the bead more precisely.

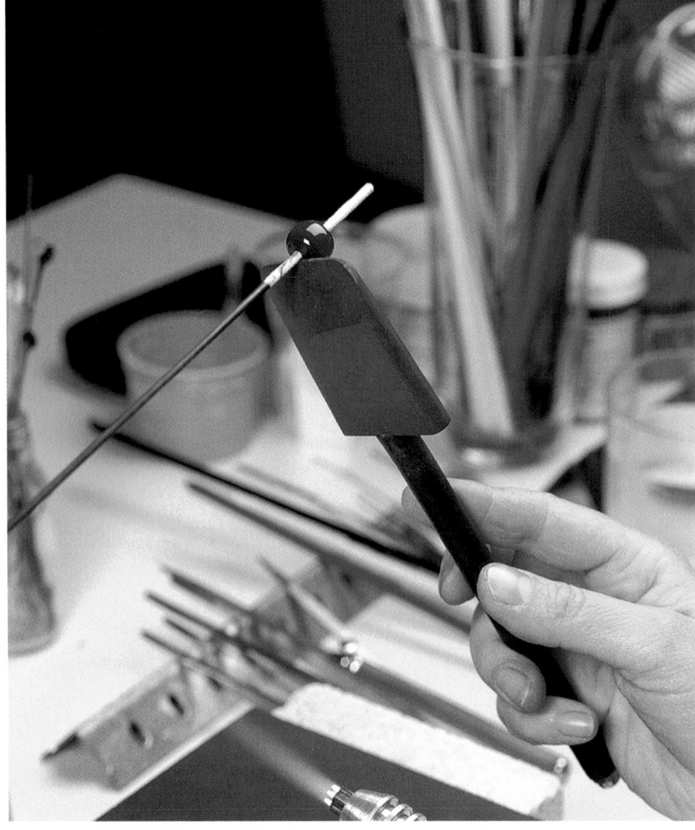

## Cooling or Annealing

Once the bead or glass object has been shaped, it must be protected from sudden cooling. An annealing phase reduces the tensions that can arise during cooling. Beads are annealed in an electric annealing kiln at a temperature range of between 878° and 950°F (470°-510°C) for about two hours, depending on the type of glass used. After that time, the bead is allowed to cool in the closed kiln until it reaches room temperature.

The annealing oven is used only when very complex or highly decorated beads have been exposed to the fire for a long time, or when large beads are created. Small beads don't require annealing; instead, they simply need to be placed in a container of vermiculite, a non-flammable heat insulator , and allowed to cool down slowly.

◀ **1.** A kiln capable of reaching a stabilizing temperature of 950°F (510°C) is adequate to assure proper cooling for any beads that may require it because of their size or complexity.

▲ **3.** Finally, the bead is put into water to dissolve the releasing agent stuck to it so it can be released from the mandrel.

▲ **4.** The end of the mandrel is held tightly, and the bead is removed from it. Simply give the bead a couple of twists while keeping the mandrel from turning.

▲ **2.** Once the bead is done, it is put into a container of vermiculite for a period of at least two hours, until it has completely cooled.

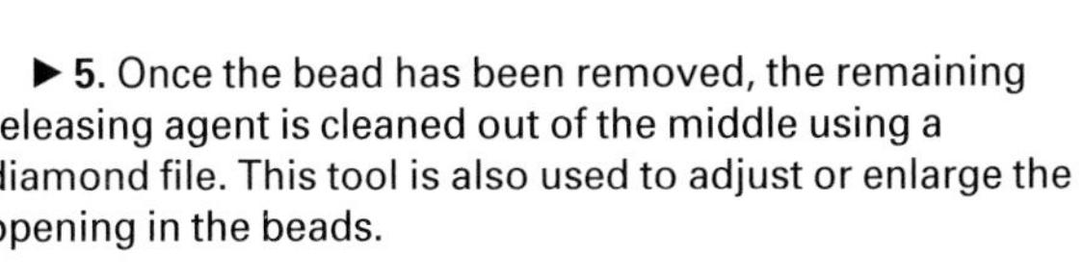

▶ **5.** Once the bead has been removed, the remaining releasing agent is cleaned out of the middle using a diamond file. This tool is also used to adjust or enlarge the opening in the beads.

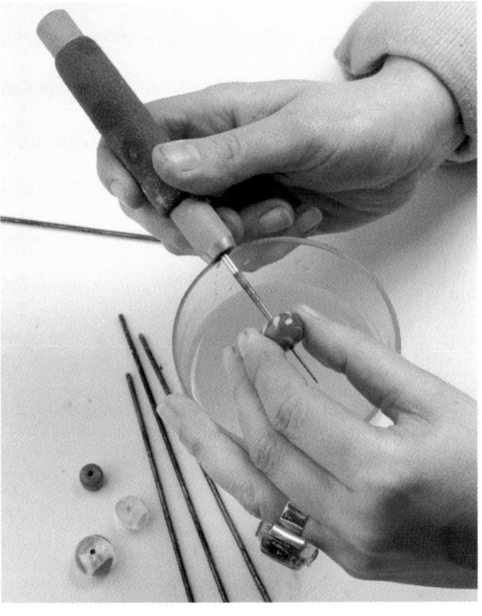

▲ **6.** The diamond file is always used with water; that keeps the bead from heating up through friction and possibly breaking.

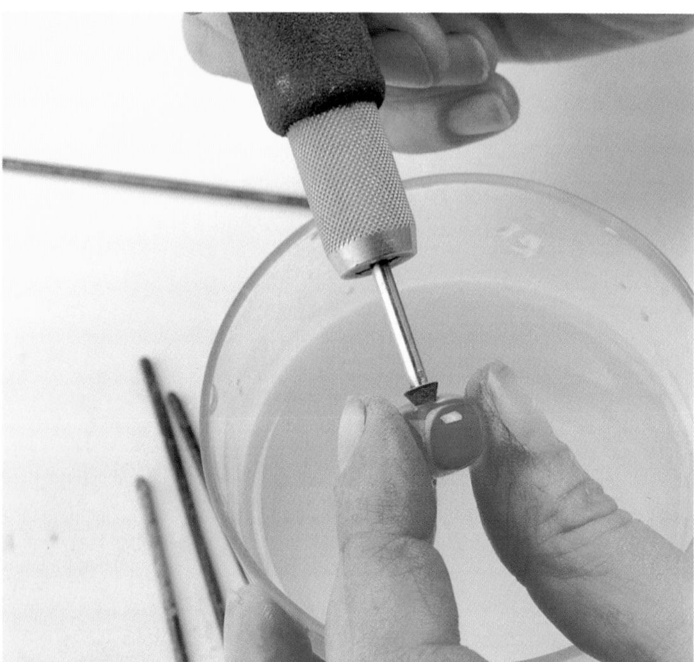

◀ **7.** After removing all of the releasing agent from the inside of the bead, the two entry holes are filed using a conical diamond burr.

◀ **8.** Here are the results produced by Susana Aparicio Ortiz using the combing technique.

## How to Make Different Shapes

When the bead is melted on the mandrel, its shape can be modified in many ways. One simple modification that's easy to perform involves flattening it slightly. This can be carried out after making the bead by any of the techniques explained further in this book. After flattening the bead there will be some small marks on the surface of the glass due to the cooling caused by the contact with the squashing pliers; as a result it will be necessary to slightly remelt the surface before annealing the bead.

◀ Once the bead is melted on the mandrel, it can be flattened to give it a four-sided appearance. Either press the bead onto the marvering pad, or use a special stylized flattener as shown in the photo.

▲ Flat beads made using the *twister* technique by Susana Aparicio Ortiz

◀ A glass bead mounted on a ring made by Carlos Reano and Susana Aparicio Ortiz, 2003

## Making a Bead Using the Combing Technique

When the bead is melted on the end of the mandrel, it is ready for the addition of other colors by means of various techniques explained in this chapter. In this instance, the combing is produced by first applying lines of glass from different colored threads onto the pearl located on the mandrel, then using awls to drag them around the melted surface of the glass to create beautiful effects.

▲ **1.** To begin, the bead is built up a little more by applying a ring of glass around the center to produce more volume.

▶ Combed beads in which blue glass has been applied over white, by Susana Aparicio Ortiz.

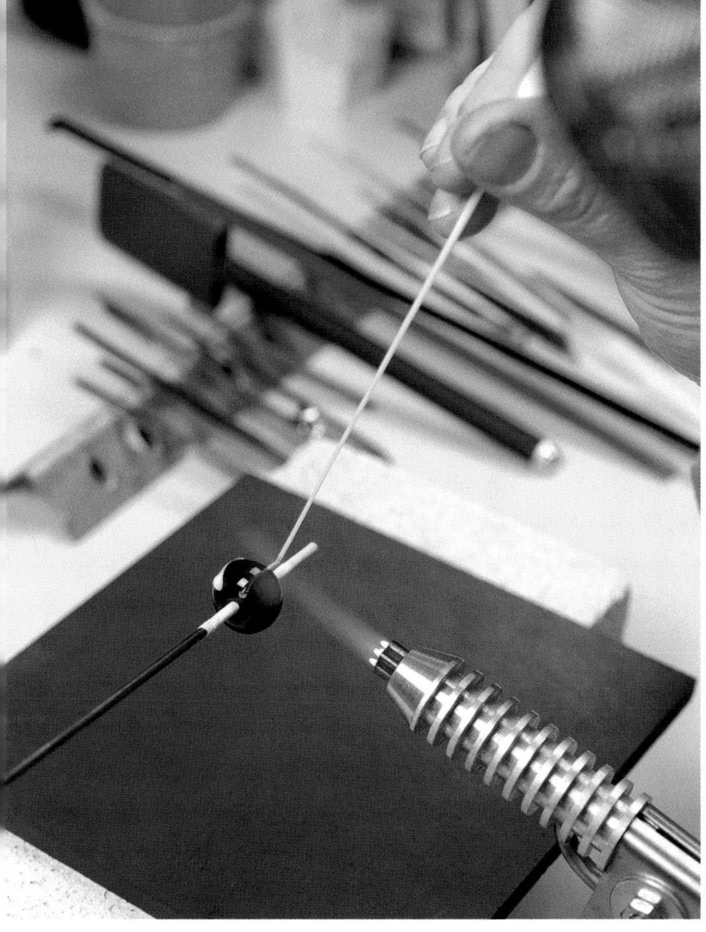

▲ **2.** Lines of white glass thread are applied, and then the bead is melted once again.

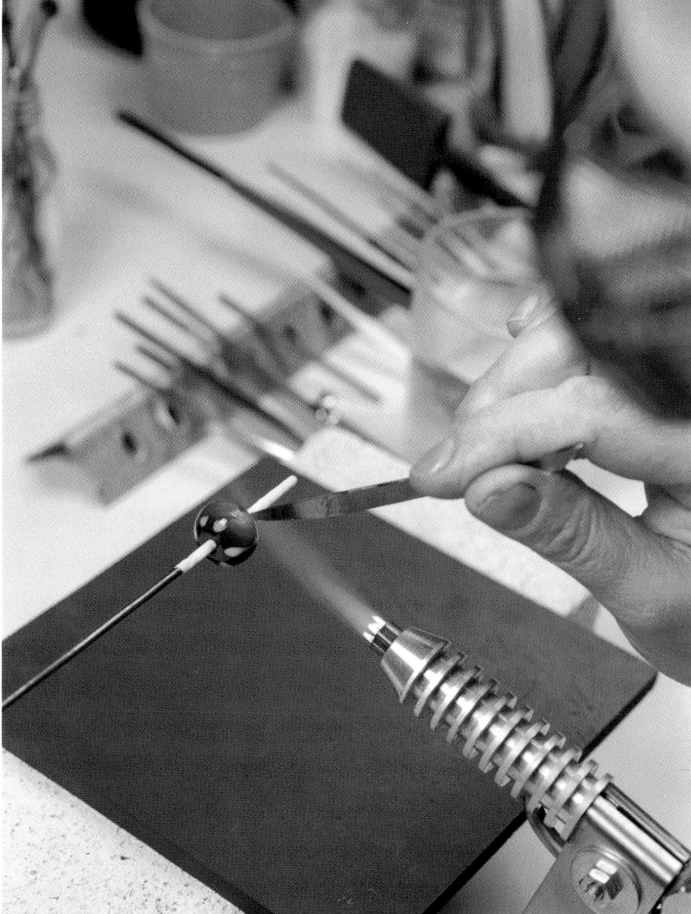

▲ **3.** The colored lines are dragged over the surface of the bead with the point of a steel awl to create interesting and attractive combing effects.

## Work Techniques

Now that the basic bead-making technique has been explained, it's time to learn how to produce more stylized beads. Susana Aparicio Ortiz next demonstrates four essential bead-making techniques that can be used to create an infinite number of variations and produce some very original effects. The technique for applying the glass is the same, as are the preparation of the materials and the positioning and movement of the hands.

### The Eye Technique

One of the simplest ways to decorate a bead, the eye technique involves the successive application of uniform droplets of glass that are melted on the surface of the bead.

◀ **1.** Begin by heating the mandrel and the end of the rod. In this instance white was chosen as the base color for the bead.

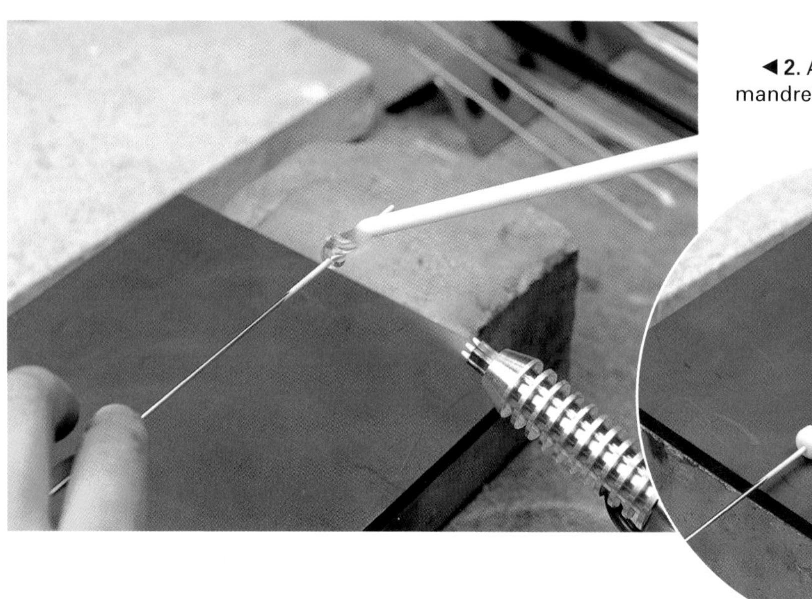

◀ **2.** Apply the end of the melted rod onto the mandrel as it turns evenly.

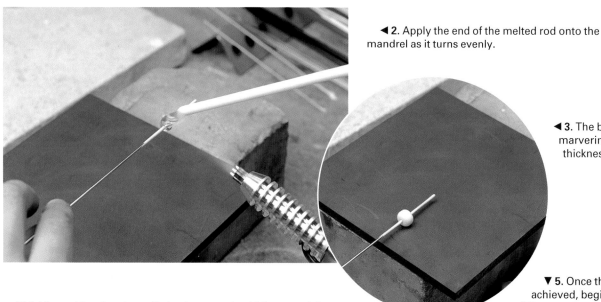

◀ **3.** The bead is rolled over the marvering pad to even out its thickness, then melted again.

▼ **4.** More white glass is applied to increase the thickness and the volume of the bead.

▼ **5.** Once the desired thickness is achieved, begin to melt the end of a different colored rod; in this case, red.

▲ **6.** Several even dots of red glass are deposited in a regular pattern all over the bead.

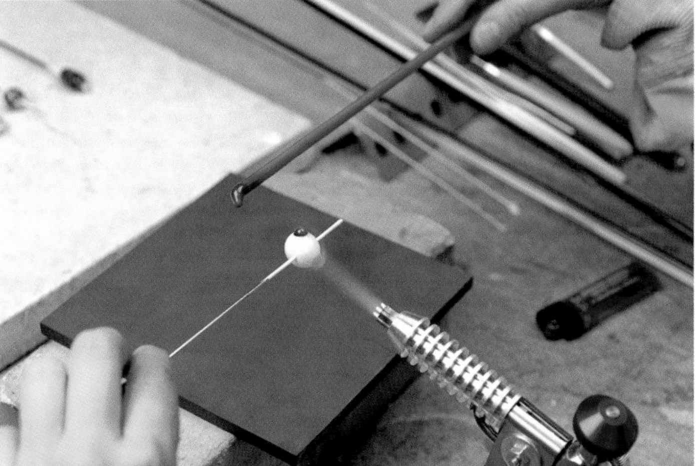

▲ **7.** To cut off the rod with the torch flame, simply place the rod onto the body of the bead and gently lift up on it.

◀ **8.** The drops of red glass spread out over the surface form projections that have to be melted into the bead by turning it in the flame to produce an even surface.

▲ **9.** The same process is repeated by taking a fine stringer of white glass and applying the white onto the melted red drop, then melting the entire bead once again. Once that's done, the bead is put into the vermiculite or into an annealing kiln until it has completely cooled.

▶ **10.** Bead made using the eye technique, by Susana Aparicio Ortiz.

◀ **1.** To produce this effect, begin by making a small bead.

▼ **2.** Next, a belt of glass is added around the bead to create the desired thickness.

### Bubble Inclusions

Another simple way to decorate a bead is to create a controlled air bubble inside the melted points on the pearl and cover them with transparent glass. This process produces a curious decorative effect when repeated all over the bead.

▶ **3.** As in the previous technique, several points of melted white glass are deposited onto the surface of the bead, and the glass is cut using the same flame when the rod is removed.

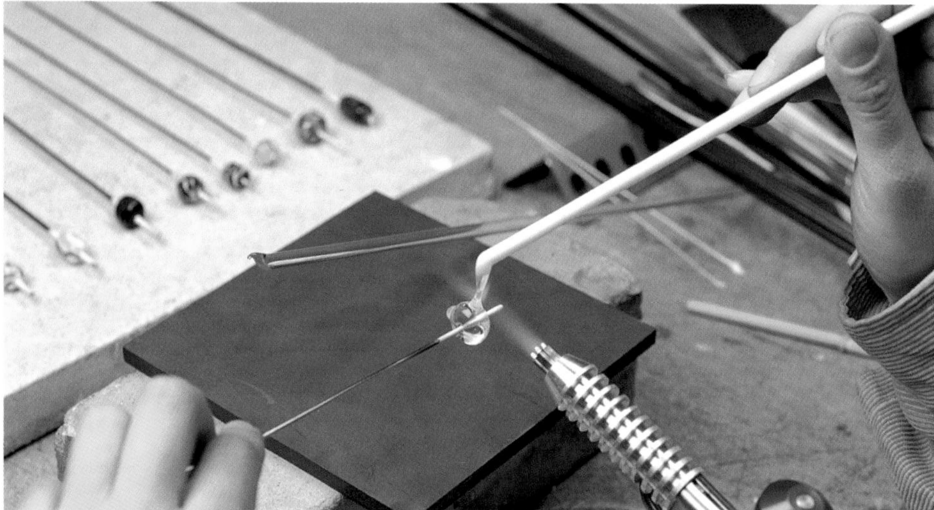

▼ **4.** The bead is melted once again to even up the surface.

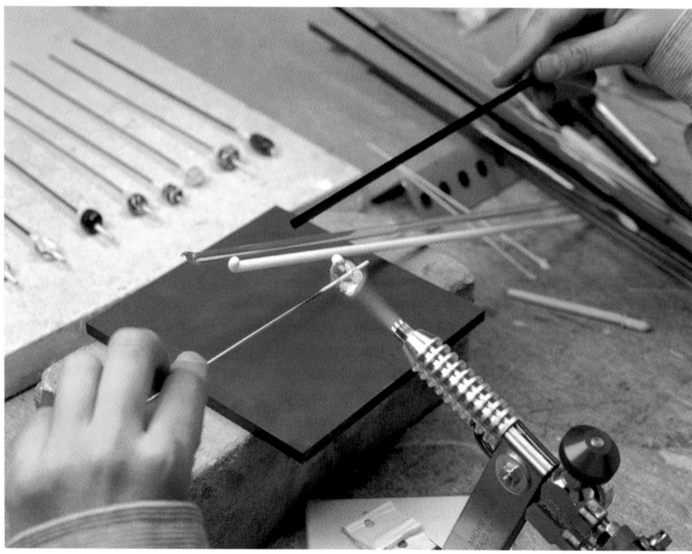

▼ **5.** Now a new point of color is applied on top of the white sleeve, and the whole assembly is melted once again.

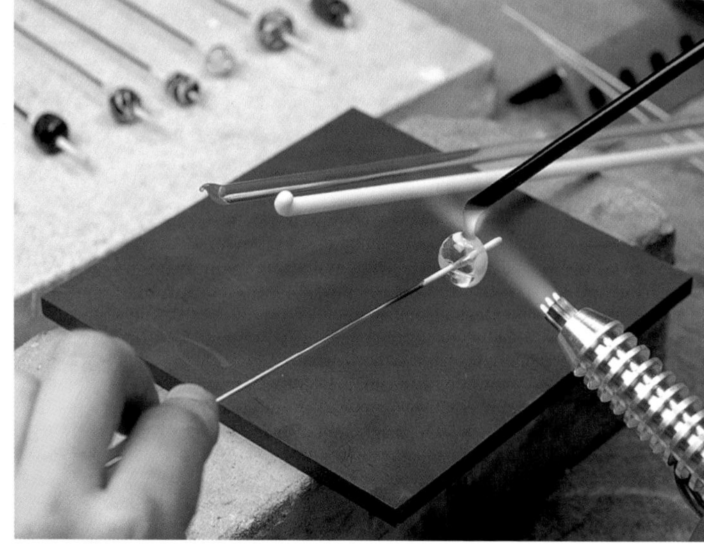

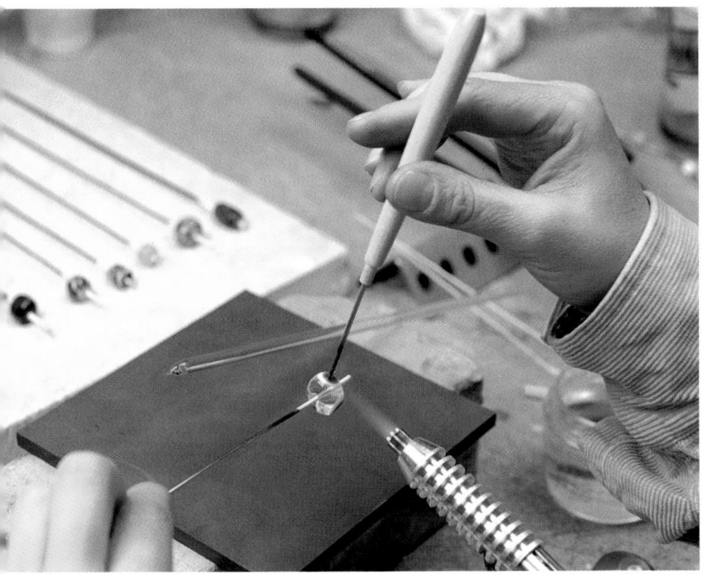

▲ **6.** The point of a steel awl is dipped into water and then jabbed into the center of a colored point to create an air bubble. The process is repeated to create more bubbles.

▲ **7.** A drop of transparent glass is applied to each bubble, and the bead is melted once again.

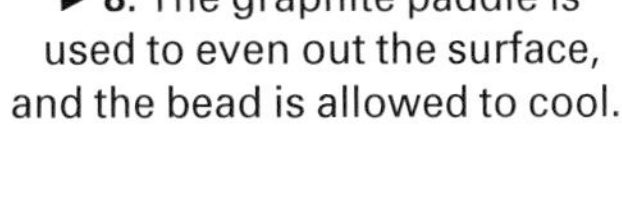

► **8.** The graphite paddle is used to even out the surface, and the bead is allowed to cool.

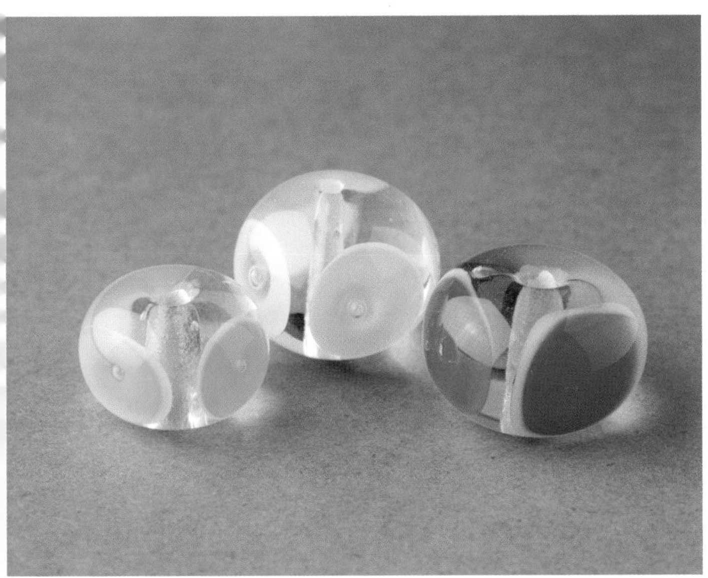

▲ **9.** Beads with bubbles on a transparent glass background made by Susana Aparicio Ortiz

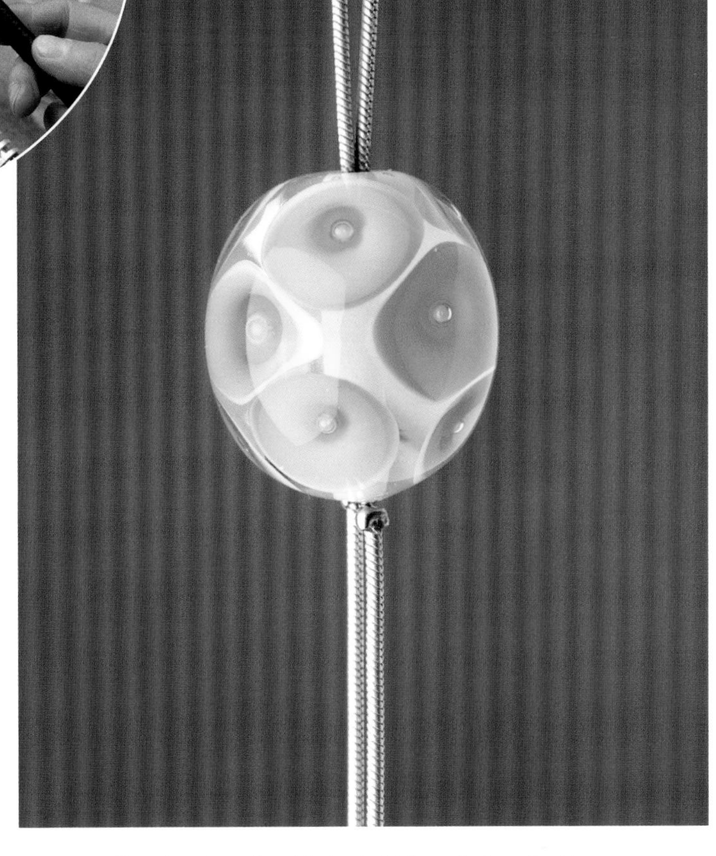

▲ **10.** Glass bead made with the bubble technique by Susana Aparicio Ortiz

### Technique for Making Pagoda-shaped Beads

This term is applied to cylindrical beads to which glass bands or thick stringers of any color are added. The form suggests a pagoda because of the elongated shape and the protuberances that are evident when the bead is held vertically.

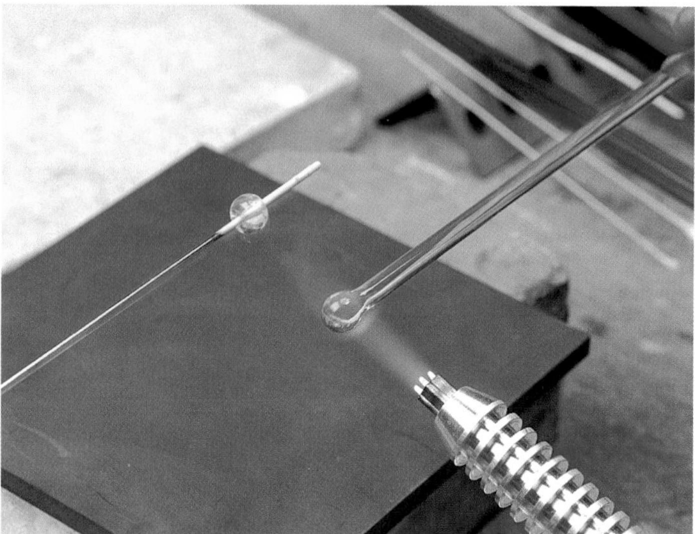

◀ **1.** First, transparent glass is loaded onto the mandrel to create a small circular bead.

▲ **2.** Next, successive transparent glass belts are made at the ends, rather than on top of the initial bead, in order to produce the length in what will be the body of the bead.

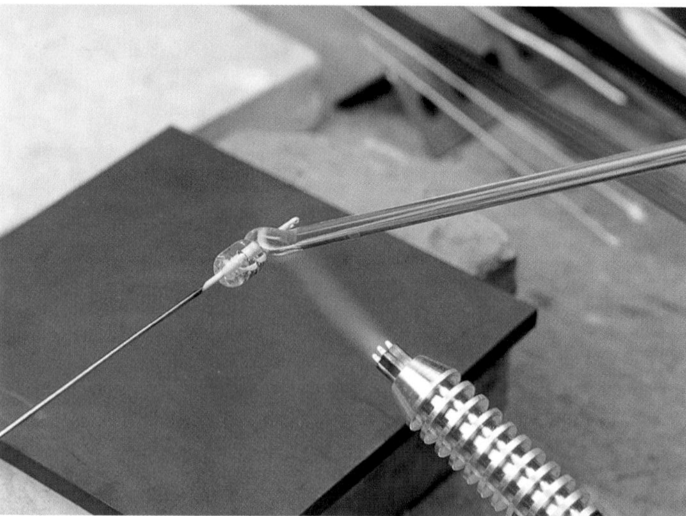

▲ **3.** Proceed in this manner until a transparent glass cylinder is formed.

▲ **4.** In order to even out the surface of the body of the bead, it is rounded on the marvering pad.

◀ **5.** Before adding a new colored rod, it is heated at the end until it takes on the consistency of thick honey.

▲ **6.** Next, a first glass belt is applied round the transparent body of the bead without melting it.

▼ **7.** It's important to apply the glass evenly in order to create a consistent thickness all around the bead. To ensure that, the turning motion by the hand holding the mandrel must also be even.

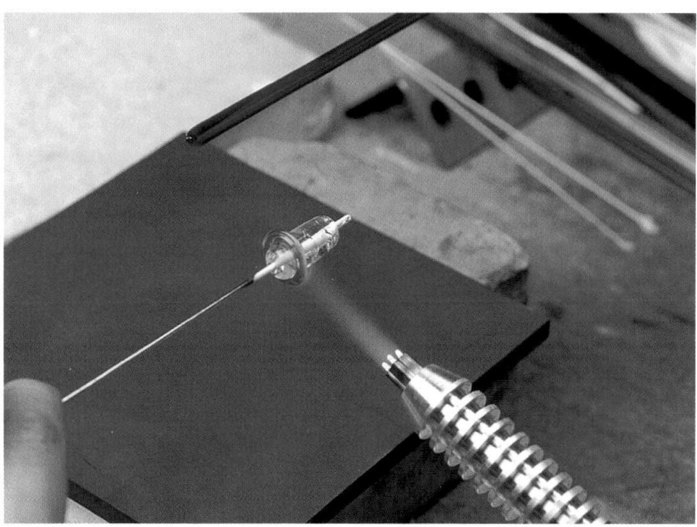

► **8.** A new colored belt is applied in the same way.

▼ **9.** The last belt is applied.

► **10.** Different beads made using the pagoda technique, by Susana Aparicio Ortiz

### The Twister Technique

This technique gets its name from the movement of a colored glass stringer thrust onto a bead while making small twists to create whirls. This requires quick, precise hand movements and creates an attractive effect.

▲ **1.** As before, an initial glass ball is made on the mandrel; in this instance an opaque yellow rod is used to make the first half of the bead.

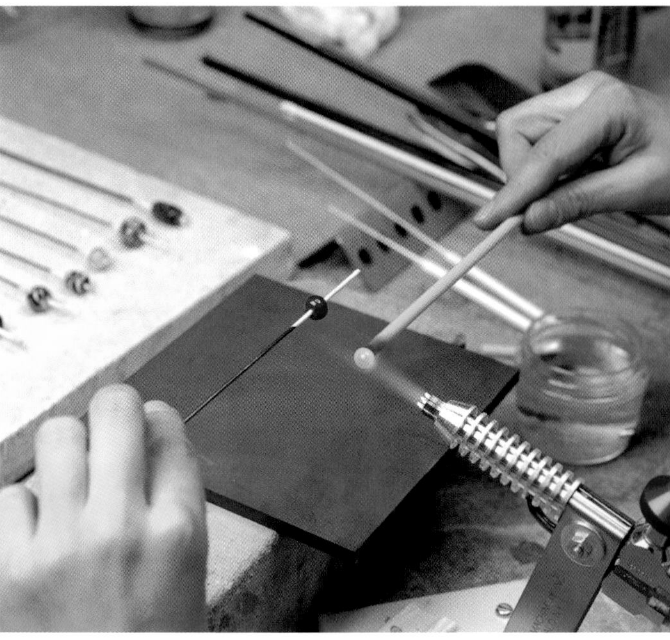

▲ **2.** The end of the rod is heated to the application temperature.

▲ **3.** Successive belts of glass are applied. As they melt, they form a cylindrical bead of greater size.

▲ **4.** To even out the shape of the bead, it is rolled evenly over the marvering surface; this produces a bead with a uniform body.

◄ **5.** Now the end of an opaque green rod is heated to make the other half of the bead.

▲ **6.** Successive belts of green glass are applied to produce a bead made up of two halves of different colors.

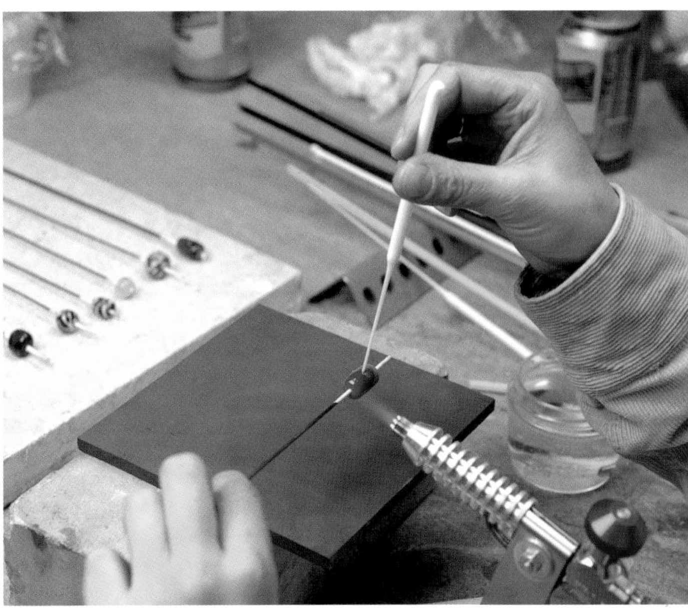

▲ **7.** The bead is heated at the point where the two colors meet, then a fine glass rod is jabbed in. Swivel the glass stringer a half-turn. This will create the effect of a small swirl once the stringer melts.

▼ **8.** Flattened bead made using the *twister* technique, by Susana Aparicio Ortiz, 2002

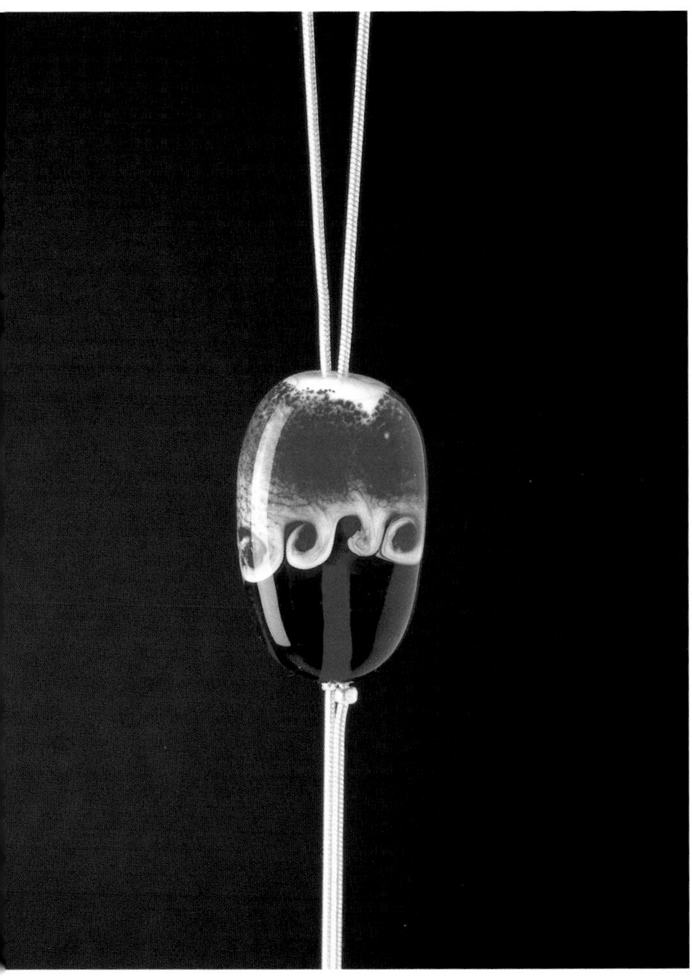

▼ *Calm Sea,* 2003. Bead made by Susana Aparicio Ortiz using the *twister* technique. The gold setting is the work of Carlos Reano.

# Polymer Modeling Clays

Polymer modeling clay is a synthetic material that is easy to find in any shop that sells craft, school, or art supplies. Sold in the form of small, individual blocks or as sets for children, they are well-suited for making various kinds of figurines and ornaments. Their consistency is similar to that of ceramic clay; one of their greatest advantages is the broad spectrum of colors available, plus the combinations of colors that can be produced by alternating different types and brands of polymer clay. It is easily modeled in a raw state, then fired in an oven—a kitchen oven is sufficient—at 266°F (130°C). The result is a rigid, durable material with great color quality that can be manipulated, painted, or cut.

At first glance it may seem the material has construction limitations and excessively bright colors. However, polymer modeling clays can be converted into an excellent artistic medium with infinite sculptural possibilities, once you learn how to use it properly and how to apply it in conjunction with metal sheets and internal frameworks.

## Characteristics

Polymer modeling clays are made from a combination of various types of polyvinyls—especially vinyl polychlorine or PVC—along with a series of specific products such as plasticizers and others that act as fillers and give the polymer good malleability before being fired. The percentage of plasticizer and added products determines the feel of each clay in raw form, as well as its hardness and color once it's fired. As a result, every brand of modeling medium has properties that make it unique and specific to each project.

## Brands of Polymer

One known brand, especially in the United States, is Sculpey, from the Poliform company. This is a soft clay that is easy to model, and it's available in a broad range of colors, including metallic and pearlescent shades. There are several formats, such as SuperSculpey in somewhat translucent flesh tones, and Sculpeyflex, which retains it flexibility after firing. A liquid format, Sculpe III, comes in a range of colors based on th pigments of oil painting. It is an exceller polymer clay that is very malleable an scarcely needs preparation before firing.

Premo is another brand that has a fee similar to Sculpey, but it's a little harder t model than Sculpey III. This stiffe consistency is excellent for millefiori projects which are created by rolling tubes an threads of different colors of polymer clay Premo has the advantage of being quit tough after firing, and of retaining most of it shape when it is modeled. It comes in a wid range of colors including special shades an those with shiny effects.

Fimo is perhaps one of the most popula brands of polymer clay. It is made in tw different consistencies: Fimo soft, which i smooth like Sculpey and hardly needs an

▲ Fimo classic requires kneading befor use, but once it has been prepared correctly becomes an excellent polymer modeling cla that can be used to create detailed works.

◀ Polymer brooches featuring *Sebastian, the Unnatural Child.* Creation of Carles Codina i Armengol

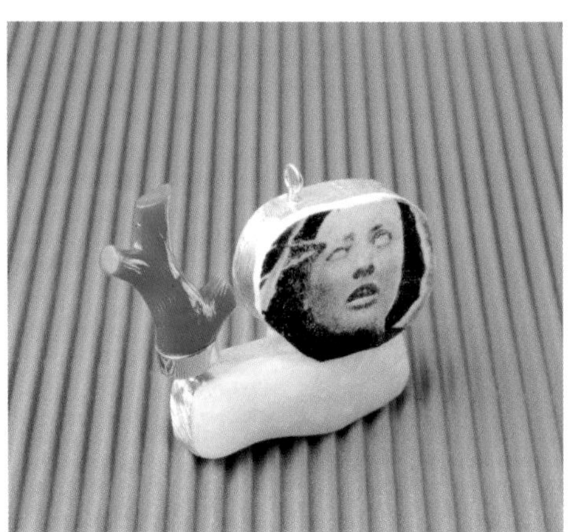

▲ Pendant made from silver, imprinted Fimo, and red coral; work by Carles Codina i Armengol

▲ Because it is soft and pliable when purchased, Sculpey III needs little initial preparation.

rior conditioning; and Fimo Classic, the most opular. It is harder and needs intensive onditioning prior to use, although you can uy a product that will soften it. Fimo Classic as a dense consistency, and requires a ertain amount of preparatory kneading. It is a ood choice for precision work because of its xcellent modeling qualities and consistency ı the raw state, and because it can be cut leanly with a knife. Once it's fired, it is hard nd retains its color extremely well.

► Flexible polymer clays retain good flexibility and resistance once fired.

◄ Granitex offers a series of polymer clays in different colors that look like granite and resemble different qualities of stone.

## Kneading and Mixing

Polymer modeling clay requires proper neading in order to produce the right lasticity, increase its strength, and prevent racks during firing. Sculpey doesn't need his conditioning, but at times it's a good idea ɔ knead it lightly by hand before using it.

Kneading also is used for mixing colors for he purpose of lightening or darkening a tone. lthough it's possible to knead by hand, it's ractical and advisable to use a pasta making nachine instead. This small device makes it ossible to knead the polymer properly and roduce sheets of a specific thickness that an later be used in any kind of project.

The polymer clay that requires the most preparation is Fimo Classic. It can be softened with a little paraffin oil or any other mineral oil. It is simply cut into small pieces using a knife, or even a kitchen meat grinder. Add a few drops of oil before kneading firmly. This same method can be used to mix it with another color. Although not advisable, Fimo Classic can be mixed with other colors from other brands.

► **1.** The kneading machine is actually a kitchen device for making pasta. It is also used for mixing and kneading polymer, as well as producing sheets of different thicknesses. It is cleaned with alcohol.

◄ **2.** A piece of material is broken off and, if desired, a little bit of another color is added to change the tone.

◄ **3.** The clay is first kneaded by hand, then put into the kneading machine through the largest opening; a thin sheet is produced.

▼ **4.** The sheet is rolled up and put into the pasta machine once again; this assures proper kneading of the material.

◀ **5.** The process i repeated several times, depending on the type of polymer clay used.

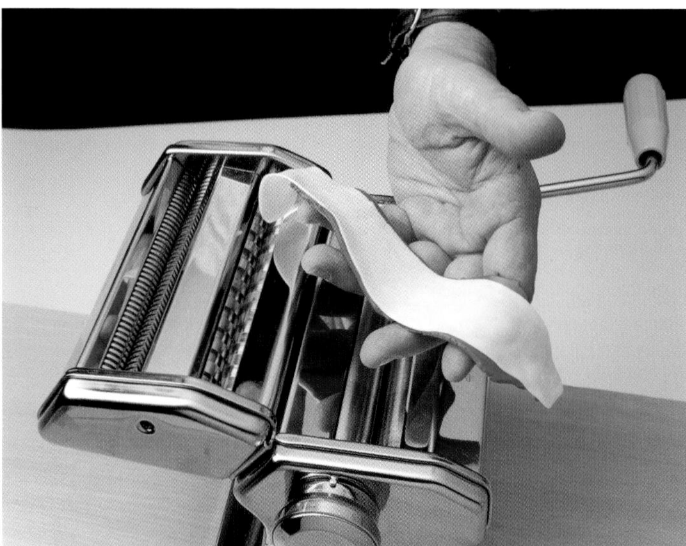

◀ **6.** To mix in a color, repeat the kneading process with the additional color, then run both colors through the pasta machine together.

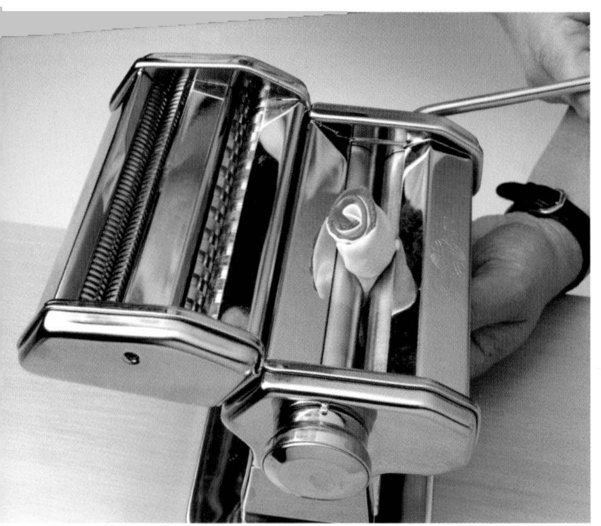

▲ **7.** Repeat the process several times.

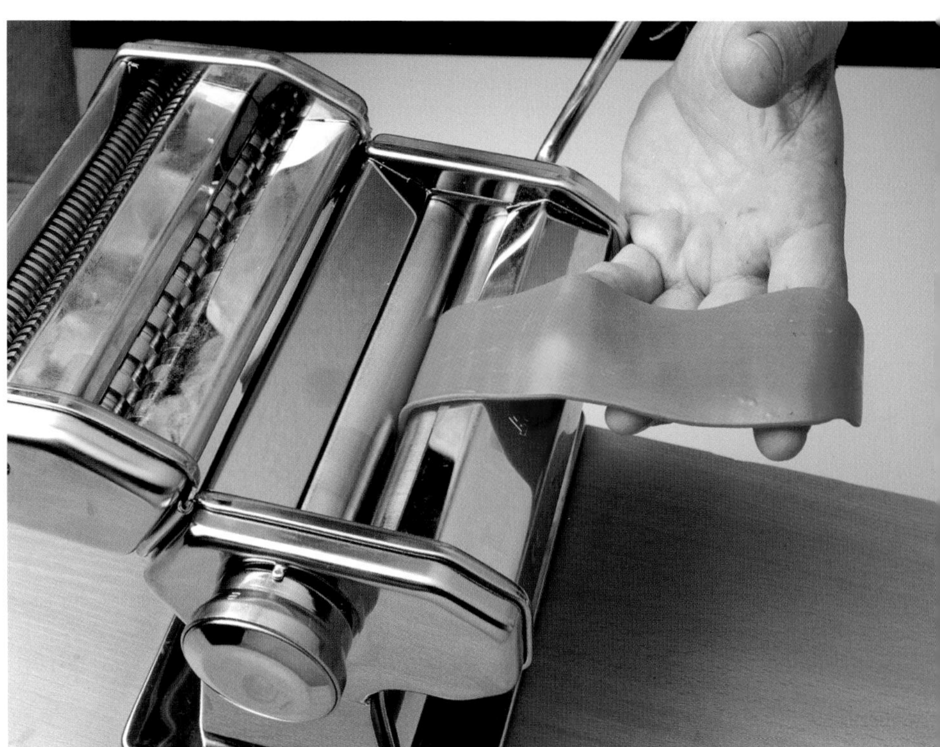

▶ **8.** The rollers of the pasta machine can be adjusted to reduce the thickness of the sheet produced.

▶ 9. One accessory this machine makes possible to produce e threads of clay that can be used to create n interesting texture or creating brooches and rings.

◀ 10. Gently compress the mass of polymer threads and shape carefully, then fire the polymer clay in the oven for 30 minutes at 266°F (130°C).

▶ 11. To turn into a pin, simply glue a clasp to the back of the piece. Colored threads also can be mixed together, or the surface of the solidified clay can be painted.

## Work Process

In working with polymer clay, choose a smooth, nonporous surface on which to work, such as glass or smooth marble. That way the material will be unaffected by the texture of the surface, and it will turn out smooth, shiny, and easy to clean.

Always begin working with the lightest color and with clean hands, as the colors contaminate one another through contact. It's also essential to clean the surface and the tools every time the color is changed to avoid compromising the colors.

Polymer clay is very easy to cut, imprint, and manipulate. Any tool can be used, such as a hobby knife, toothpicks, awls, different plastic or metal paddles. It's easy to shape it once it's been wedged or kneaded properly. It is manipulated directly with the fingers and cleaned up with moist towelettes, such as baby wipes, plus a little hand cream. Latex gloves should not be used.

Proper storage of polymer clay is also important, since light causes the product to age, and any excess heat can harden it. The best way to protect polymer clay is to place it into a resealable bag or container and keep it in a cool, dark place.

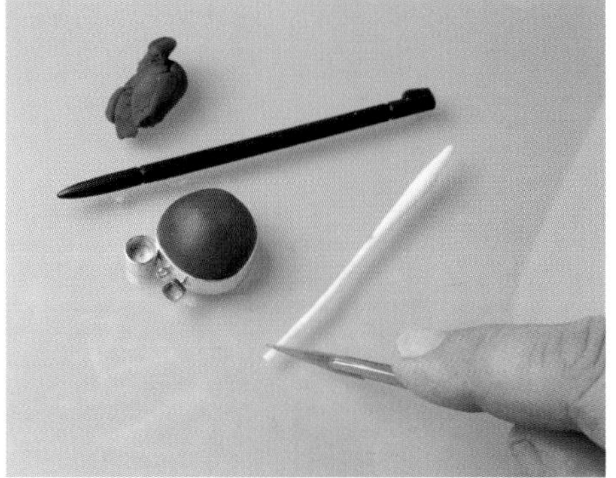

**A Polymer Clay Brooch**

▲ 1. Once the polymer clay has been wedged, it is formed into a ball. This is put into a soldered silver setting and pressed in and shaped with the fingers. The fine white polymer thread is made by stretching it out on a flat piece of glass.

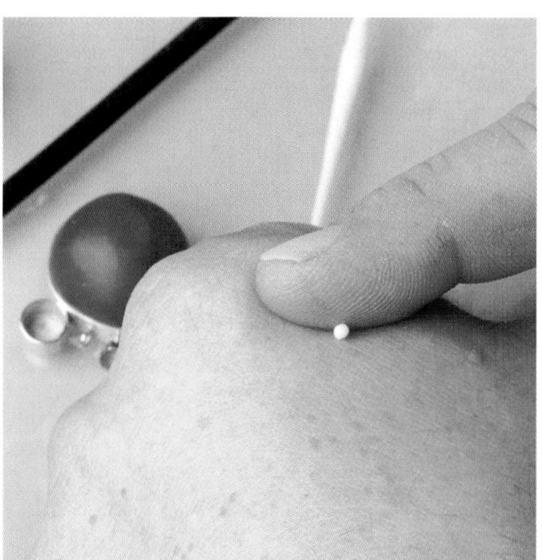

▲ 2. A scalpel is used to cut off small sections of white polymer clay and make tiny spheres.

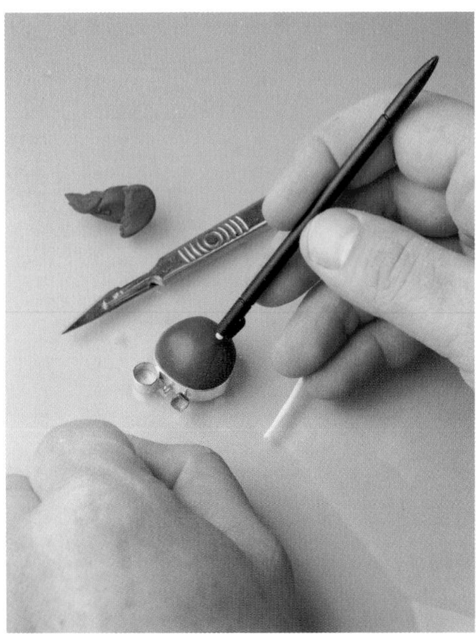

▲ **3.** Using the back of a punch, the crude balls are placed onto the surface of the main piece of violet polymer clay.

◀ **4.** Then the balls are pressed into the main body.

◀ **5.** The center of the white spots is pierced using the point of the prick punch, and the piece is fired in the oven for 35 minutes at 266°F (130°C).

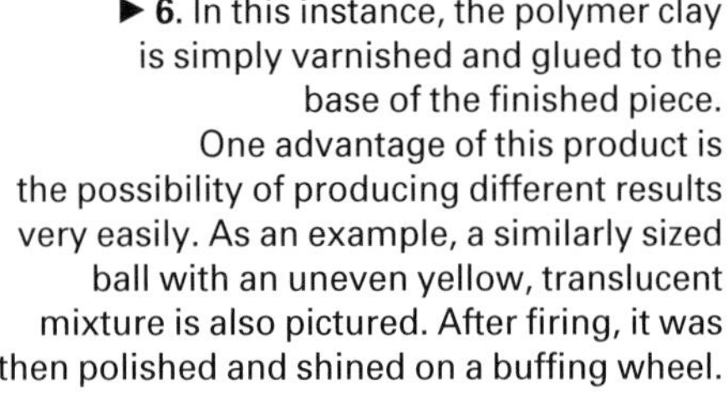

▶ **6.** In this instance, the polymer clay is simply varnished and glued to the base of the finished piece. One advantage of this product is the possibility of producing different results very easily. As an example, a similarly sized ball with an uneven yellow, translucent mixture is also pictured. After firing, it was then polished and shined on a buffing wheel.

# Firing

Polymer modeling clay hardens permanently when it is heated for a specific period of time at a certain temperature. Allow about 15 minutes of firing for each ½ inch (6 mm) of thickness. Most pieces require an average firing time of about 10 to 30 minutes, based on size. A thick piece obviously requires more firing time than a thin one.

One of the most common firing problems occurs when the polymer clay burns or warps excessively inside the oven due to the imprecise temperature control of many kitchen ovens. (If a programmable jewelry kiln is used, there won't be many problems, since this is a precise and reliable device.) Using a kitchen oven may mean that the real temperature is different from the one indicated by the dial. One way to determine if the temperature needs adjusting is to test it by placing a sheet of white paper in the oven for 30 minutes at 266°F (130°C). If the paper remains white, the temperature has not exceeded 266°F (130°C). On the other hand, if the paper is somewhat darkened, the temperature needs to be lowered.

Some colors and color combinations, especially ones that have been mixed using a translucent base, change slightly after being fired. Thus, it is worthwhile to do a preliminary test before firing the piece in order to avoid undesirable results.

Polymer clays are nontoxic in both handling and firing; avoid breathing in potential smoke caused by excessive heat to a project piece. In no case should polymer be fired in an oven along with foods.

▲ Any kitchen oven will work for firing polymer. The important thing is to observe the temperatures and the times indicated by the manufacturer on each packet of clay.

## Techniques

There are many books and magazines devoted to polymer modeling clay projects. One common project is making necklace beads from strips of various colors and combining different-shaped stringers so that when they are cut up they function as necklace beads or some other item.

By combining different shades of polymer it is possible to produce colors that resemble lapis lazuli, coral, jade, and turquoise. It is also possible to add gold leaf and other materials, such as pigments. Once fired, they can be engraved, filed, and drilled. Because the material is plastic, it also takes acrylic paints and varnishes well.

### Stamping

Any material pressed onto the polymer leaves its mark and texture on it. One very simple and economical technique involves making rubber stamps from drawings done on satin-finish paper and imprinting the polymer with the resulting rubber stamp that has first been moistened in colored ink. Once the piece is fired, it will remain imprinted with the ink on the surface.

The seal and the texture to be imprinted must be sunk deep into the clay to produce clearly defined shapes. The thicker the clay, the sharper the impression, and the more durable the piece.

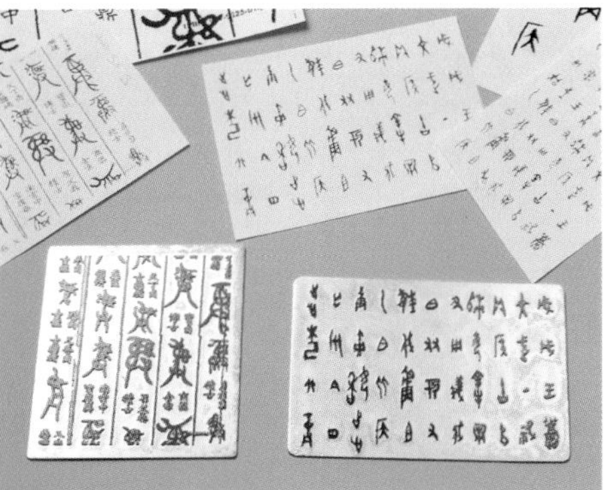

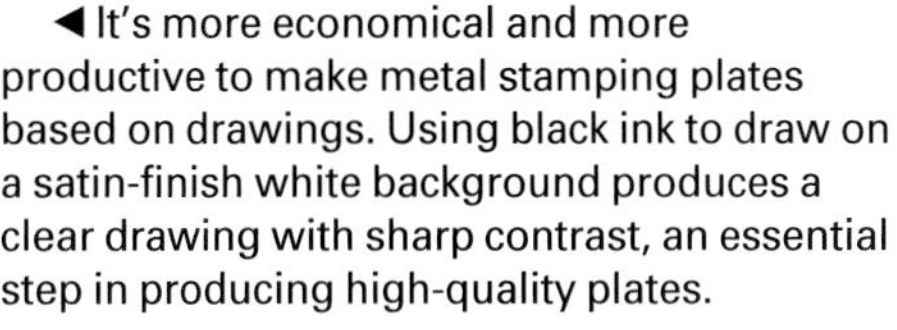

◀ It's more economical and more productive to make metal stamping plates based on drawings. Using black ink to draw on a satin-finish white background produces a clear drawing with sharp contrast, an essential step in producing high-quality plates.

▶ Generally, the plate is made by a photogravure company; then raw polymer clay is pressed into the desired part of the photoengraved plate.

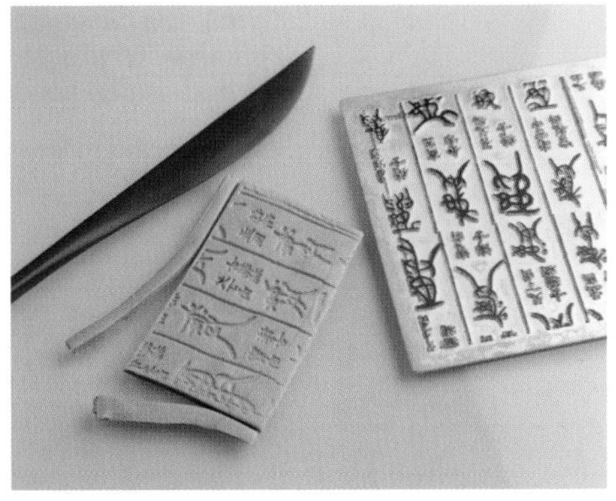

▲ Once the plate is made, select the part to be used by trimming away the rest.

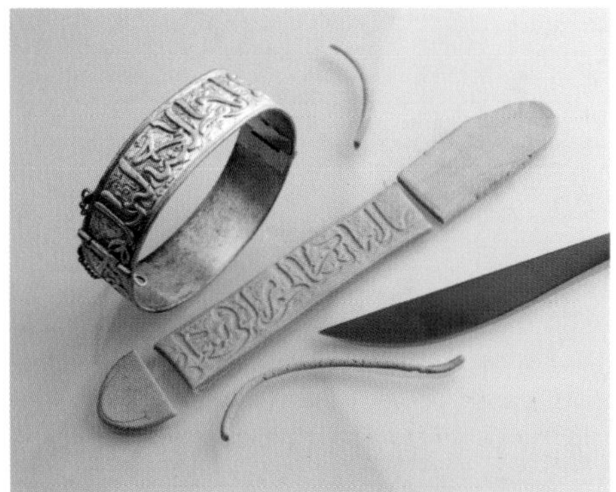

▲ Any hard material is a candidate for making an impression.

### Color Gradations

There are many ways to produce color gradations. The basic process involves cutting out a square of each color from a sheet of polymer, then cutting each one on a diagonal. Next, triangles of the same color are superimposed and laminated in a pasta machine to produce a rectangle. Once that's done, the rectangle is folded in the middle to form a new square, and put through the pasta machine again along the fold. After running the piece through the pasta machine several more times, the result is a progressive gradation.

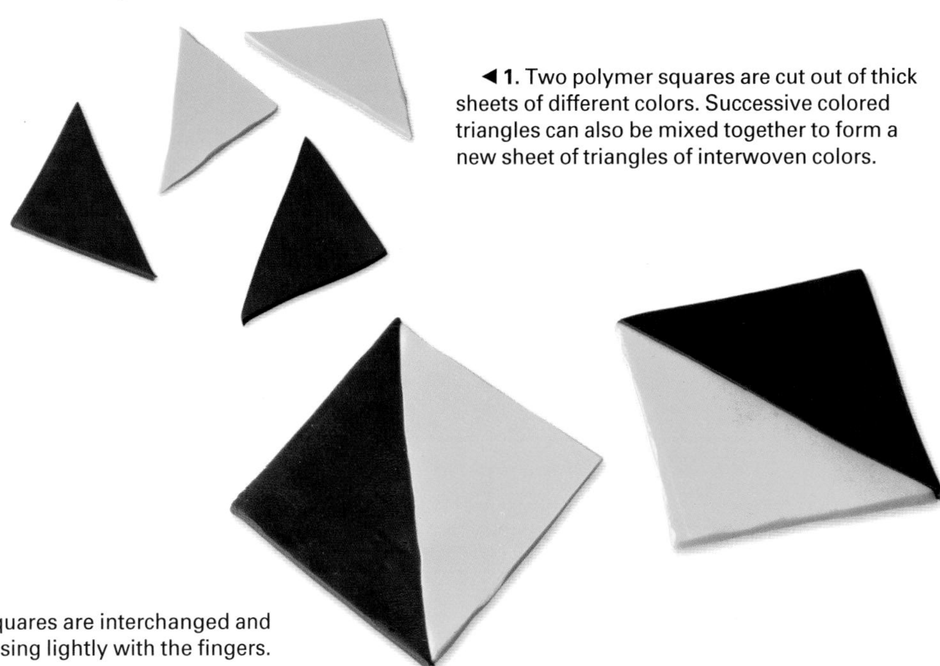

◀ **1.** Two polymer squares are cut out of thick sheets of different colors. Successive colored triangles can also be mixed together to form a new sheet of triangles of interwoven colors.

▶ **2.** The squares are interchanged and joined by pressing lightly with the fingers.

◄ **3.** The two squares are superimposed so that the same colors match up.

▼ **4.** The square is now laminated in the machine to produce a rectangle.

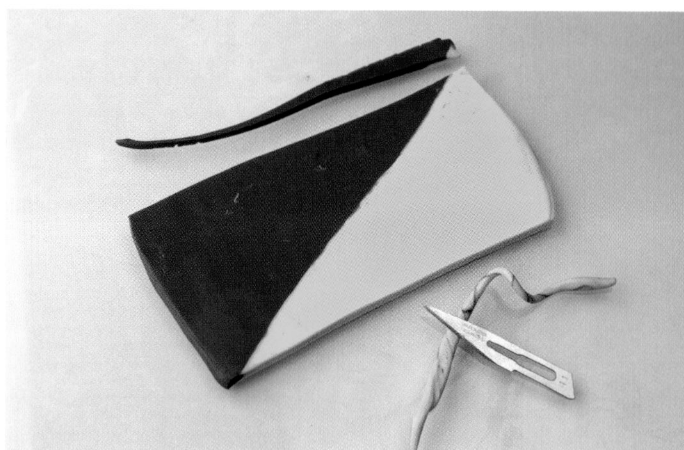

◄ **5.** The rectangle is folded in the middle to make a square, and is laminated once again to produce a new rectangle. The sheet is fed into the machine by the edge where the fold is located.

▲ **6.** The process is repeated until the desired color gradation is achieved.

▲ **7.** In order to combine colors manually, several thick sheets are cut at an angle. Detail of the cut.

► **8.** A diffused effect is created by sliding a finger over the joint area.

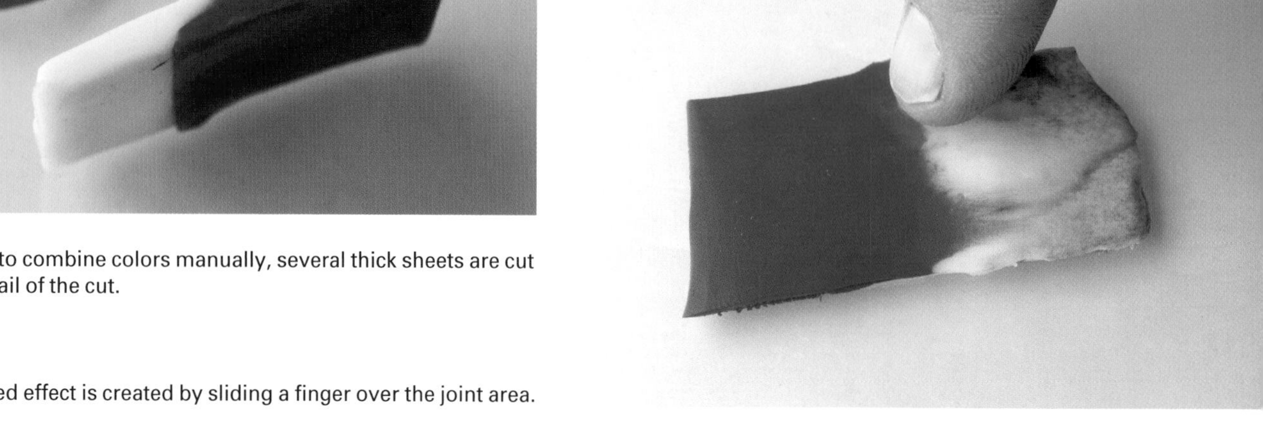

### Imprinting Images onto the Polymer Clay

It's easy to transfer images to polymer, but remember that the picture will be reversed unless the initial photocopy was made from a previously inverted image. Here, an imprint of a black and white image is used, but it is possible to follow the same procedure using color photocopies.

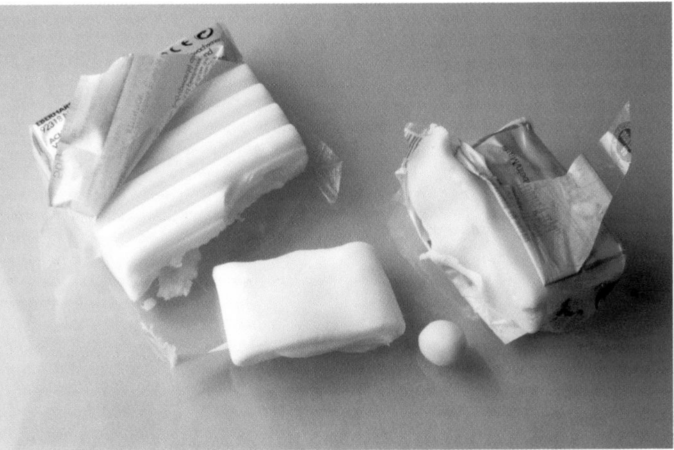

◀ **1.** It's preferable to choose a polymer clay in white or a very light color so the image will stand out clearly against the light background.

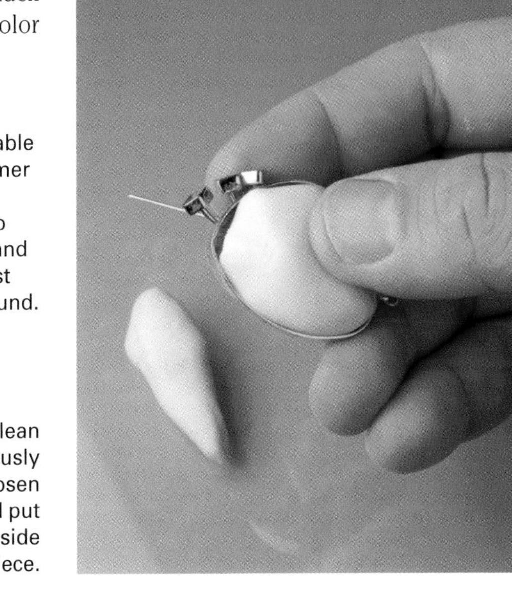

▶ **2.** With clean hands, vigorously knead the chosen polymer and put it into place inside the piece.

▼ **3.** A high-contrast photocopy is made using plenty of ink. It's a good idea to do several trials to get the desired contrast.

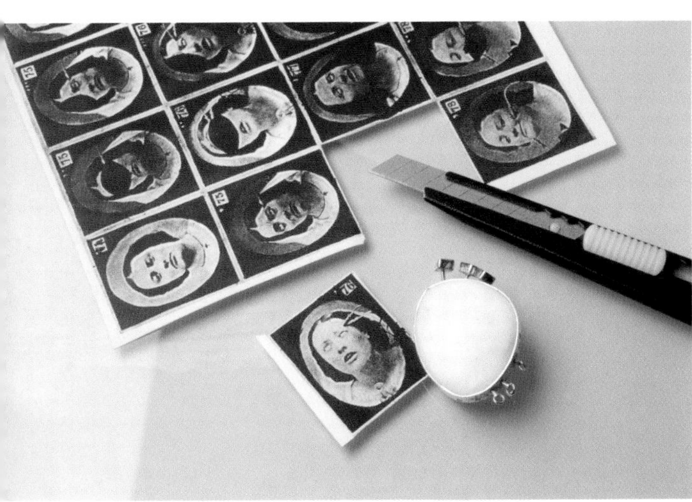

▼ **4.** The surface of the polymer clay is moistened with a little eucalyptus oil.

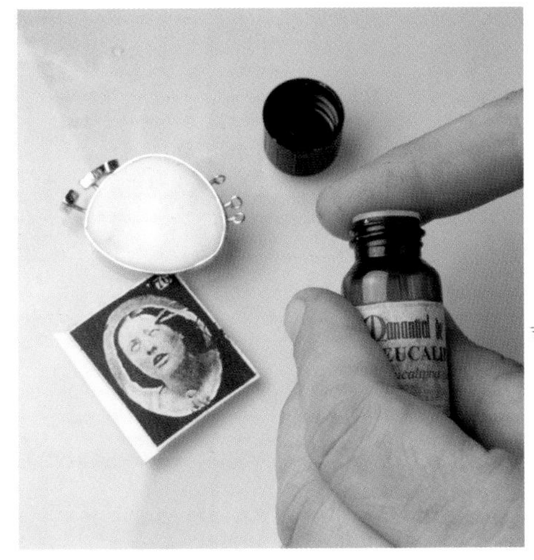

▼ Pendant made by Carles Codina i Armengol

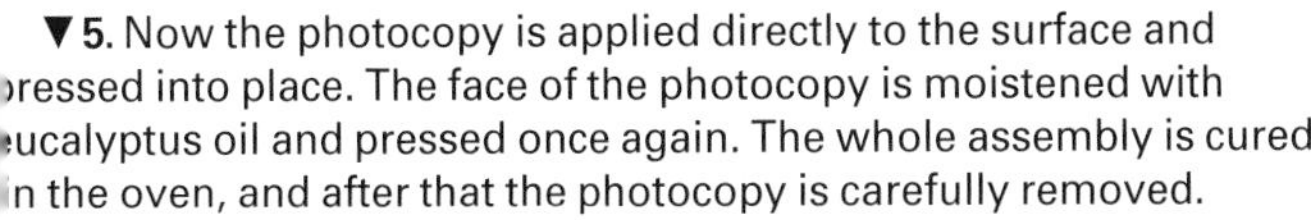

▼ **5.** Now the photocopy is applied directly to the surface and pressed into place. The face of the photocopy is moistened with eucalyptus oil and pressed once again. The whole assembly is cured in the oven, and after that the photocopy is carefully removed.

▲ **6.** The remaining elements of the pendant are added. Brooch made by Carles Codina i Armengol.

# Finishes

Once polymer modeling clay has been properly cured and cooled, it can be filed, engraved, and drilled. Since this is a plastic surface, it also can be painted with acrylic or similar paint, although it's most common to retain the original color of the paste.

The material can also be sanded to a very smooth finish and then carefully polished. The sanding is done by subjecting the polymer to an increasingly fine series of sandpapers. The polishing wheel is used in the same way and with the same abrasives as for polishing plastics, making sure that the surface of the piece doesn't become too hot through friction from the polishing tools.

Once the polishing is completed, the piece can be varnished. Several companies make varnishes that harden and protect surfaces. If working with a plastic surface, apply a water-based acrylic varnish of the type commonly used on wood and paper. The varnish will hold the mass together a little more, since it penetrates and hardens without causing deterioration. There are also floor varnishes that work just as well on polymer projects.

It is also possible to apply colore synthetic powders and very fine sifte metallic powder to polymer pieces. These ar applied with a brush before curing the paste and then the piece is varnished.

Gold leaf can also be applied either befor or after curing, as long as a mordant varnis that prevents separation is used. Anothe technique that produces interesting spottin effects involves impregnating the varnish wit pigment and applying it to the polymer.

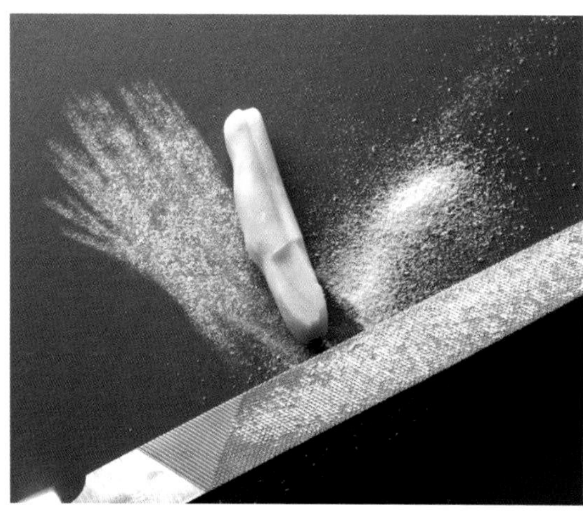

◀ The polymer can be filed, polished, and drilled. One very interesting finish involves leaving the texture of the file on the completed surface.

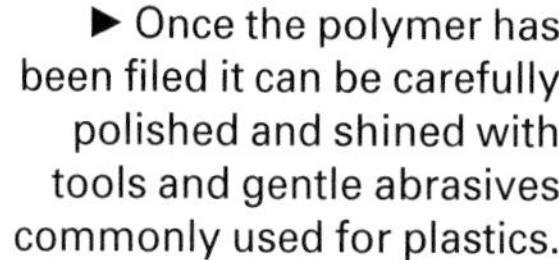

▶ Once the polymer has been filed it can be carefully polished and shined with tools and gentle abrasives commonly used for plastics.

**Metallic Patina**

A series of products makes it possible to produce different colored patinas similar to the oxidation that occurs naturally on metals. The method used involves applying a base coat in the form of a coat of paint of the desired metal (bronze, iron, copper, etc.), then adding an acid that reacts with and oxidizes the metal.

Using this method, for example, iron oxide can be applied to decorate a surface of plastic or any other material that has been treated with a base of the desired metal. This process is good for aging and oxidizing objects made of plastic, resin, wood, and rust-resistant metals; the effect is so real that it's difficult to distinguish from true oxidation.

◀ An imprinting varnish, a metallic paint, and the acid or salt that causes the reaction and produces a surface patina. Once the surface has been prepared, one of the desired metal bases is applied. Next, a patina is added. Different shades of oxidation will result, depending on the base selected.

▶ To oxidize with iron oxide, first apply a thick coat of liquid iron and let it dry.

## METAL BASES AND SHADES OF OXIDATION

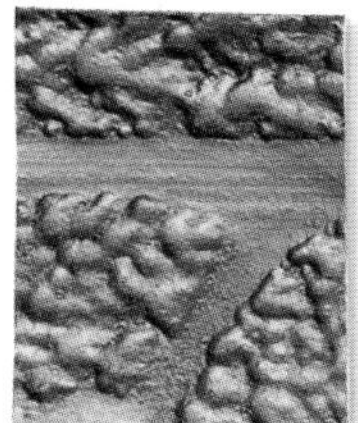
Copper colored base

Golden base

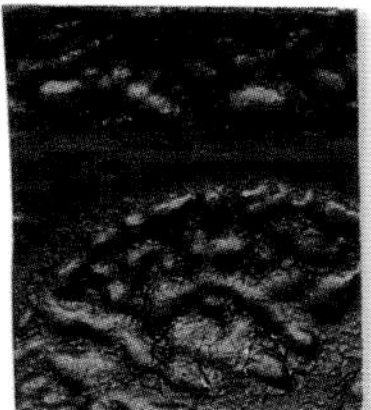
Dark bronze base

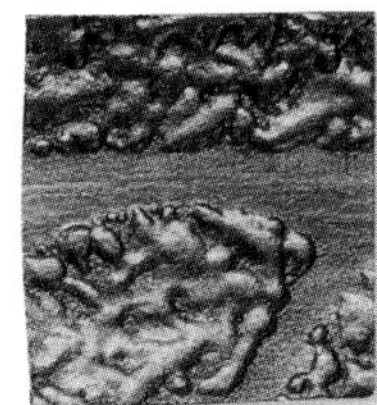
Light bronze base

Iron base

Light base

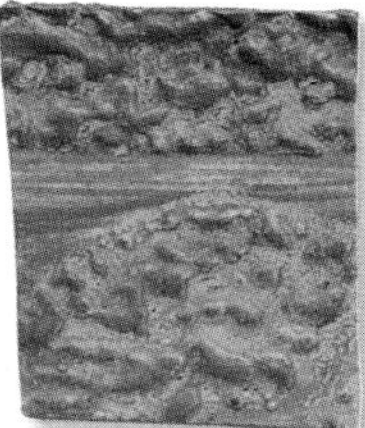
Green patina on copper-colored base

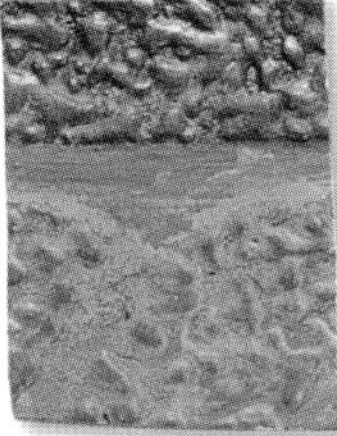
Green patina on golden base

Green patina on dark bronze

Green patina on light bronze

Oxidation solution on iron base

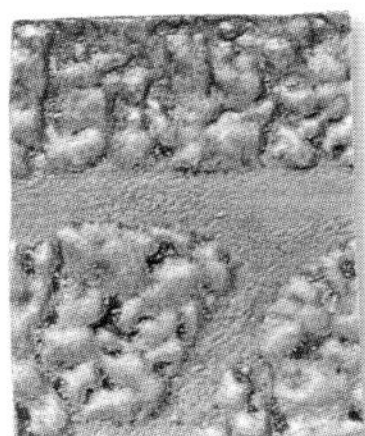
Black finish on light paste

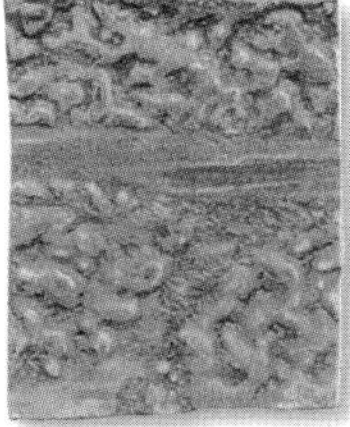
Blue patina on copper-colored base

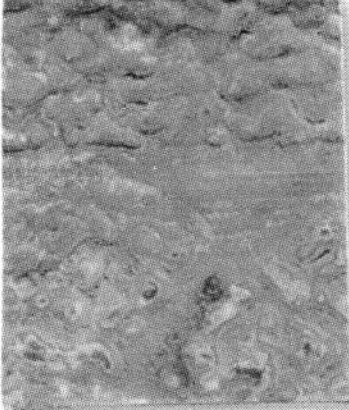
Blue patina on golden base

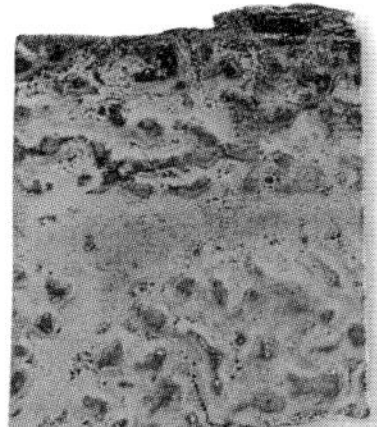
Blue patina on dark bronze

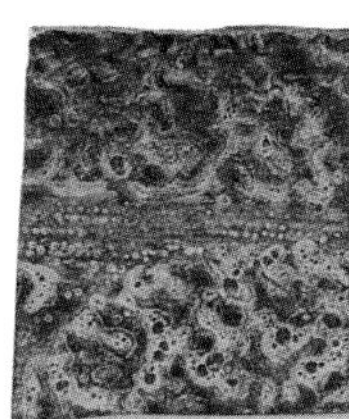
Blue patina on light bronze

Red finish green patina on golden base

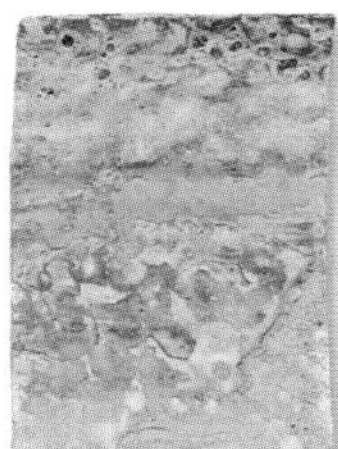
Black finish green patina on copper- colored base

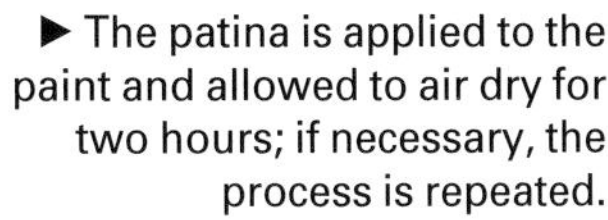
▶ The patina is applied to the paint and allowed to air dry for two hours; if necessary, the process is repeated.

◀ Various items made of polymer and polyester oxidized using iron oxide

▶ Brooch-pendant with iron oxidation by Carles Codina i Armengol

## Polymer Brooch

There are countless objects from the goldsmith's art immortalized in the paintings of every era, and some of them have been idealized and reproduced by various painters. This is the basis for the following project: interpreting an object based on a painting and using the means at our disposal. The main material used is colored polymer and everyday materials from the home or studio. Rather than attempting to make a faithful reproduction of the original, the goal is instead to interpret it, capture the main features and dominant colors from the painting, and make an object that ultimately will perform a distinct function in a different context.

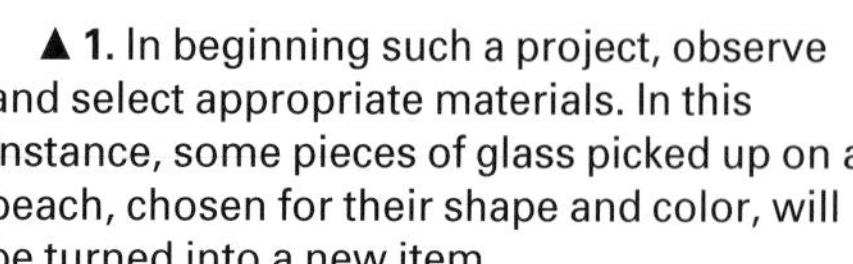

▲ **1.** In beginning such a project, observe and select appropriate materials. In this instance, some pieces of glass picked up on a beach, chosen for their shape and color, will be turned into a new item.

◀ **2.** Just as the painter interpreted or imagined a shape, reinterpret what is seen using materials that approximate the graphic image through their color or texture such as pieces of glass, needles, synthetic pearls, and a sheet of metal.

◀ **3.** Once the approximate dimensions of the final product are determined, cut out a sheet of metal and decide which clasp to solder or glue into place.

▼ **4.** In this instance, the polymer clay is ochre Sculpey III, which is very close to the golden shade. Make a plate and a thick rod and fit them to the metal plate to create the shape in the photo.

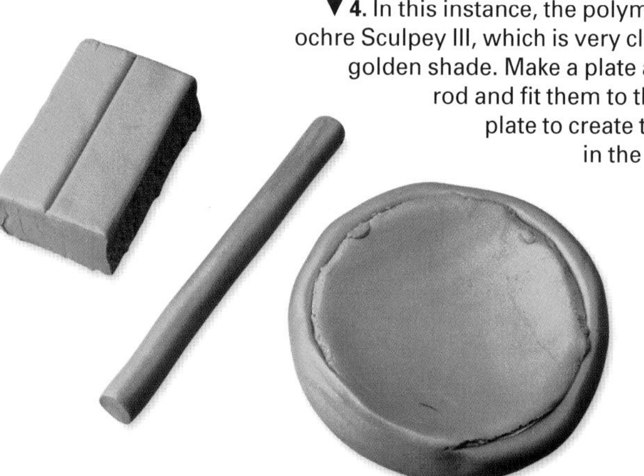

▼ **5.** The polymer is shaped with the fingers. The outer settings for the red pieces of glass are made, then inserted into the polymer.

▲ **6.** The mountings are made from small pieces of polymer, and the stones are arranged and pressed into the polymer.

▲ **7.** Imitation pearls are pressed into place. Once all the elements are arranged, they are removed from the piece so the polymer can be baked. That way the location of the pieces of glass and the pearls remain in the polymer. Later on, when the polymer is removed from the oven, the elements will be put back into place.

▲ **8.** The polymer is cured for 40 minutes at 266˚F (130˚C) and allowed to cool.

▶ **9.** The polymer is too uniform in color and doesn't look like the desired antique; it has to be painted unevenly on the inner surfaces and certain other areas to improve the overall appearance.

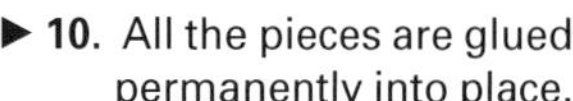

▶ **10.** All the pieces are glued permanently into place.

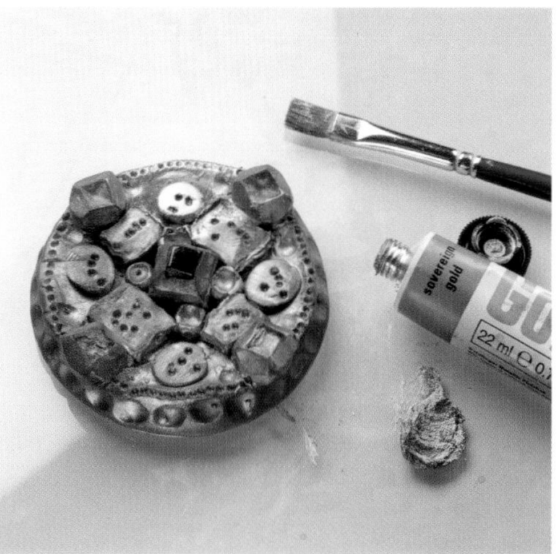

◀ **11.** To age the piece visually, apply asphaltum diluted in turpentine, which will soften the shade. The asphaltum blackens the background and improves the finished appearance of the object. Once it is dry, a coat of water-based acrylic varnish is applied to the piece.

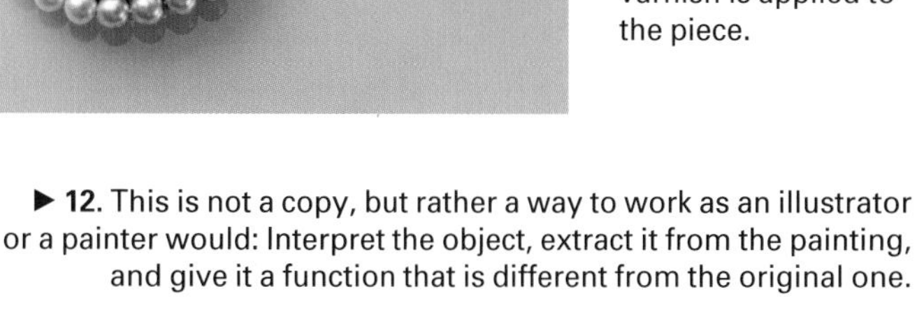

▶ **12.** This is not a copy, but rather a way to work as an illustrator or a painter would: Interpret the object, extract it from the painting, and give it a function that is different from the original one.

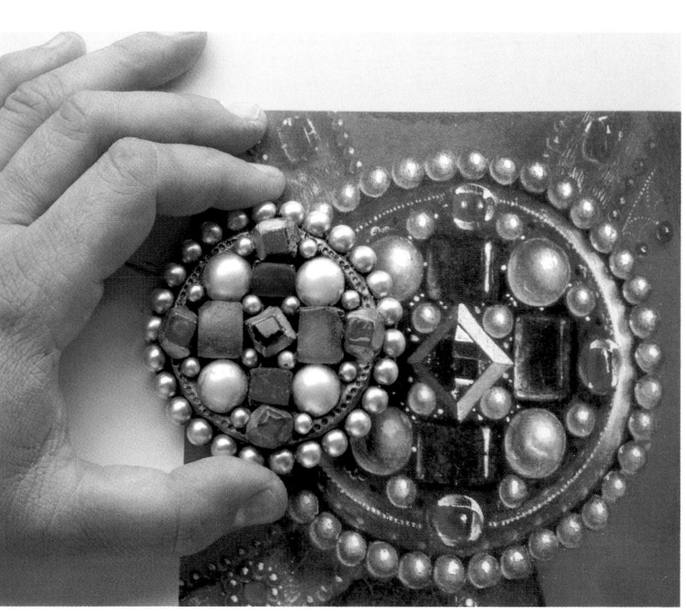

# *PLASTIC MATERIALS*

*Plastics are fairly new materials that, because of their characteristics, low cost, and ease of production, have become indispensable items in our daily lives. Plastic resins are a major group among these plastics and the ones most frequently used for ornamental objects, since they produce high-quality color and a broad spectrum of shades.*

## Plastic

In general, plastic is a light, strong material that softens when it is heated without losing cohesion, and can be reshaped when it cools again. It is also a good thermal and electrical insulator that resists most acids and solvents.

◀ Celluloid belt buckle made between 1920 and 1930. Celluloid was one of the first synthetic plastic materials used to make items of adornment.

### Monomers and Polymerization

Plastics are compounds made up of large organic molecules known as monomers. Each monomer is comprised of carbon and hydrogen atoms that combine to produce long polymer chains. These are used to make such plastics as polyethylene, polypropylene, ABS, and polystyrene. Polymerization is the process of making long chains from a basic unit or monomer that keeps repeating; organic polymers are those compounds that may be deformed in many ways, such as by thermofusion, injection, and extrusion to produce the desired shape.

The plastic molecules come from diverse origins. There are natural polymers such as horn, amber, and tortoise shell, which have been widely used in jewelry for centuries. In addition, cellulose, wax, and natural rubber are considered natural polymers. There are also semi-synthetic plastics, which originated from modifications to natural polymers; examples are cellulose and casein (a milk protein), along with some other chemical products. Finally, there is a large group made up of the plastics whose molecules are totally synthetic in origin, since they come from polymers produced from hydrocarbons extracted from crude petroleum, such as polyethylene, nylon, and others.

### Types of Plastic

There are basically two types of plastic, based on how the enormous polymer chains that make them up are arranged:

**Thermoplastics:** These are plastics whose chains of atoms are arranged in linear, ramified form. When they are heated or subjected to pressure, the atoms come together and take on different shapes that eventually harden by cooling. This happens because the bonds among the different chains are weak and can be broken by pressure or heat so they can form new shapes.

**Thermo-stable Plastics:** These are polymers whose chains are interlaced and tightly bonded because of the reaction used to produce them. Heat is used in these reactions, sometimes along with catalyzing agents. Examples of these are the epoxy resins, polyurethanes, alkyds, and polyesters, which will be further discussed later in this chapter.

◀ Rings made of silver, carnelian, and resin applications; creation of Silvia Walz, 2002.

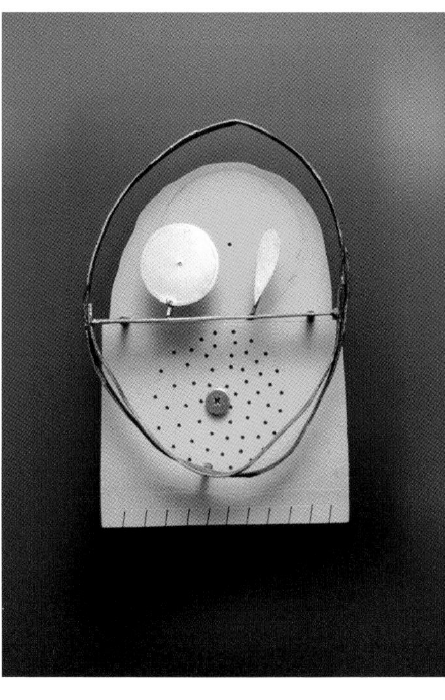

▲ *Wind Line,* 2002. Brooch made of silver, alpaca, wood, and plastic; creation of Ramon Puig Cuyàs.

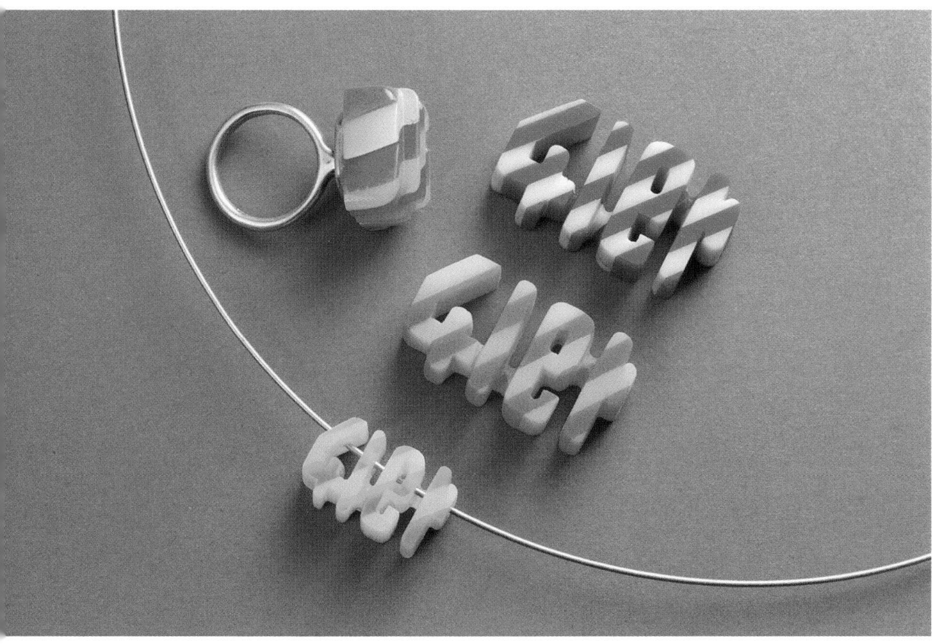

▲ Pieces made by gluing different layers of methacrylate together, by Hans Leicht, 1970

## he History of Plastics

The first known plastic was discovered by e American Wesley Hyatt in 1869. The aterial was patented under the name of **elluloid,** and used to manufacture various bjects, even though it had two serious rawbacks—it was flammable and ecomposed easily, especially if exposed to unlight. The first truly synthetic and stable esin was patented in 1907 by the Belgian eo Hendrik Baekeland. This was a rmaldehyde phenol—popularly known as **akelite**—and was the first plastic produced y humans using chemical products.

This new and revolutionary material was sed to make many items, including jewelry nd ornaments that today are in high emand among collectors. During this same eriod rayon, cellulose nitrate, and ellulose ethanoate, among others, were lso developed.

### Nylon and Teflon

A decisive step in the evolution of plastic as the discovery that plastic is comprised of acromolecules. This fact led to more esearch, which bore fruit between 1920 and 930 with the appearance of new ompounds such as cellulose acetate and inyl polychloride, better known as PVC. nother noteworthy development was ethyl polymethacrylate, which was arketed under the name of Plexiglass.

A few years later, in 1935, Wallace Carothers and his team advanced the plastics industry even further when they synthesized an artificial silk that was superior to rayon, and nylon was born. Two years later the first polyester resins were developed, and in 1938 polytetrafluorethylene—which was marketed in the 1950s under the name of Teflon—was developed. In 1941, J. Whinfield and J.T. Dickson discovered polyesters.

### Polyethylene and Polypropylene

Plastic seemed like an innovative and revolutionary material, but at the same time it gained a reputation of being a low-quality material because of its ephemeral use. It wasn't until WWII and the appearance of new plastics, along with new applications for them, that plastic's image received a tremendous boost. Unsaturated liquid polyester was one of the materials that, when used in conjunction with fiberglass, produced a new material that was much stronger, lighter, and cheaper than many others used up to that time.

During WWII, plastic became a good substitute for many raw materials that were in scarce supply. This necessity led to the development of synthetic rubber; nylon replaced many textile fibers; polyesters were used in the military industry; and during the post-war era the polycarbonates, acetates, and polyamides were developed. Plastic was even capable of replacing some metals, and it was ideal for working under certain conditions. Polyethylene was developed in 1953, and polypropylene came on the scene in 1954; these are two of the most common plastics today.

### From 1960 to 1990

The 1960s were pivotal years in the development of plastics and their ornamental use. The industry made great strides in this field, accompanied by an appreciation of the aesthetics of plastics. Some truly innovative projects were completed up to that time: Plastic furniture, pieces of jewelry, clothing, shoes, and sculptures were made of plastic. But with the onset of the oil shortage and a greater environmental consciousness in the 1970s, plastic was called into question. But that didn't keep many contemporary jewelers from using it in their creations, and that continued well into the 1980s, a time when new plastics with very attractive characteristics were introduced.

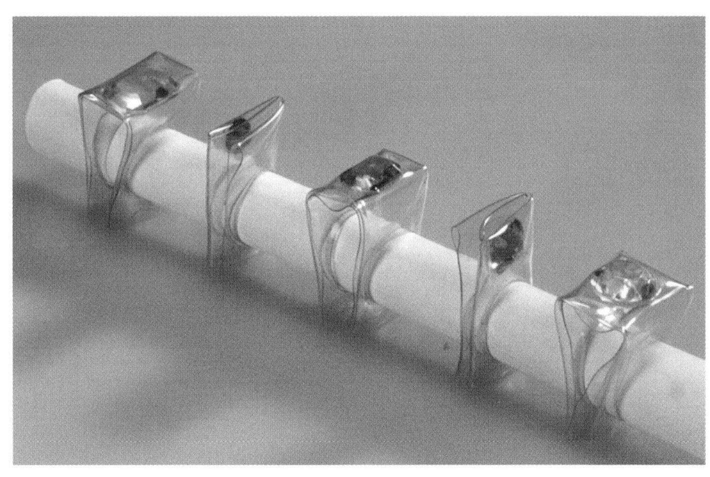

◀ Plastic rings with precious stones made by Judith Hoefel. Photo by Petra Jaschke

# The Plastic Resins Group

Of all the various types of plastics, plastic resins are the ones most commonly used in making jewelry, costume jewelry, and other accessories. Resins are liquid polymers that turn into solids when certain agents are mixed in, whether catalysts or hardeners. These agents set up the bonds that provide rigidity, making it possible to use these resins to create many different objects.

Polyester resins and epoxies are used the most; the latter shrink less than the polyester resins and, because they are transparent, they are good choices for projects like the ones in this chapter. Polyurethanes are ideal for casting in molds; they can also be colored, they shrink very little, and they have other excellent qualities for making ornamental and useful items.

## Polyester Resins

Polyester resins are used in the plastics industry for making such things as paints, varnishes, and textile fibers. Used in conjunction with fiberglass, they produce an excellent material for making automobile bodies and boat hulls, for example. They belong to the system referred to as polyester-vinylester: a group of resins made up of polyester resins, vinylester resins, gel coats, plus various special polyester putties.

**Polyester-Vinylester Resins**

Vinylester resins offer very good adhesion plus great resistance to chemical products and high temperatures, so they are excellent for producing laminates when reinforced by fiberglass. They are used in a way similar to polyester resins, and are generally applied with the same accelerators and catalysts.

Gel coats are resins that are used for exterior coverings; they are not appropriate for pouring, since they are very viscous. They commonly are applied on vertical surfaces as protection for fiberglass against moisture.

Putties also belong to the polyester group; they are used mainly to repair and join pieces of damaged polyester. They dry naturally and are easy to sand.

The polyester resins used in projects in this chapter, like the epoxy resins and the polyurethanes, turn into solids with the addition of catalyzing agents. Along with accelerating and hardening agents, they cause the material to harden when mixed properly. Generally, the accelerator used in work with polyester resin is cobalt octoate (6%); added in the proportion of 0.3%, it speeds up the polymerization of the polyester and vinylester resins.

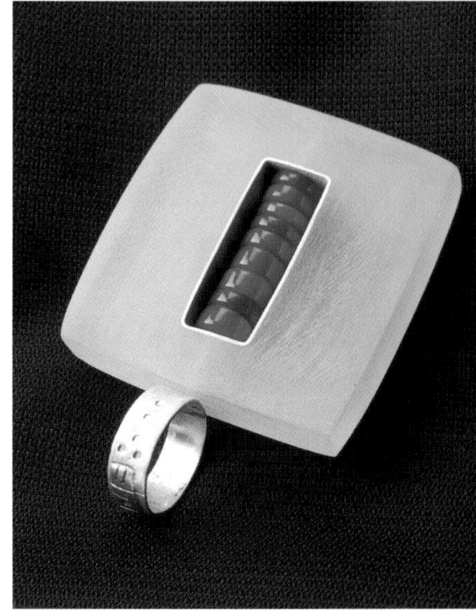

▲ Pendant made using transparent matte polyester resin, by Carlos Reano

**Hardening of the Resin**

The resin used for projects in this chapt has an accelerator mixed in with it; on catalyst needs to be added. This is meth ethyl ketone peroxide in liquid form, and it known as MEK Peroxide. This is one of th most commonly used catalysts in work involving polyester resin, but there are other such as Butanox M-50 and Butanox LPT. Th resin used here is transparent and colorles although at first it may appear slightly bluis that color vanishes, however, when it is mixe with the catalyst. The reason for choosing th

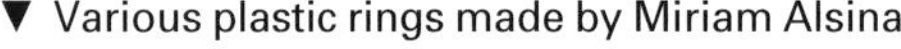

▼ Various plastic rings made by Miriam Alsina

▲ Polyurethanes are included in the group of plastic resins. Polyurethane is prepared in equal parts, and it reacts very quickly. That's why it's a good choice for making models that will subsequently be reproduced, as well as for making many items for daily use. Additionally, it can be tinted, and finished similarly to polyester resins.

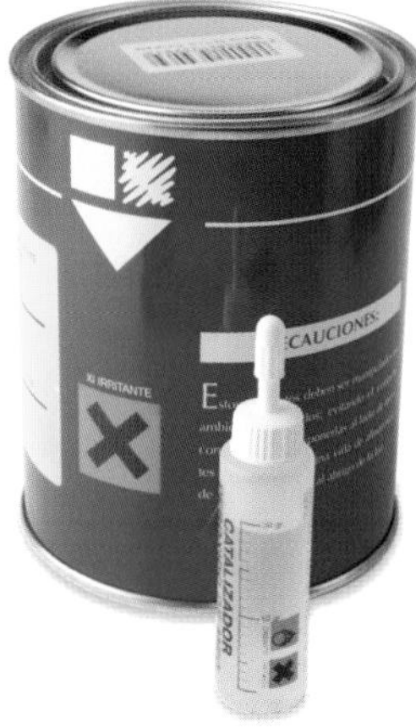


▲ All polyester resins need the addition of a
talyst. In this instance MEK peroxide is used.
he quantity added must always be in exact
roportion to the amount of resin used. To
revent overheating, add less catalyst, but not
ss than two percent. Adding too little catalyst
ay produce problems in the final product,
ıch as discoloration or improper hardening.

## Work Area and Safety

Before starting to work with resins, become familiar with the potential hazards that doing craft work with plastics entails. Generally, final products made of hardened, finished plastics pose no health threats, since they are an inert material. That's not true, however, while the plastic is being worked, for some monomers used in the manufacture may produce cancer. It's certain that resins are toxic when inhaled, so be sure to work in a well-ventilated area and use a powerful exhaust fan that assures proper aeration of the workspace.

It's also important to mention that plastics, and resins in this instance, are not biodegradable materials, so they have to be recycled as solids. Allow the leftover resin to harden before discarding it; in no case should liquid resin be poured down drains or mixed with other products without knowing how they will react.

Resins, hardeners, and catalysts must be kept away from fire and all sources of heat, since these are very flammable products. Similarly, the acetone used for cleaning up liquid resin is also highly flammable.

In order to keep polyester resin from sticking to work surfaces, protect it with newspapers or disposable cardboard. To clean up leftover liquid, wipe the work surface with a rag moistened with acetone.

esin is that it's a good one for use with
clusions of various materials, and because
f its low polymerization temperature.

In order to make the resin transparent,
olorless, and produce the ideal hardness
r subsequent manipulation, catalysts,
ardeners, and accelerators must be applied
precise quantities. Too much catalyst
ellows the resin; an excess of hardener gives
slightly bluish tint to the completed project.
emperature is another factor to keep in
ind, since at low temperatures polyester
esins take longer to harden.

On the other hand, a temperature that's too
gh causes a quick reaction in the resin. The
eal room temperature for resin to harden
roperly is around 68°F (20°C). Generally, the
esin hardens in a couple of hours, but it's not
ady to be worked with files and sandpaper
ntil it has hardened completely, a process
at may take up to a week.

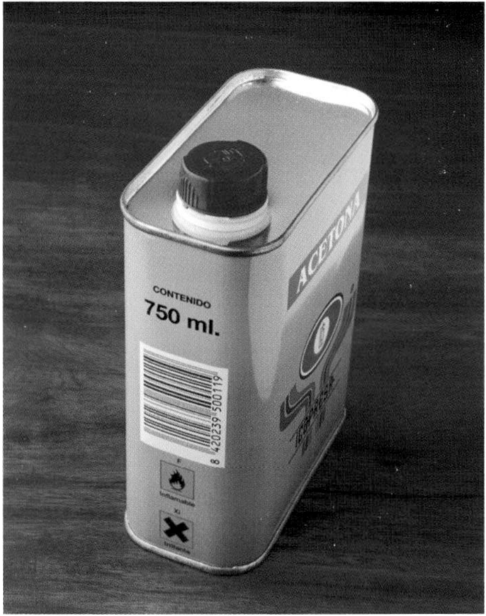


▲ Acetone can be used for cleaning up the resin and removing it from surfaces without catalyzing it. On some surfaces, such as polypropylene, it's preferable to let the resin harden completely and remove it once it's dry.

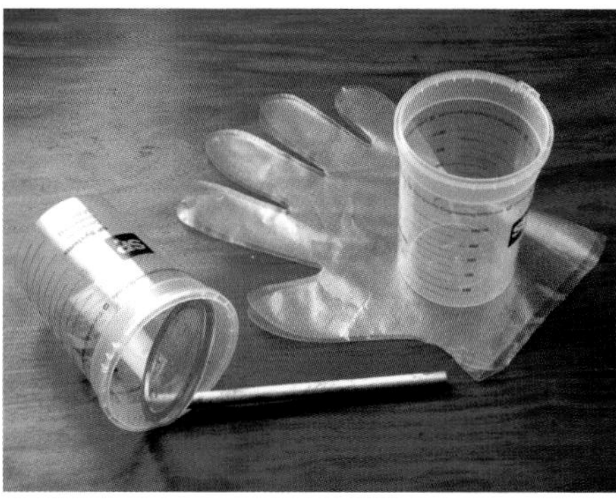

▲ It's advisable to use graduated polypropylene measuring cups. The resin won't stick to them, so once it dries it is easy to remove. Resin does not stick to melted PVC or to polyethylene; however, it can't be used in conjunction with polystyrene.

▲ Wear either non-latex, single-use disposable gloves or another more durable glove when working with resins in order to avoid direct skin contact with the resin.

► Be sure to wear a mask and use
ppropriate gloves during the polymerization
phase. In the filing and polishing stages,
wear a mask to prevent dust inhalation.

## Preparing and Coloring the Polyester Resin

Before preparing the polyester resin for casting, it's necessary to determine the amount of resin needed to fill a mold completely. To do this, fill the mold with water and pour it into a graduated test tube. Another method is to do a calculation based on the density of the resin, which hovers around 1.15. Then the mold is dried thoroughly to remove all remnants of water before filling it with resin.

Once the volume of resin has been determined, pour it into the graduated propylene container up to the calculated amount. The resin must be poured into this container slowly in order to avoid producing air bubbles. Once the resin has been weighed, add two percent of this weight of MEK peroxide and stir in gently to avoid producing more bubbles. If coloring a resin, add the catalyst to the resin first, then add the desired dye or color. Sometimes this sequence can be reversed by first adding the color and then the resin; that way the desired resin color can more precisely be produced and corrected before adding in the catalyst.

No additional hardener or accelerator is used in the project in this chapter; however, if a quicker polymerization is desired, an accelerator can be added to the mixture.

▼ **1.** The resin is poured into a graduated container up to the desired volume. Because it's important to avoid creating many bubbles, hold the side of the measuring container at an angle and pour slowly down the container's side.

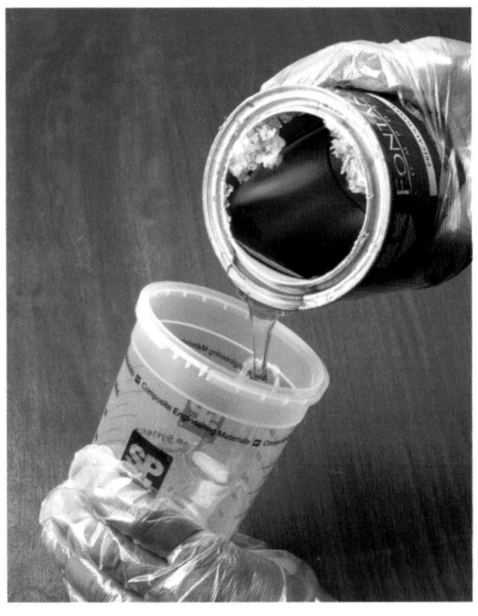

▼ **2.** First, determine the precise weight of the resin by placing it on a scale. Calculate two percent of this weight; this yields the amount of MEK peroxide that must be added.

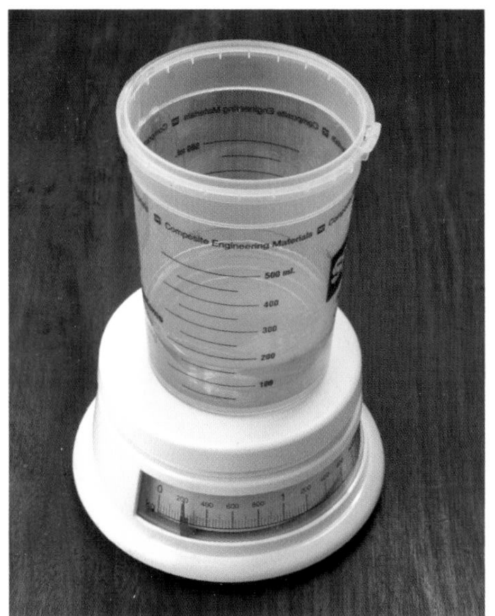

▼ **3.** Once the volume of catalyst has been determined, slowly add it to the resin. It is preferable to do this step first and then add the desired paint or dye. The bottle of catalyst has a scale that helps in calculating the volume equivalent of the weight.

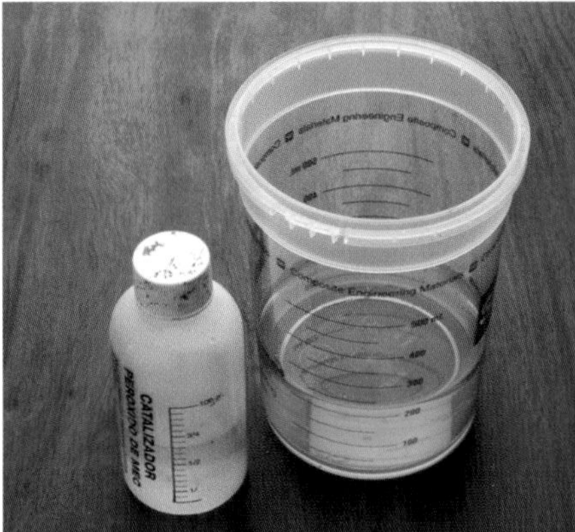


▼ **4.** Next, the tint or paint is carefully added. It's a good idea to weigh the amount of dye that needs to be added and write it down for repeating the same color or correcting it in other applications.

▼ **5.** The substance is mixed, taking care not to make bubbles, and then set aside for about 10 minutes before it starts to catalyze. The room temperature should be about 68°F (20°C).

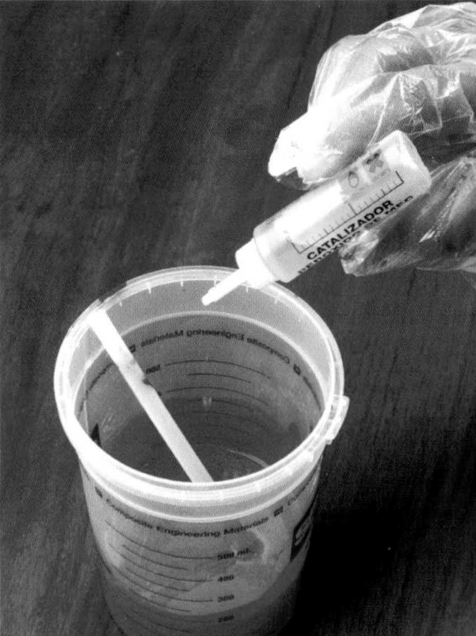


▲ **6.** Sometimes it is preferable to add the dye to the resin first; that way the shade of the desired color can be more effectively adjusted. Add the catalyst once the desired shade is reached.

# Making Bracelets from Colored Resins

This is a simple process that makes it ossible to produce a good number of racelets by using polypropylene food ontainers as molds. There are countless ottles and jars on the market that have very nteresting textures, shapes, and diameters rom which to choose. In this section, various racelets will be made from colored olyester. This is a very common technique hat works well and is inexpensive, since eftover colored resin from previous projects an be used.

◀ **1.** In preparation for this project, two plastic containers made from propylene have been chosen, one of which fits inside the other and has a diameter appropriate for use in making bracelets.

◀ **2.** Once the containers are placed one inside the other and centered, they are held in place with a piece of plasticene.

▶ **3.** Next, the first color is prepared in the way previously described, and the colored resin is poured inside the mold.

▶▶ **4.** Once the resin begins to thicken a bit (a couple of minutes), place the cover on the container.

▶ **5.** At this point, begin rotating the mold so that the colored resin moves about slowly in the pace between the two containers. It's important that the resin not be too liquid, so some nteresting and well-defined color combinations can be created.

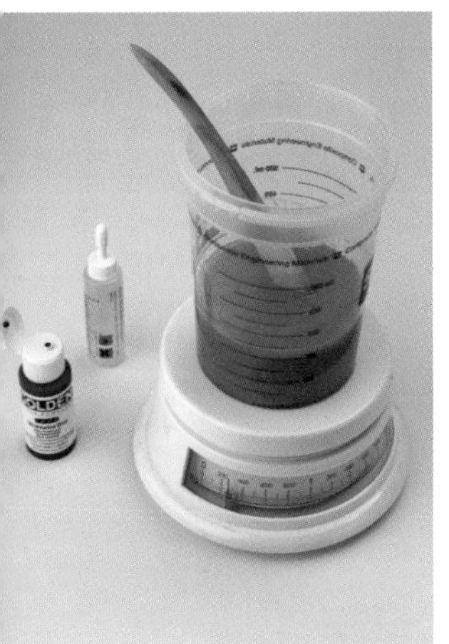

▲ **6.** Now the same process f coloring the resin is used vith different colors.

▲ **7.** The successive colors are prepared and poured into the mold until the container is completely full.

◀ **8.** A variety of containers can be used in the same way. Shown here is a striated outer container from a water bottle and an inner one made from a hexagonal baby bottle. The latter must have an appropriate diameter to fit a person's wrist. In order to use up the resin it's a good idea to have several containers ready for pouring in the leftovers from previous projects.

▶ **9.** Once the resin is completely hardened—and, depending on the room temperature, it may be necessary to wait a week to handle it properly—remove the outer plastic container, then the inside container. From this point on, the raw material is ready to be transformed into bracelets.

### Finishing Resin Bracelets

Before applying the final finish that will provide shine and transparency to the resin, the resin must be absolutely hard; this process can take up to a week. Sometimes if there are projections or areas that need smoothing up, the resin may first have to be filed. Then it is subjected to a progression of various emery papers until all scratches are removed from the surface.

One finishing method involves first using sandpaper; a couple of sheets applied in different directions in succession will be adequate. Then, the surface is further smoothed using several pieces of wet emery paper in the same way. Depending on how you want the surface to turn out, begin with a 200- or 240-grit paper, change to a second paper with a grit between 400 and 500, and finish up with a grit of 1000 or 1200.

Once the surface has been sanded thoroughly with the wet paper, it is rubbed with a scouring pad. It is also possible to use an electric motor or polishing wheel in the sanding phases.

After the piece has been sanded it will have a matte appearance, and this is the point where the polishing begins. First, a coarse polishing compound that generally contains pumice is applied using a sewn cotton polishing wheel and a couple of brushes. Once the piece is cleaned, the resin is shined using several polishing wheels, preferably with an open or fairly loose weave so the resin won't heat up from the speed of the polishing wheel. Sometimes the resin needs a final polishing. In that case, a paste with a high wax content is used; it is applied usin very light cotton wheels that make it possib to attain a high surface polish on the resin.

▲ **1.** Once the resin has hardened completely, the various rings can be cut out. Using an electric carpenter's saw quickly produces straight, clean cuts.

◀ **2.** Using an electric belt sander with a coarse belt works well to remove a large quantity of resin and shape the bracelet quicky, remembering to continually change the direction of sanding.

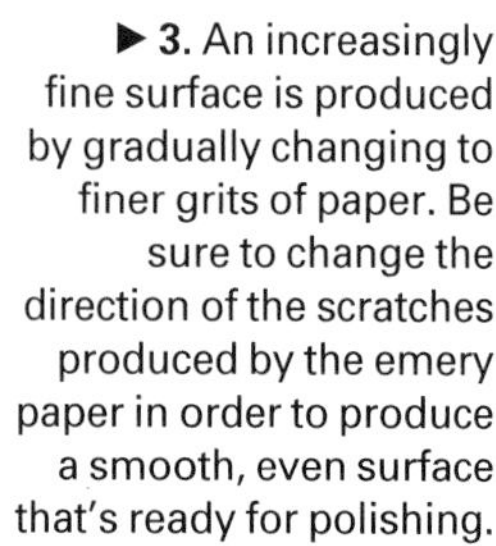

▶ **3.** An increasingly fine surface is produced by gradually changing to finer grits of paper. Be sure to change the direction of the scratches produced by the emery paper in order to produce a smooth, even surface that's ready for polishing.

▲ **4.** It's preferable to finish rounded shapes y hand, moistening with water all the pieces of mery paper that are used in finishing the resin.

▲ **5.** There are a number of tools that work well for polishing the inside of the bracelets.

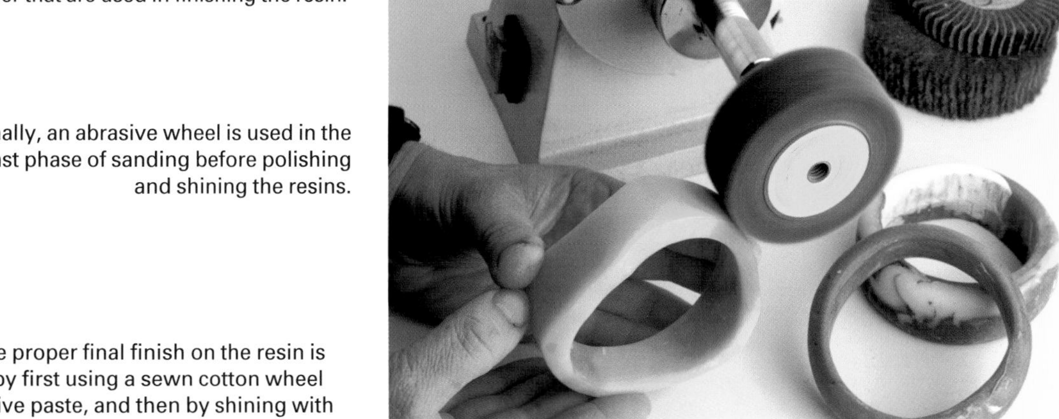

► **6.** Finally, an abrasive wheel is used in the last phase of sanding before polishing and shining the resins.

▼ **7.** The proper final finish on the resin is chieved by first using a sewn cotton wheel nd abrasive paste, and then by shining with n unsewn cotton wheel to which the olishing paste has been applied.

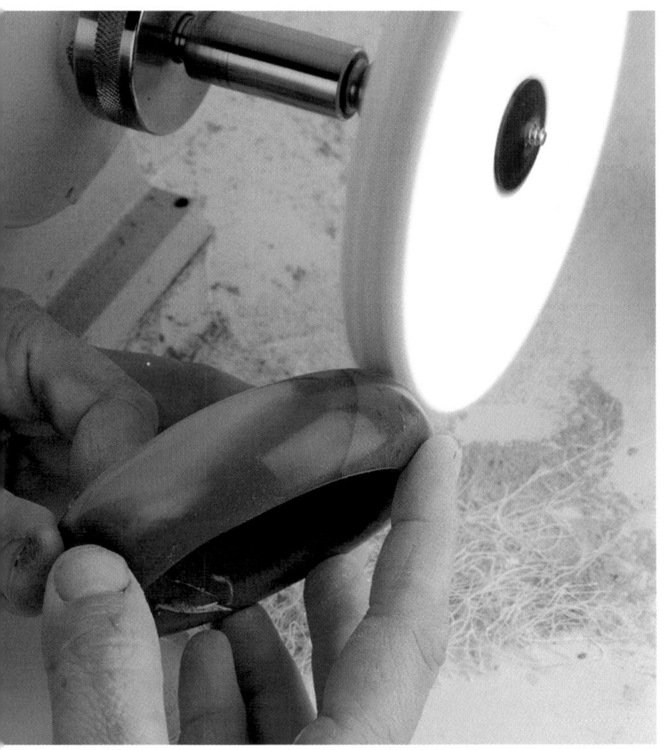

▼ **8.** Completed resin bracelets by Carles Codina i Armengol

## Inclusions

In addition to dyeing the resin with opaque colors, it is also possible to produce interesting transparent shades by dyeing it with inks or even certain liquid watercolors. It's also possible to put a variety of materials and objects as inclusions into a clear or slightly transparent resin. However, it is very important to be familiar with the properties of the material to be used as an inclusion to avoid a negative reaction when it contacts the resin. If in doubt, do a contact test before putting the object into the resin. In order to do a project like the following one, prepare the resin as previously described and then fill a plastic syringe with it.

▲ **1.** The shape of the object to be reproduced has been created in polyurethane foam, and then a silicone mold was produced. Plastic objects will be incorporated inside this mold as an illustration of what constitutes an inclusion.

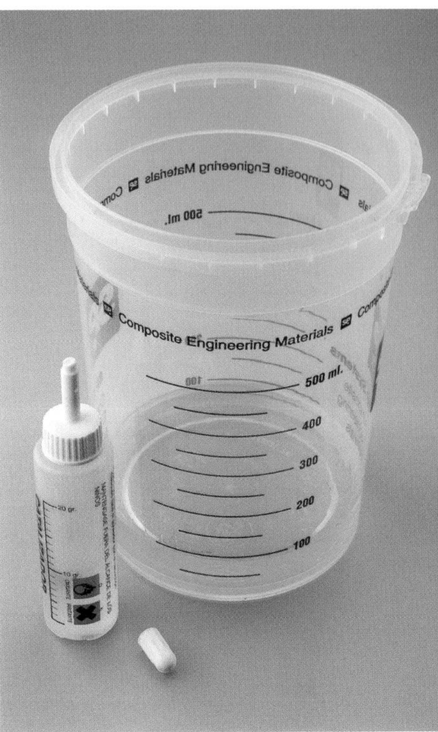


▲ **2.** The clear resin is prepared by calculating the volume of resin desired and adding two percent by weight of MEK peroxide.

▲ **3.** Normally the resin releases fairly well from this silicone, but when the model is complex it's advisable to use a releasing agent specifically for resins.

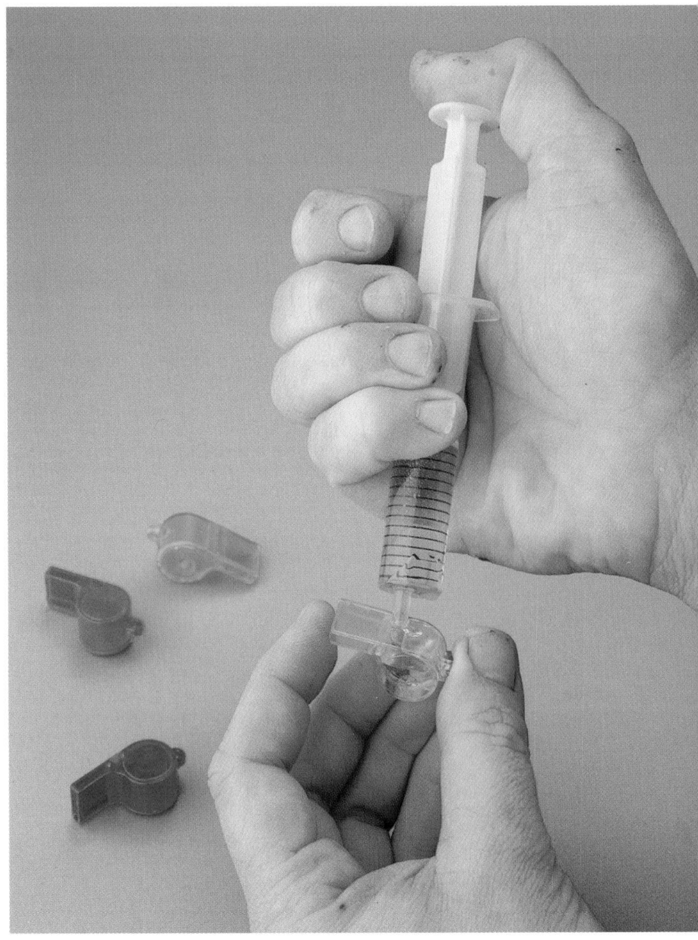

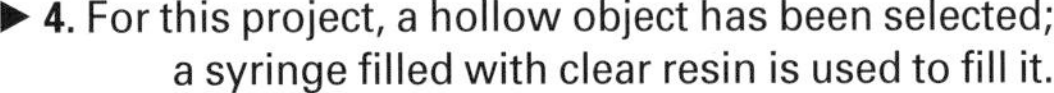

▶ **4.** For this project, a hollow object has been selected; a syringe filled with clear resin is used to fill it.

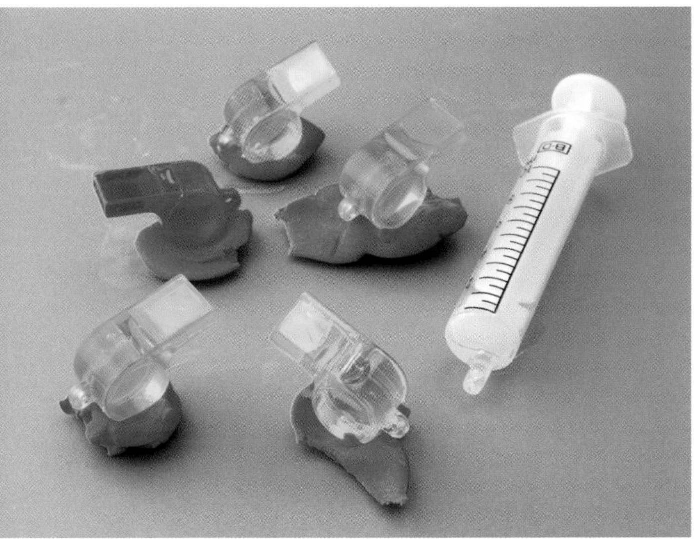

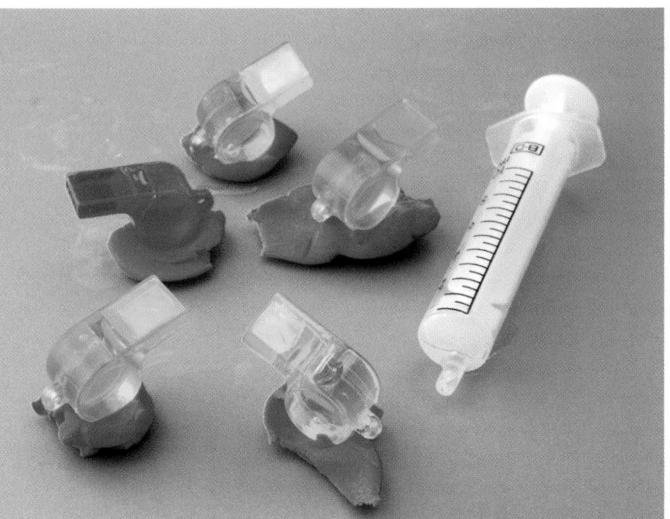

▲ **5.** The resin is allowed to catalyze with the object placed on a piece of modeling clay so that it remains immobile during the process.

▶ **6.** A small amount of clear resin is put into one half of the mold and allowed to dry covered with the other half of the mold. That way, contamination in the form of dust does not stick to the resin.

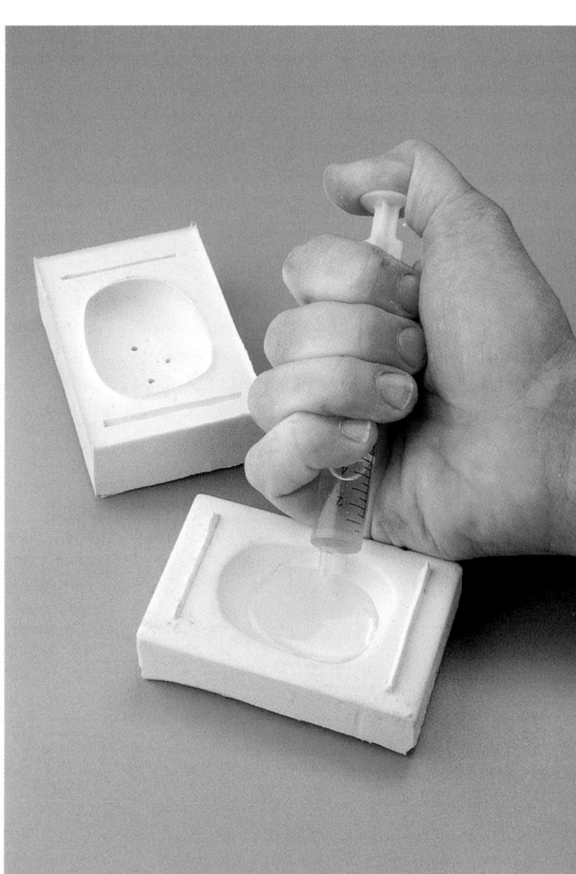

◀ **7.** Once the first layer is dry, the various items to be used as inclusions are put inside and the mold is closed.

▲ **8.** This mold is held together using simple office staples stuck into all eight ends.

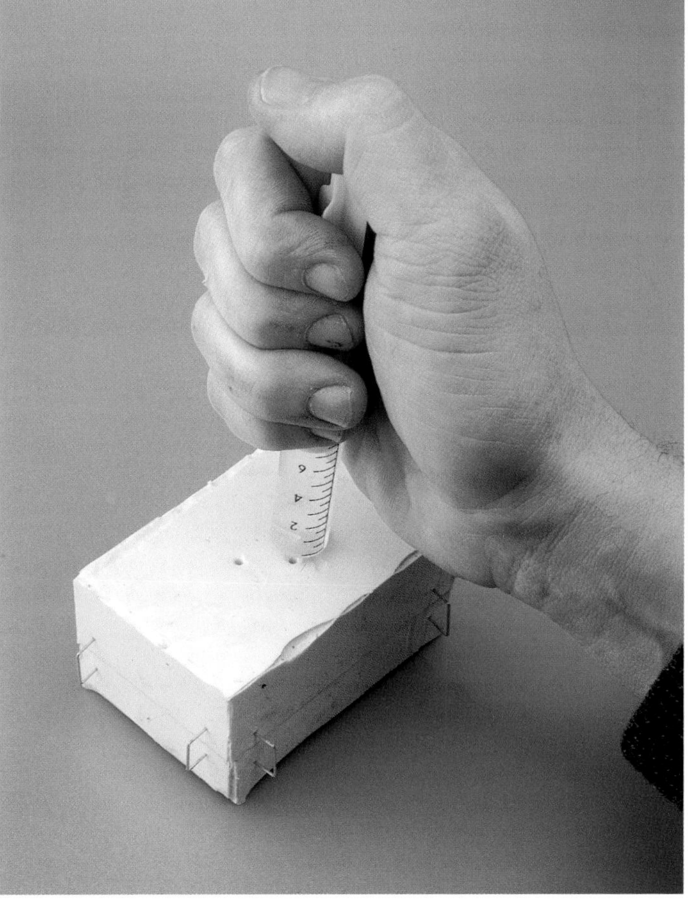

▲ **9.** More clear resin is prepared and inserted through the holes in the top of the mold.

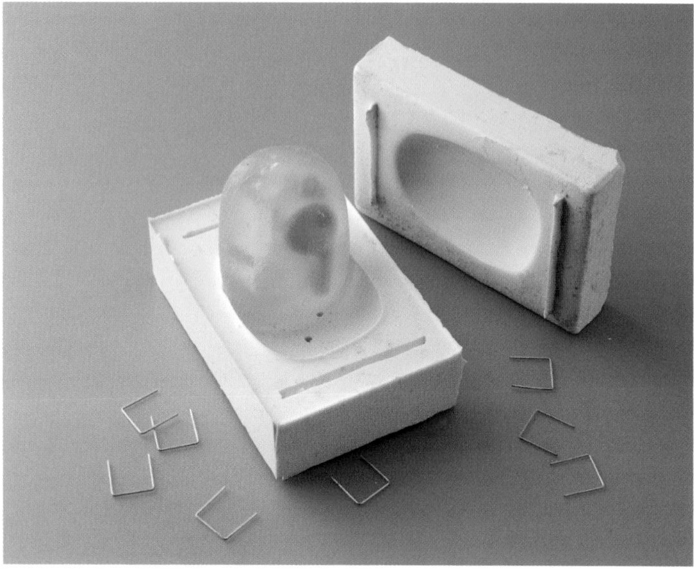

▲ **10.** Once the assembly is dry and the mold is opened, the resin's surface can be finished.

▲ **11.** The resin is smoothed with a progression of wet emery papers up to a grit of about 1200.

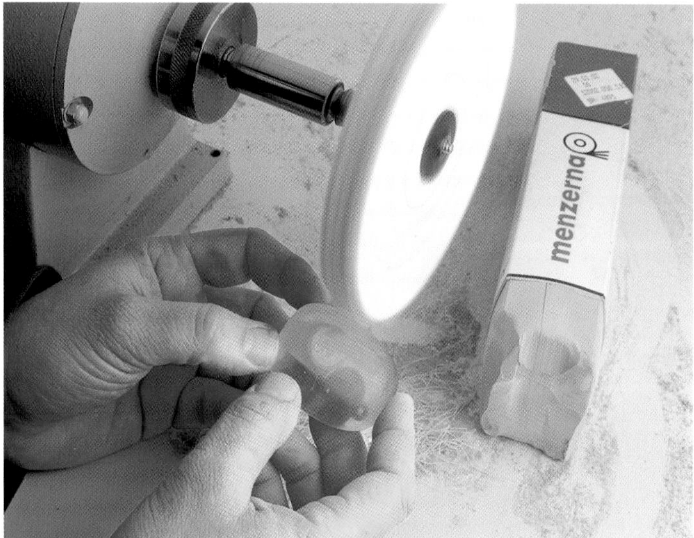


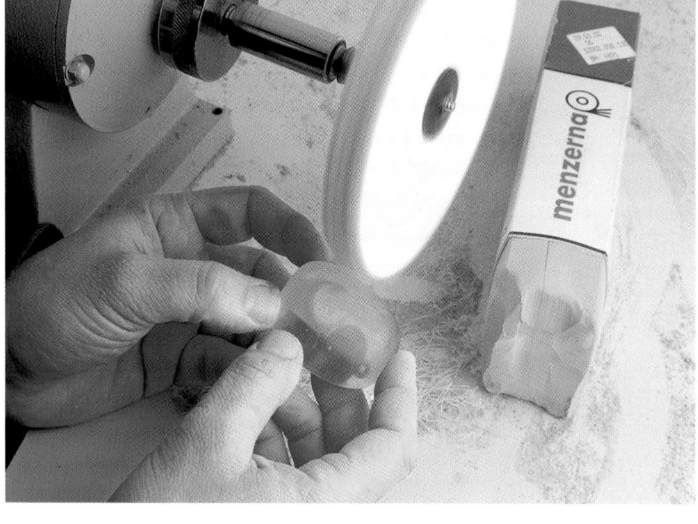

◀ **12.** Next, the piece is polished and shined using abrasive paste to produce the proper surface polish.

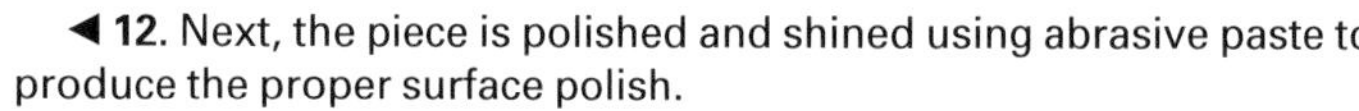

▼ **13.** Once the surface is perfectly polished, it is cleaned to produce the best possible finish.

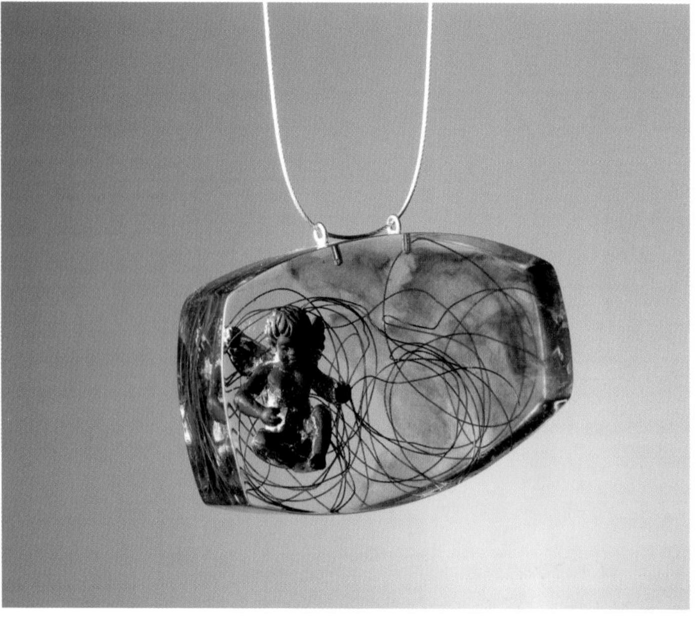

◀ Polyester resin pendant with inclusions of various silver elements, by Carles Codina i Armengol

# Enameling with Polyester Resins

Synthetic resins can be used for filling up the spaces or cells in numerous decorative objects made for the purpose. Resins are also used in jewelry and costume jewelry applications, since they can be joined to many metals without having to apply heat. Another factor in using them is their speed of application and low cost.

▲ Silver pendants made using polyester resins, by Carlos Reano

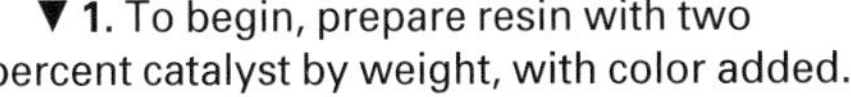

▼ **1.** To begin, prepare resin with two percent catalyst by weight, with color added.

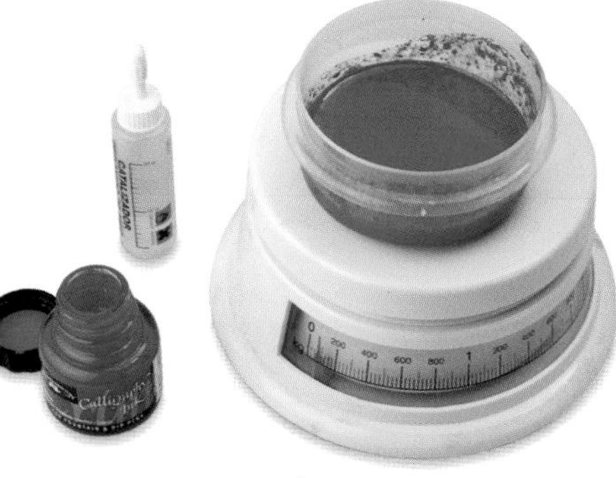

▼ **2.** The resin is drawn into a plastic syringe, taking care to avoid producing bubbles.

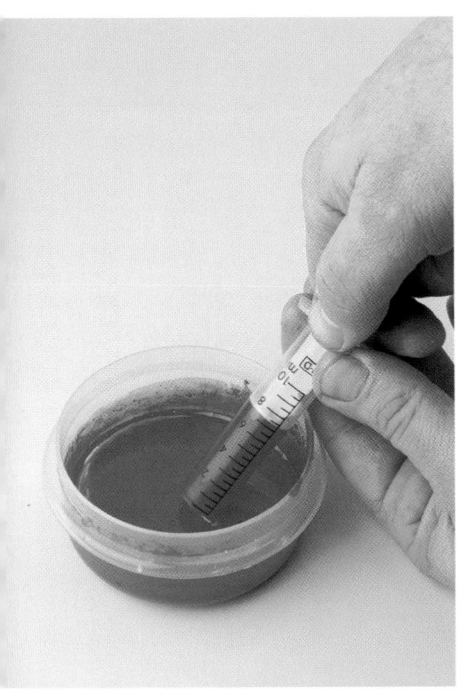

▲ **3.** The next color is prepared by mixing a natural, dry pigment directly into the resin; it is likewise put into another plastic syringe for transferring the resin to the inside of the mold. Repeat the same process of making separate syringes for each color to be used in the project. When using syringes, it's still a good idea to wear gloves.

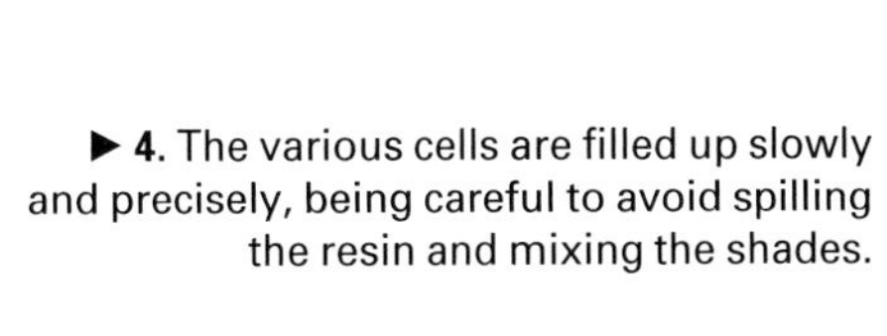

► **4.** The various cells are filled up slowly and precisely, being careful to avoid spilling the resin and mixing the shades.

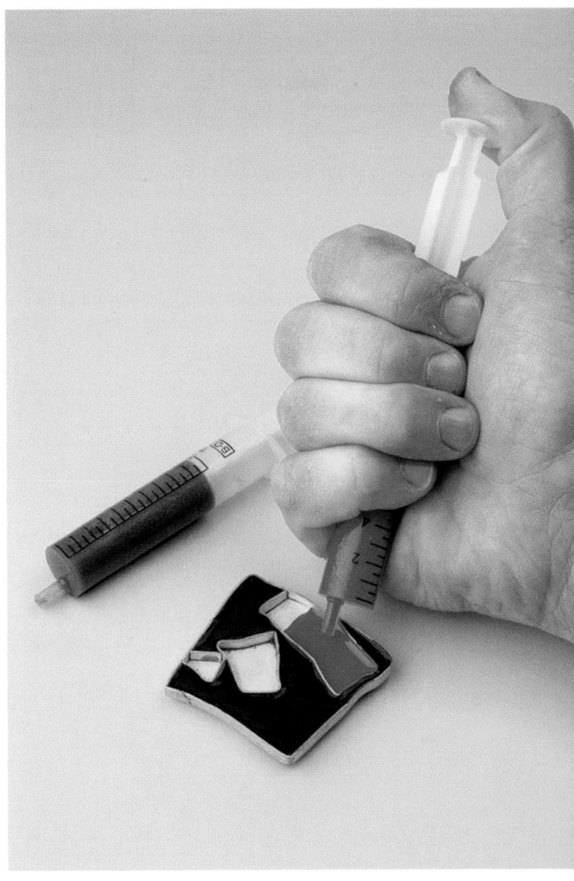

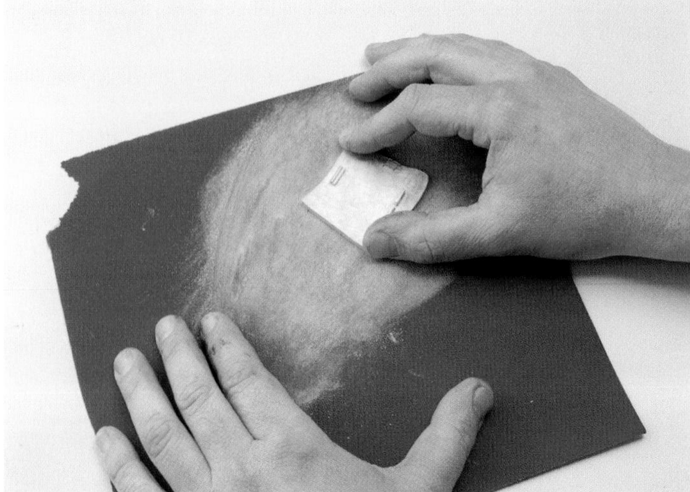

◀ **5.** The resin must be thoroughly dry before moving on to the polishing stage. First using a very coarse paper to even up the surface, the grit of the emery paper is then progressively reduced to about 1000 or 1200.

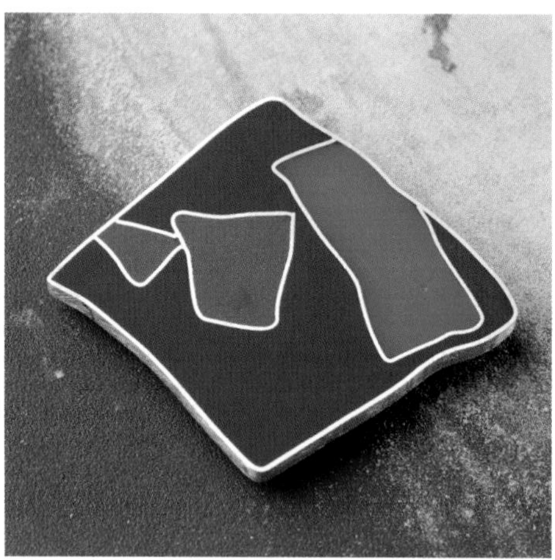

◀ **6.** The surface must be smooth and free of scratches before beginning the polishing stage. If the fine polishing with emery paper is done well, it can sometimes be the final finish, and it may be even more interesting than a perfectly polished piece.

▲ **7.** Here is the piece after polishing and shining. Creation of Carles Codina i Armengol

---

**Inclusions in Polyester Resins**

▼ **1.** There are many ways to work a surface filled with resin. One way involves removing parts of the surface resin by using a grinding bit or burr, or some similar tool. Whether in the shape of the strokes shown in the photo or a definite design, simply fill up the cavities with different colors of resin and wait for them to polymerize before sanding.

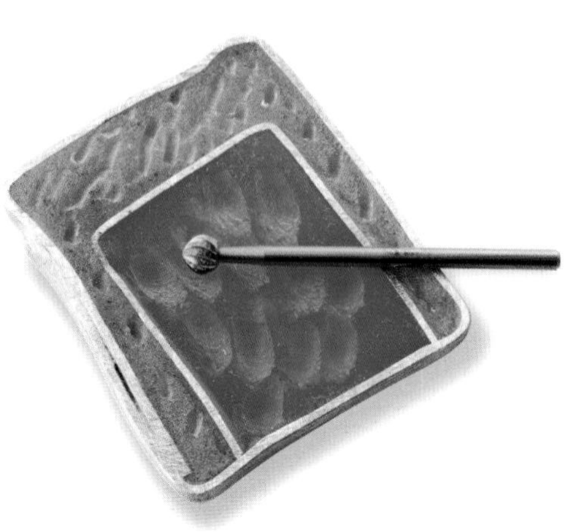

▼ **2.** In this instance, black resin is applied with the syringe. Once it's dry it will be removed by evening out the piece as previously described.

▲ **3.** Here's the finished piece, after evening it out and polishing the surface.

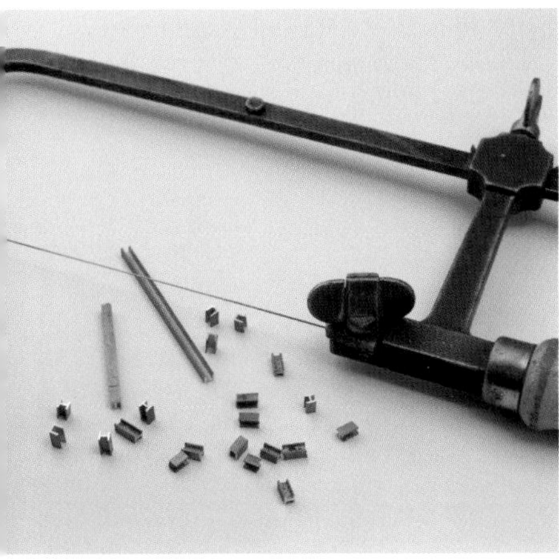

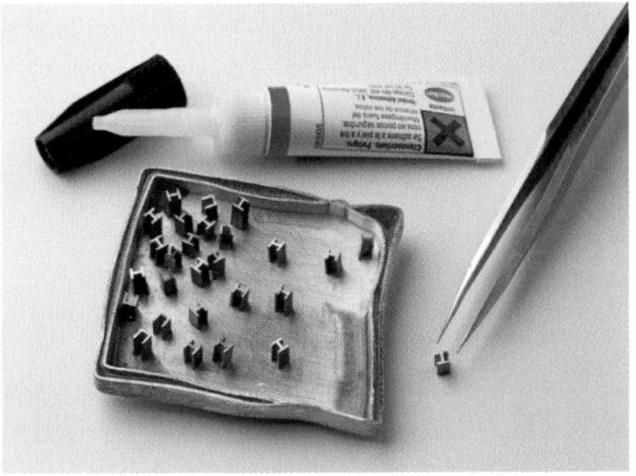

▲ **2.** The various pieces of brass are filed and glued onto the base of the metal.

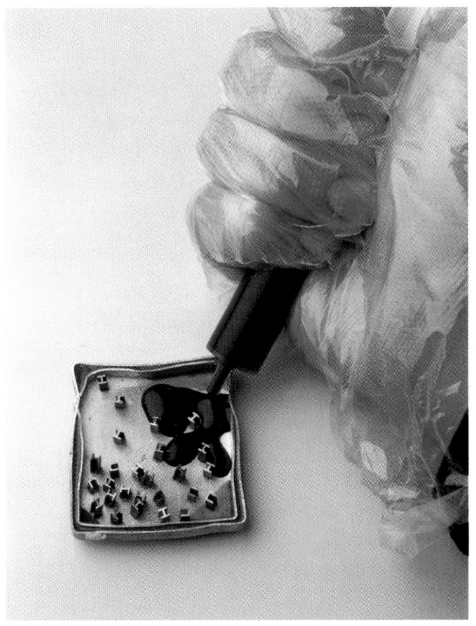

**Inclusions of Other Materials**

▲ **1.** Inclusions of plastics, shells, wood, and various metals can be put into the resin. Shown here are small pieces that have been cut from a brass shaft.

▶ **3.** Once the glue is dry, the cells are filled with the colored resins prepared in advance.

▶ **4.** Every space must be filled by the resin. Once it is dry, the entire surface is smoothed and polished with emery paper.

▶ **5.** Here is the finished brooch with the surface polished and shined. Creation by Carles Codina i Armengol

▶ Another variation involves mixing colors before they have polymerized. Here, pieces of silver tube are glued onto the surface, and one part is filled with resin. Then, before the resin has polymerized completely, new colors are added, and the resin mixes in a totally random way.

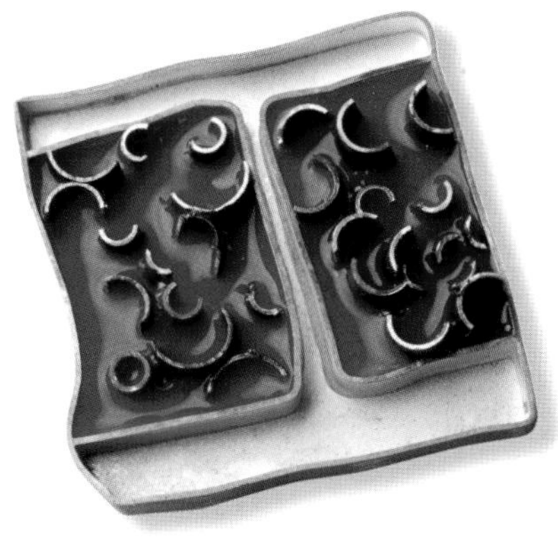

▶ Here is the result after polishing and shining with emery paper. Creation by Carles Codina i Armengol

# Epoxy Resins

The epoxy resins are part of a large group of compounds known as thermostable plastics. These are strong, solid materials derived from resins that react chemically with a catalyst. Epoxy resins (or epoxy) are appealing for both their strength—which allows for the creation of finer, lighter elements than those made with polyester—and their ability to adhere perfectly to any surface. Because of these characteristics, as well as the great variety of possible changes in their chemical makeup, many manufacturers produce and use these resins with colors that are commercially available. These products may be applied like a cold enamel on any surface.

## Resin Pendants, by Miquel Rubinat

This section details the making of a series of silver pendants inside which various colored epoxy resins have been applied, and colors manufactured using epoxy resin as a starting point. Based on these color preparations, which are easily found in craft stores, the initial colors can be adapted to individual taste and personality. The end result is jewelry distinguished by the spectrum of colors used, improved transparency, and uniqueness.

▼ Various manufacturers produce and market colored epoxy-based resins, but sometimes they are not appropriate for projects like the one that follows. Here artist Miquel Rubinat modifies the color shade by adding a greater quantity of clear resin to a basic color. This creates a broader spectrum of shades. Once the desired shade of colors is achieved, the colors are weighed in order to create a chromatic scale.

◀ **1.** The resin is poured into a container, preferably of glass. The can is held as illustrated, and the glass container is tilted slightly to minimize the creation of air bubbles.

▶ **2.** Color is added to the resin until the desired shade is reached, and then the special catalyst for epoxy resin is added, in this case in a proportion of 50 percent by weight. For example, two grams of enamel are mixed with one gram of catalyst.

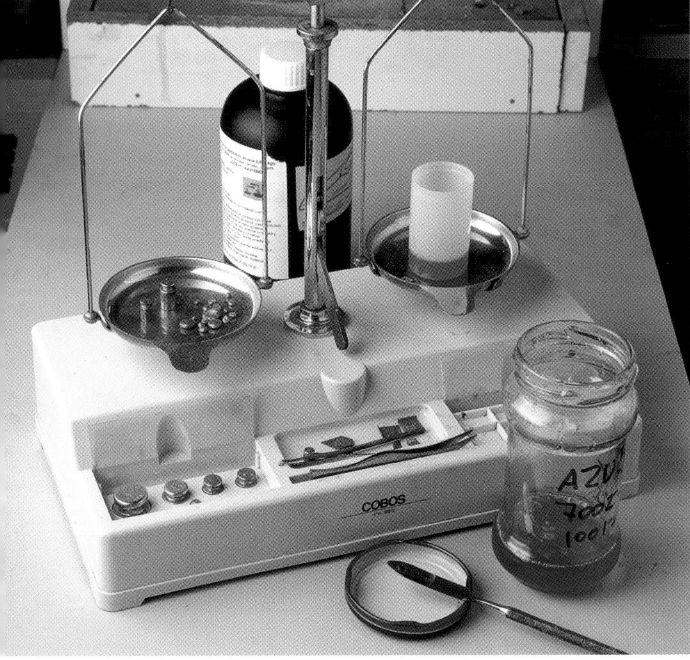


▲ **3.** When the desired color shade is reached, the quantity of resin in the mixture is weighed precisely and written down for later use in determining the correct amount of catalyst to be added.

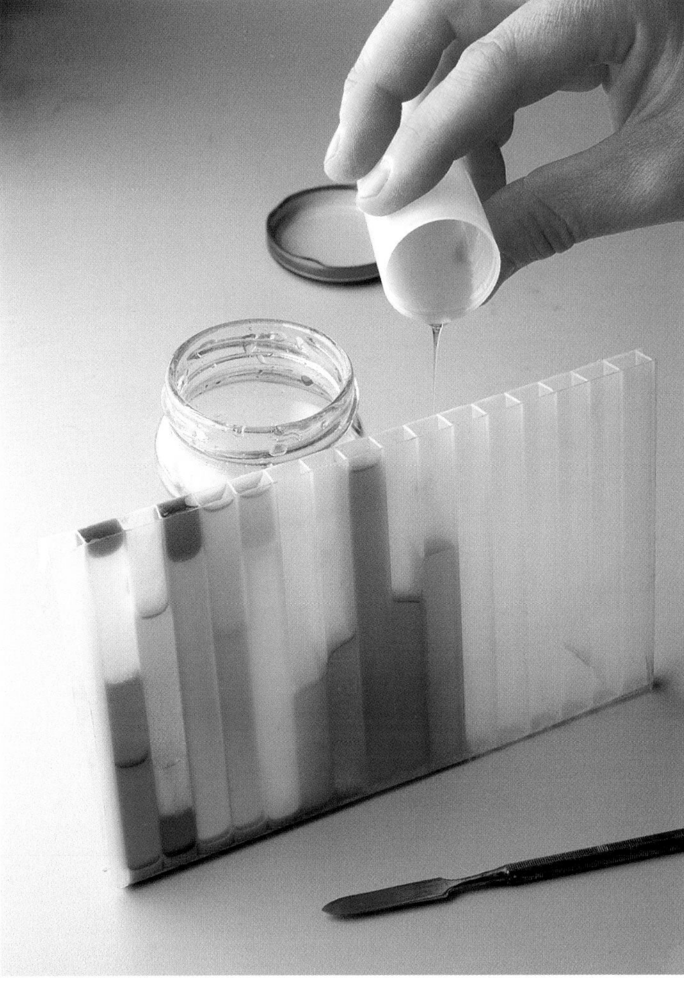

► **4.** Once the resin is mixed with the catalyst, it is slowly poured into a polycarbonate form; this is a material to which the resin does not stick, and from which it can be extracted easily.

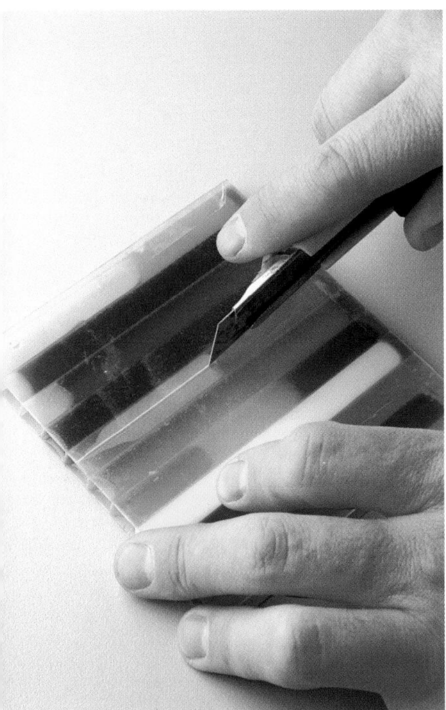

▲ **5.** After the resin has dried for a minimum of 36 hours, it is removed from the polycarbonate mold by cutting lengthwise along the compartments and folding them over forcefully until the mold opens.

▲ **6.** Once the mold is open, a hobby knife is used to remove the epoxy from the inside. There are many different types of molds; the important thing is that the resin doesn't stick to them.

▲ **7.** Several slices of resin half as large as a die are cut out with a saw; then they are filed on their base to make them flat.

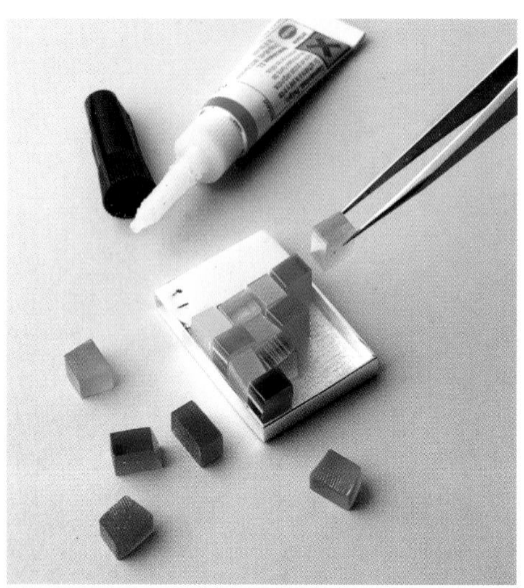

◀ **8.** Cyanoacrylate glue is used to cement the pieces of resin inside the brooch and to prevent the pieces from moving around when the new resin is put in.

▲ **9.** Once the pieces are in place, the clear resin that will fill up all the corners and unite the different colored pieces is prepared.

◀ **10.** Cellophane tape is used to construct wall around the piece to prevent overflow when an excess amount of resin is poured in. This new resin is poured inside in such a way that all spaces are filled up and no bubbles ar created inside the form.

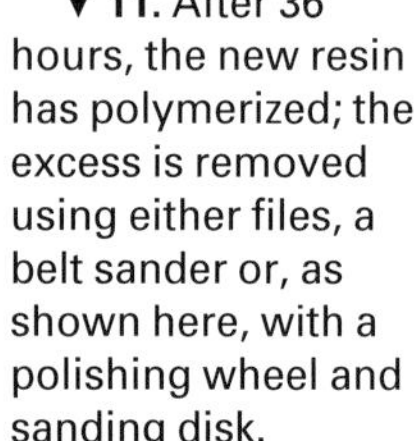

▼ **11.** After 36 hours, the new resin has polymerized; the excess is removed using either files, a belt sander or, as shown here, with a polishing wheel and sanding disk.

▼ **12.** As with all projects involving resins, the finishing follows a progression of wet sandpapers until arriving at the finest possibl emery paper. Then comes the polishing and buffing phase.

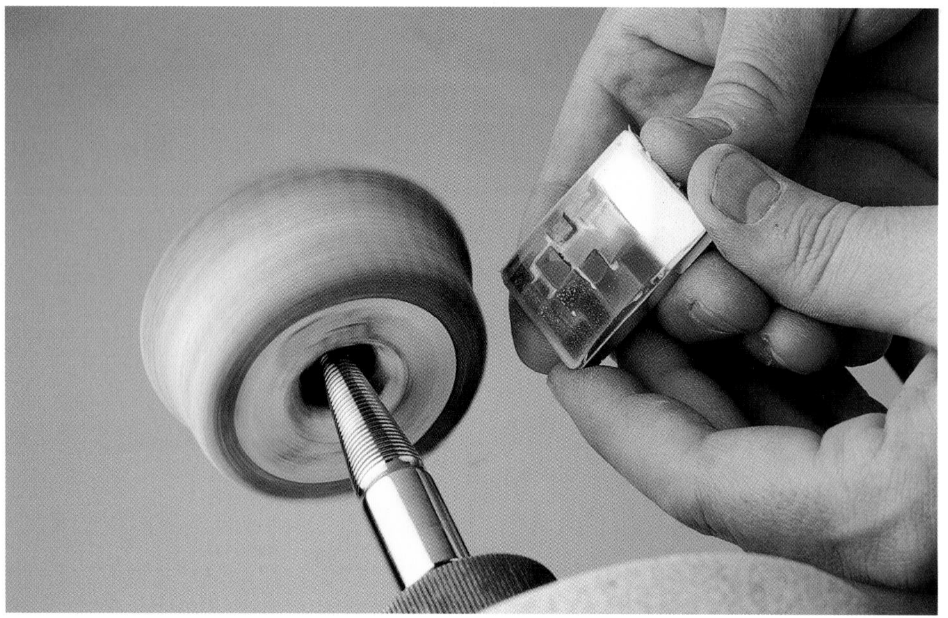

▲ **13.** First, the resin is subjected to an initial polishing with fairly hard, seamless cloth wheels. Next, special polishing paste for plastics is applied, then the entire piece is cleaned thoroughly.

▲ **14.** Polishing compound is applied to a sewn cotton wheel, and the surface of the resin is polished. Finally, the piece is cleaned with soap and water, or an ultrasound device is used for the final cleaning.

► **15.** Once the polishing phase is complete, there should be no visible scratches on the surface, and the shine should be perfectly even.

▲ **16.** Final result of the epoxy resin brooch made by Miquel Rubinat.

◄ Epoxy resin brooches made by Miquel Rubinat

# Molds

Polyester resins are generally applied by pouring or casting inside a mold; thus it's essential to use some support or structure that allows containing these resins and giving them shape while they polymerize.

There are lots of things that can be used to make molds, including modeling clay, plasticene, clay, wax, plaster—virtually any object or surface that accepts a pour of resin inside it. Various types of plastic, glass, and certain metals also can be used. Additionally, certain porous materials such as featherweight board or wood can be used as long as a separator is used before pouring the resin. Separator keeps the resin from sticking to the mold and makes it easier to remove the model; it also improves the appearance of the resin when it's taken out of the mold.

In any case, the molds must always be perfectly clean and dry, and the resin should be poured on a flat, stable surface.

## A Silicone Mold Made of Featherweight Board

The following project shows how to produce silicone molds. Silicone is an organic compound derived from the silicon that was developed during WWII. This is a compound that remains stable in the presence of heat and oxygen, and it is this quality that makes it more durable and permanent than other organic substances. Silicones are very useful in working with polyester resins, since they make it possible to construct extraordinary and complex molds for casting the resin.

One very easy way to make a polyester copy of any object involves first making a silicone mold of the object. Begin by constructing a simple framework from a sheet of featherweight board. In this instance, various plastic balls used for dog toys will be used to produce several brooches.

▲ **1.** First, cut one of the selected balls through the middle, making a clean cut that will allow the hemisphere to sit perfectly on the smooth surface of the featherweight board.

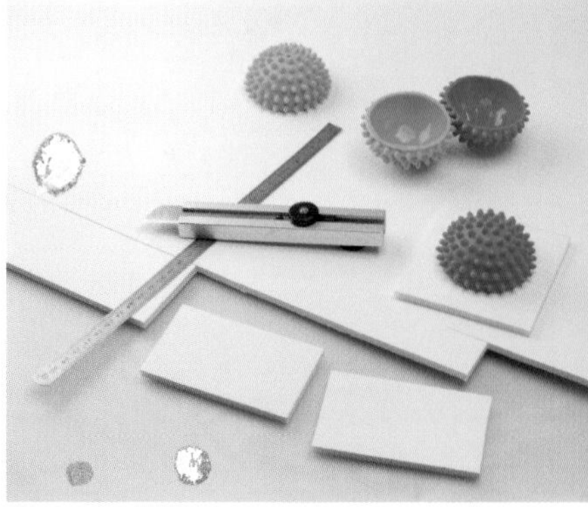

▲ **2.** Because silicone is fairly expensive, try to maintain a minimal amount of space between the object and the wall of the framework. The base should be cut no more than ½ inch (1.3 cm) larger than the size of the ball.

▲ **3.** Use a hobby knife to cut out the sidewalls that will be assembled to form the box and support the silicone when it's poured in. Glue the walls onto the base one by one with the hot silicone glue gun.

▲ **4.** The same silicone glue applicator is used to glue the ball in the center of the lightweight board base.

▼ **5.** The box must be completely sealed, since the silicone will be poured inside the mold in a liquid state. Any hole, no matter how tiny, will cause a leak and keep the mold from filling properly.

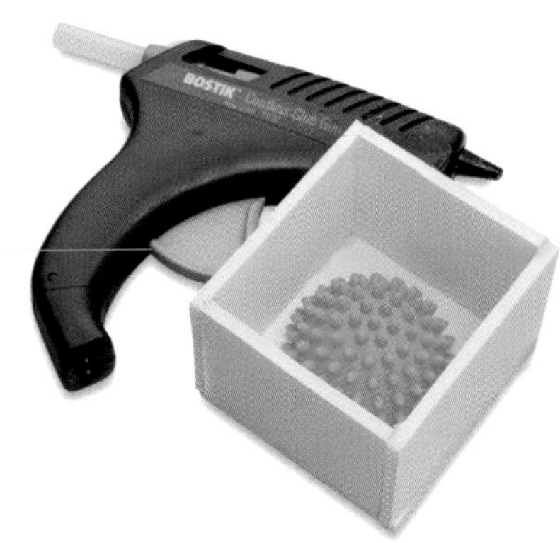

► **6.** One good way to determine the volume of silicone required is to fill the mold with water and then pour the water into a graduated measuring cup.

## ʼreparing and Pouring ʼhe Silicone

Silicone comes in a variety of forms and ·as many applications in industry as well as ı jewelry and ornamentation. For this simple roject of pouring a polyester resin casting, a ommon, semi-elastic silicone that is easily ·moved from the mold has been chosen.

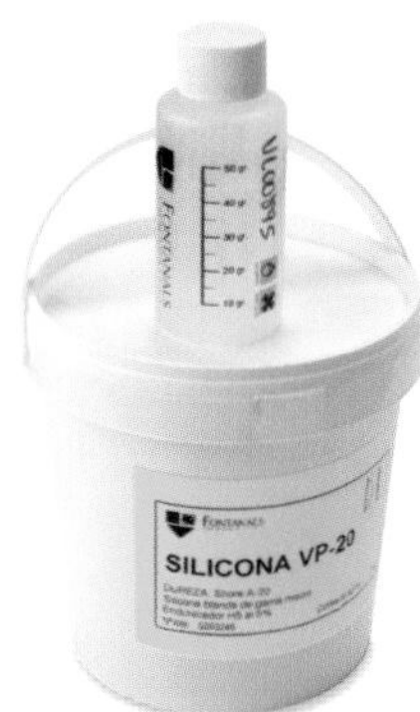


◄ **1.** In order for the silicone to harden properly, it must be mixed with a specific hardener; this is usually sold by the same silicone supplier.

▲ **2.** To mix, use a scale and a container which has first been weighed to find out the tare.

◄◄ **3.** Next, the desired volume of silicone is poured in and weighed on the scale.

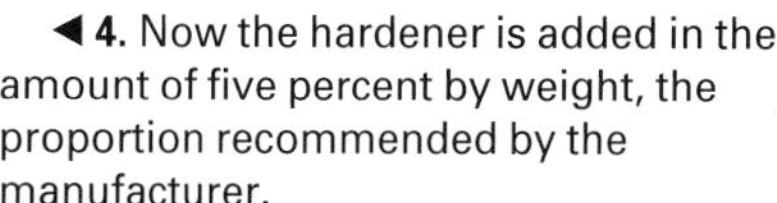

◄ **4.** Now the hardener is added in the amount of five percent by weight, the proportion recommended by the manufacturer.

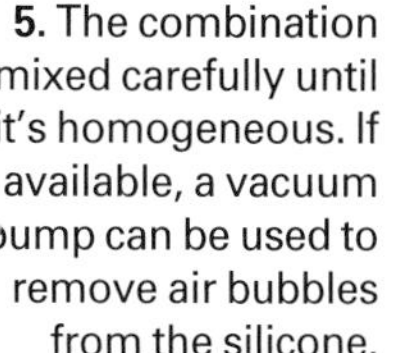

**5.** The combination mixed carefully until it's homogeneous. If available, a vacuum ›ump can be used to remove air bubbles from the silicone.

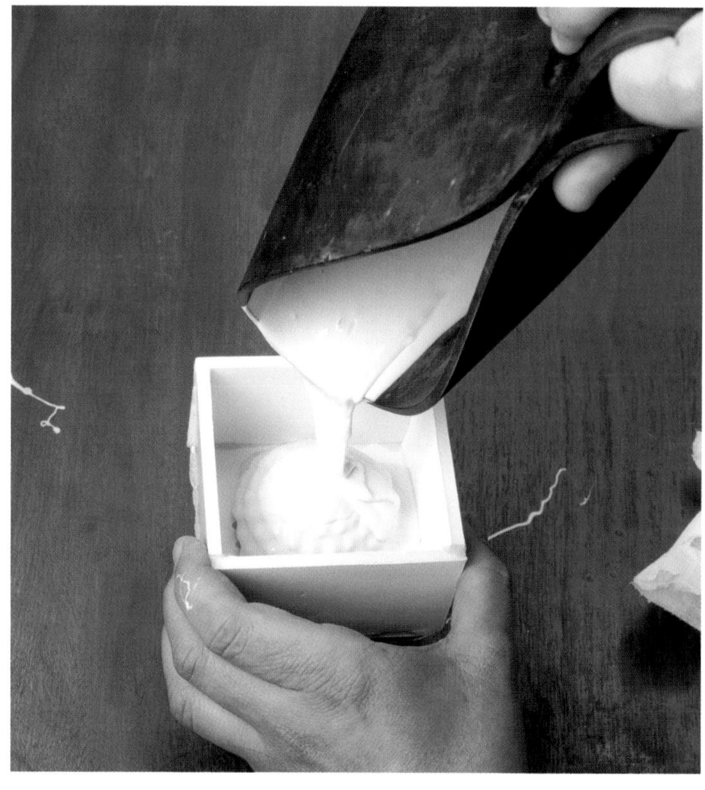

► **6.** Once the mixture is ready it is slowly poured in, making sure that the silicone reaches all the corners of the piece. The mold is kept in motion so that it fills perfectly. The mold has been filled completely; if necessary, the box is tapped lightly to help eliminate air bubbles that may exist in the silicone.

▲ **7.** The silicone is set aside in a flat, stable spot until it is completely dry, or about 36 hours. Next, the featherweight board is removed. There is no need to apply a separator to the featherweight board before pouring the silicone, since once the silicone is dry it's easy to separate from the board.

▲ **8.** Once the half rubber ball used as a mold is removed, the silicone mold is ready for pouring the polyester resin.

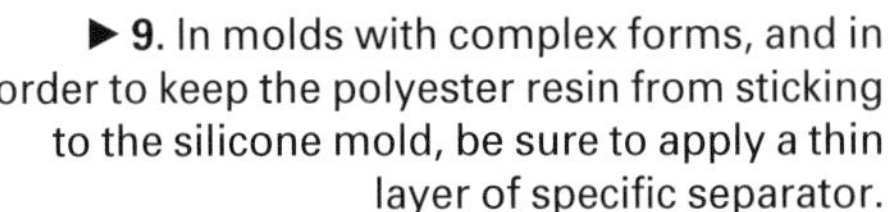

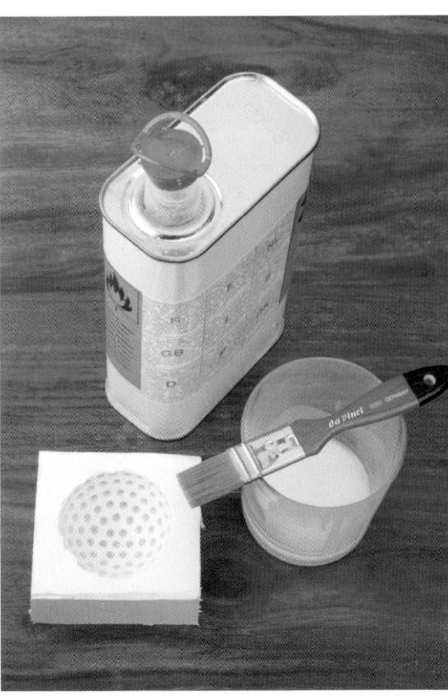

▶ **9.** In molds with complex forms, and in order to keep the polyester resin from sticking to the silicone mold, be sure to apply a thin layer of specific separator.

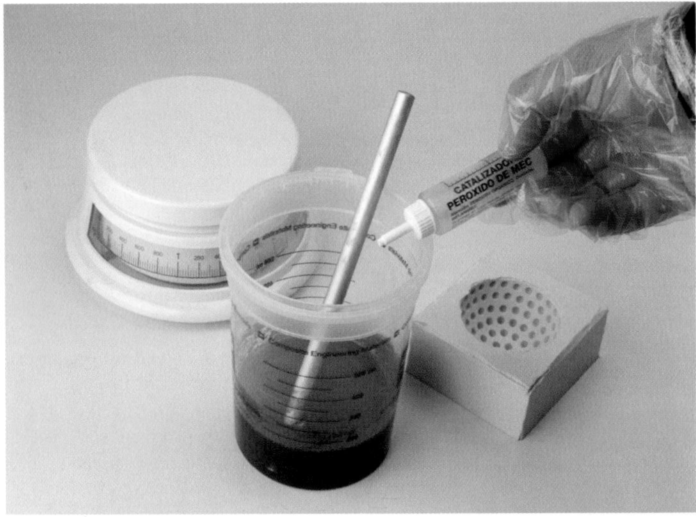


▲ **10.** The resin is prepared. In this instance, it is mixed with purple dye, then the corresponding amount of catalyst is added based on the weight of the resin.

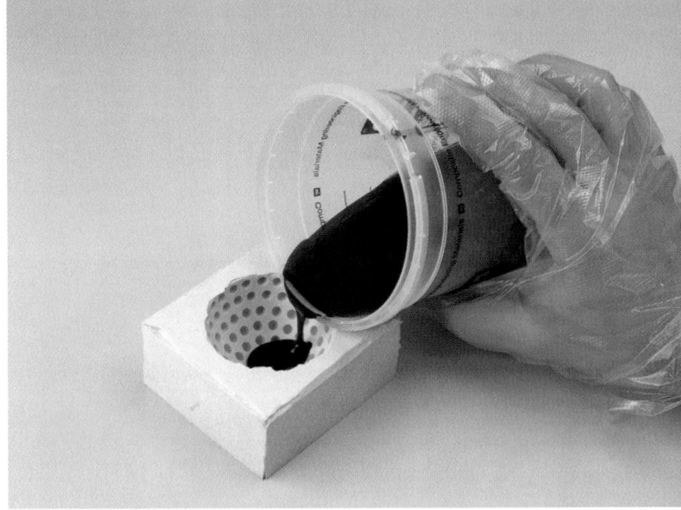

▲ **11.** Once the material has been mixed thoroughly, it is poured slowly into the mold.

◀ **12.** It's a good idea to move the mold around so that the resin, even though it's still very viscous, spreads evenly and completely.

▶ **13.**Once dry, in about 24 hours, it is carefully removed from the mold. After another 24 hours of drying time, the base is filed and sanded flat.

▼ **14.** Among the many objects that can be made are a variety of pendants and brooches, which require affixing clasps to the base of the resin with a glue made for plastics.

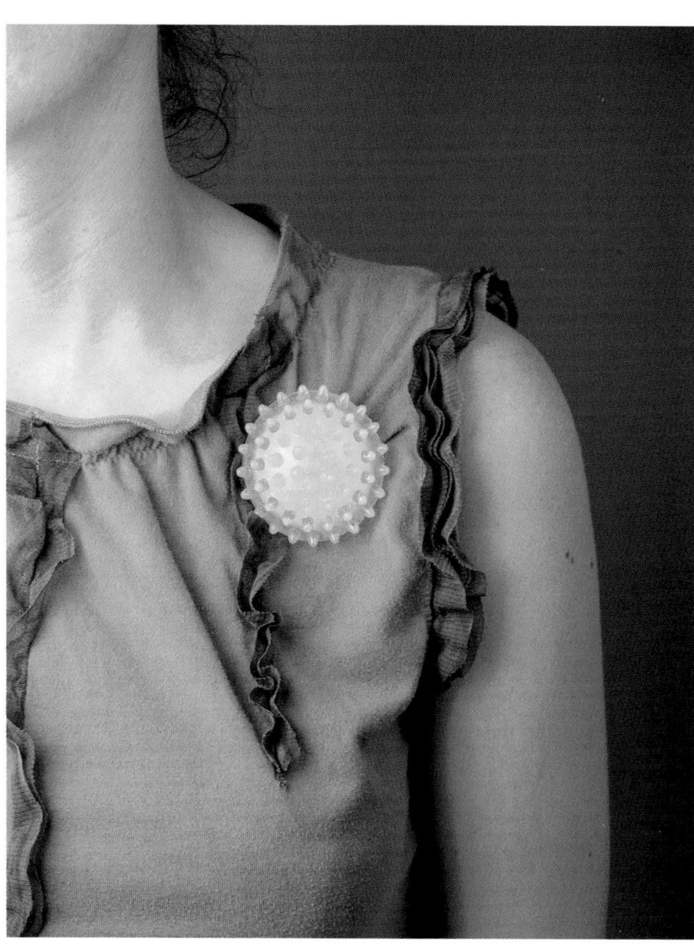

▶ **15.** One of the resin brooches made by Carles Codina i Armengol

## Another Way to Open a Mold

A silicone mold can be made from a single pour or from two separate pours as long as an appropriate separator is applied between pours so that the mold can be opened up to remove the model inside it.

Another quick way to open a mold and remove the model, even those with complex shapes, involves making a single silicone pour that completely covers the model. In this case, the model must be raised inside the framework by several hollow feet made from small plastic tubes. Their purpose is to center the model in the framework. It is also possible to inject the resin into the mold. Once the model is covered with silicone and has hardened properly, a scalpel is used to cut into it. Then a syringe filled with polyester resin is injected into one of the openings created by the removal of the small tubes.

◀ The mold has been made from featherweight board; the model, from puttied and protected polyurethane resin. Once the mold has been filled with silicone and has hardened, the model is removed by cutting into the center of the mold with a hobby knife. A toothed cut assures that the two halves will fit back together properly.

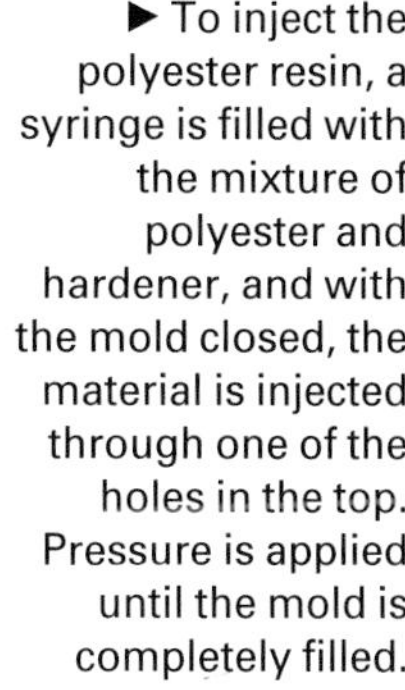

▶ To inject the polyester resin, a syringe is filled with the mixture of polyester and hardener, and with the mold closed, the material is injected through one of the holes in the top. Pressure is applied until the mold is completely filled.

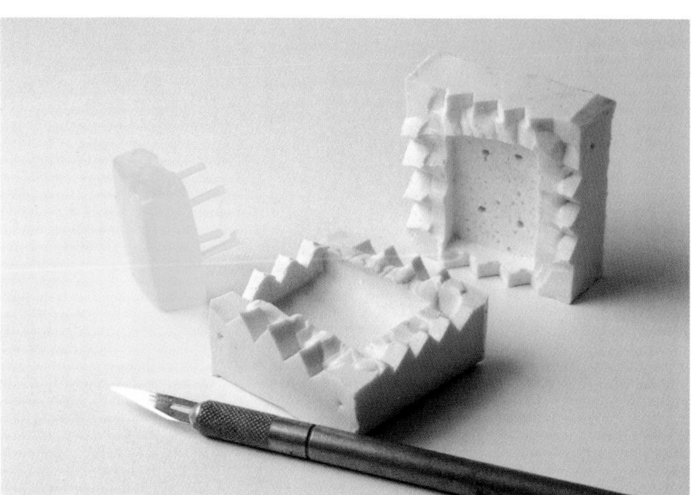

## Quick Molds on Plasticene

This is perhaps the quickest and simplest way to make a mold for producing objects with resin. Molds can be fashioned from blocks of modeling clay, various raw ceramic clays, as well as by working directly on blocks of soft wax with various tools.

▲ **1.** If using modeling clay, create a block with a uniform thickness and a surface that has been smoothed with a hand roller.

▲ **2.** Making the mold is easy: Simply press an object into the modeling medium or make a small hollow with the pads of your fingers and put an object inside it.

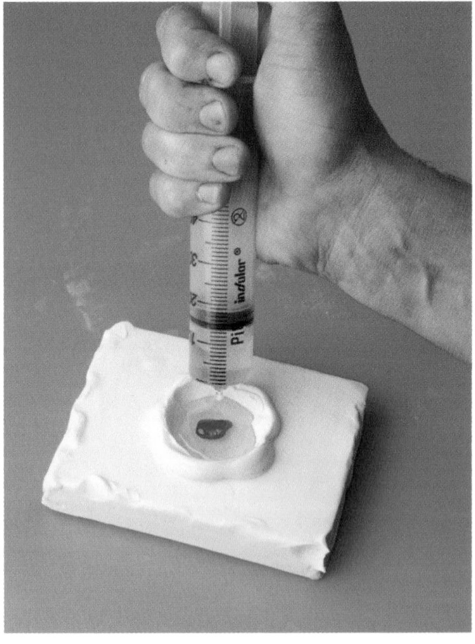

◀ **3.** The resin is prepared and put into the hollow, then left to dry for 24 hours until it has polymerized completely.

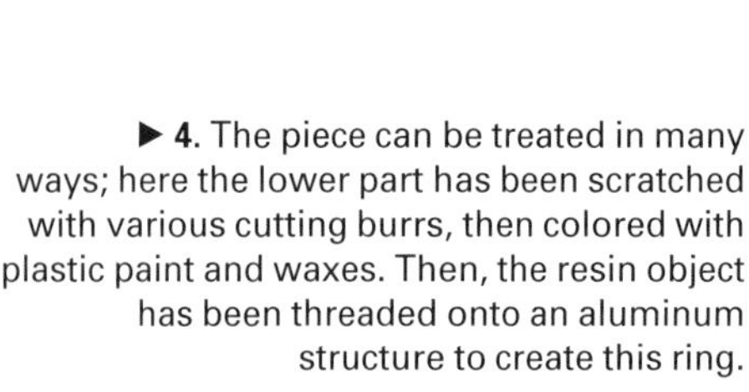

▶ **4.** The piece can be treated in many ways; here the lower part has been scratched with various cutting burrs, then colored with plastic paint and waxes. Then, the resin object has been threaded onto an aluminum structure to create this ring.

## Quick-drying Silicone

There are many types of silicones, derivatives, and uses to which they are put. There are silicones that are used in a liquid state, as well as quick-drying silicones that have a more compact appearance, to which the catalyst is added in the form of a cream (or some other form). These are used in the fields of orthodontia and dental restoration.

For this particular project, a silicone has been chosen for which the catalyst looks like a red cream. The advantage of this product is its quick-drying ability. Additionally, it is totally harmless, and it facilitates making instant molds of objects and areas that would be otherwise impossible to produce under normal circumstances.

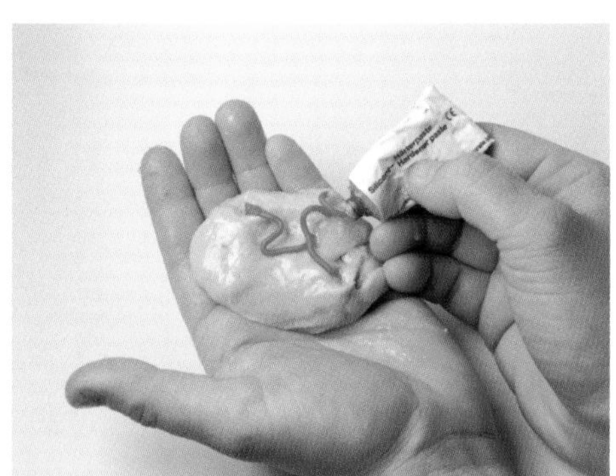

◀ The user's guide that accompanies this type of product indicates the proportion of hardener to add.

▶ Silicone and cream catalyst

▼ The silicone and hardener must be kneaded quickly and energetically. The material is then applied at once to the surface to be reproduced; after five minutes it can be removed.

# Acetate Molds

There are countless possibilities for making molds for pouring resins, and there are many materials from which molds for pouring can be made. Choosing acetate offers advantages for pouring the resin that are not available with other materials such as silicone. Acetate is an inexpensive material; it's quick and easy to use; and with a little imagination and a few trial runs it can be bent to create new, imaginative shapes. In addition, once the acetate is removed, the surface of the resin appears shiny, and that speeds up the finishing stage.

▲ **1.** To begin, several strips of acetate are cut out, taking care to cut cleanly and along parallel lines.

▲ **2.** Manually create the inner and outer shapes of the bracelets, providing a final overlap of about 1 inch (2.5 cm) to allow joining to the other end of the sheet.

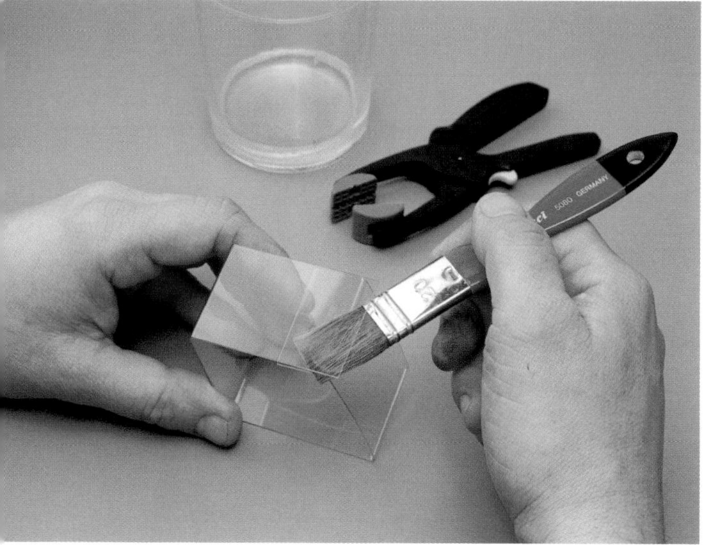

▲ **3.** Acetone is used to attach acetate to itself by moistening the surface with the acetone and applying a small amount of pressure with a clamp for a couple of minutes.

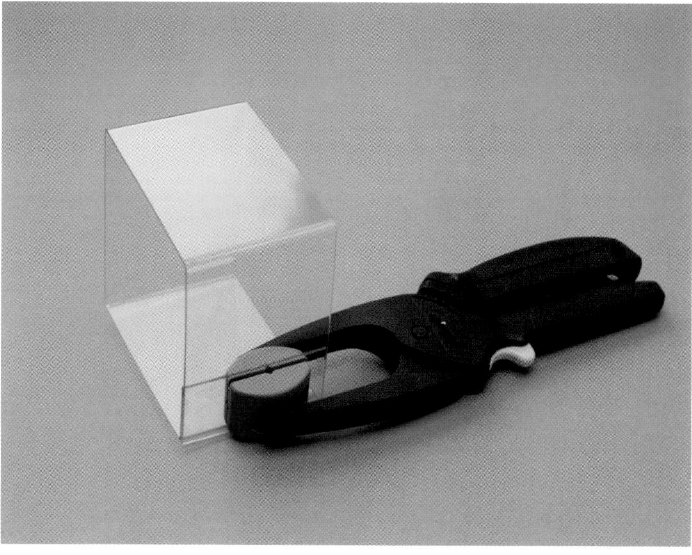

▲ **4.** The acetate that will make up the inner wall of the bracelet is made in the same manner. A shorter strip is cut out and shaped appropriately, then connected using acetone and squeezed with a clamp.

▼ **5.** Applying a small amount of pressure while clamping creates a perfect joint.

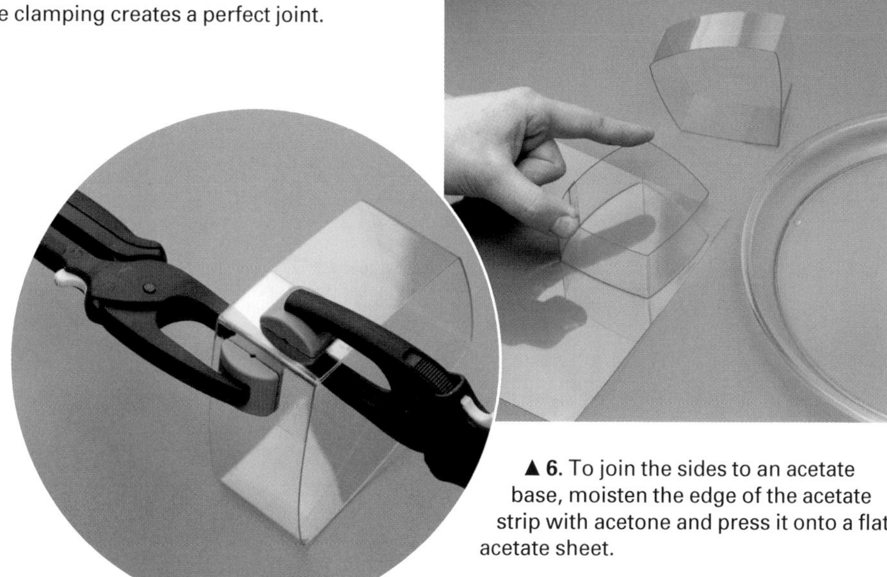

▲ **6.** To join the sides to an acetate base, moisten the edge of the acetate strip with acetone and press it onto a flat acetate sheet.

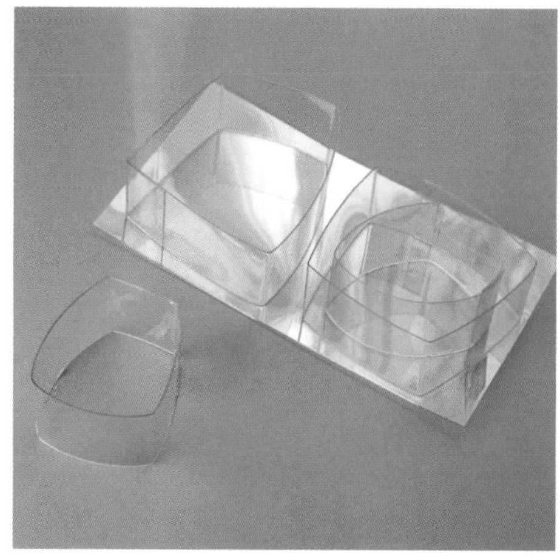

▲ **7.** It's important to maintain an even thickness and proportion between the inner and outer parts so there are no excessively thin areas that, once the space is filled with resin, would result in weak spots in the bracelet.

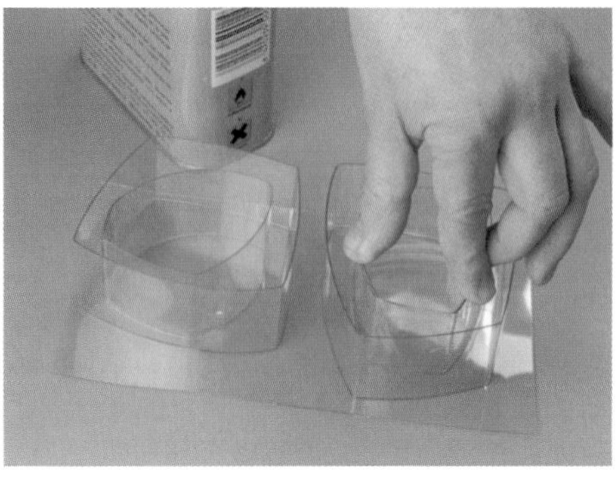

▲ **8.** All parts are glued into place on the flat sheet of acetate using acetone.

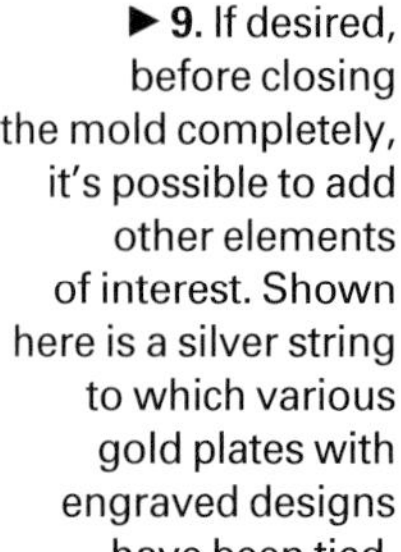

▶ **9.** If desired, before closing the mold completely, it's possible to add other elements of interest. Shown here is a silver string to which various gold plates with engraved designs have been tied.

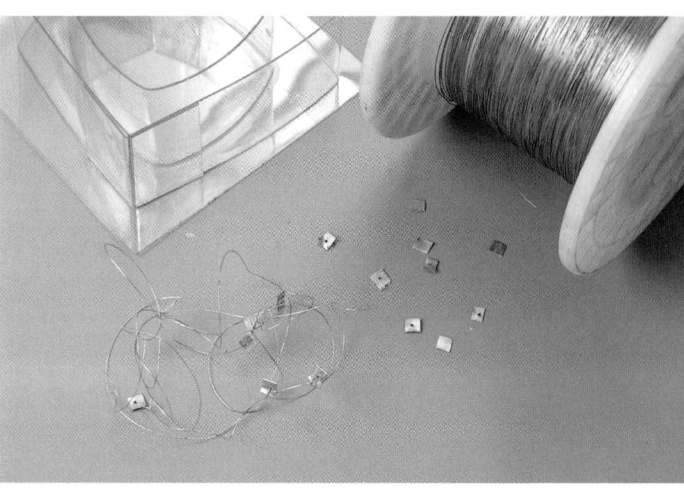

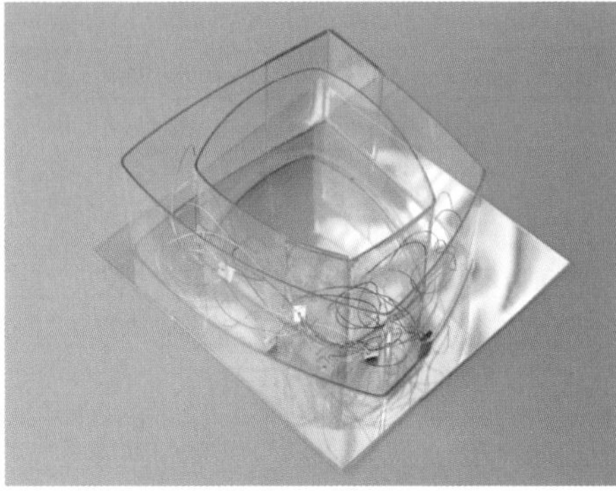

▲ **10.** The mold is sealed completely by moistening the edge with acetone and pressing it firmly onto another flat sheet of acetate.

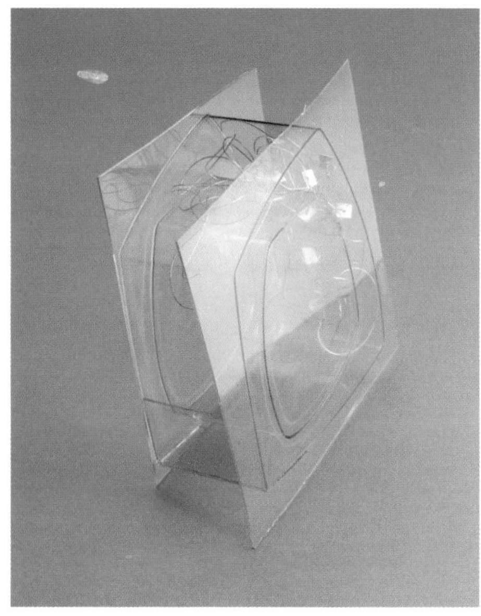

▲ **11.** Make sure there are no holes through which the resin can leak.

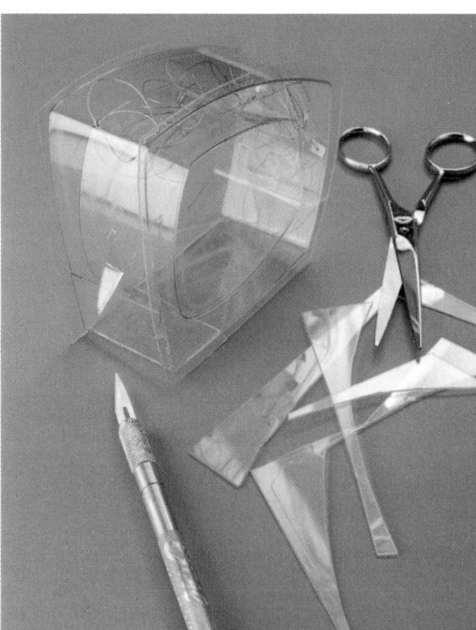

▲ **12.** The excess acetate is cut off; then a triangular cut in one side is made without removing the resulting tab; this is the hole through which the polyester resin will be injected with a syringe.

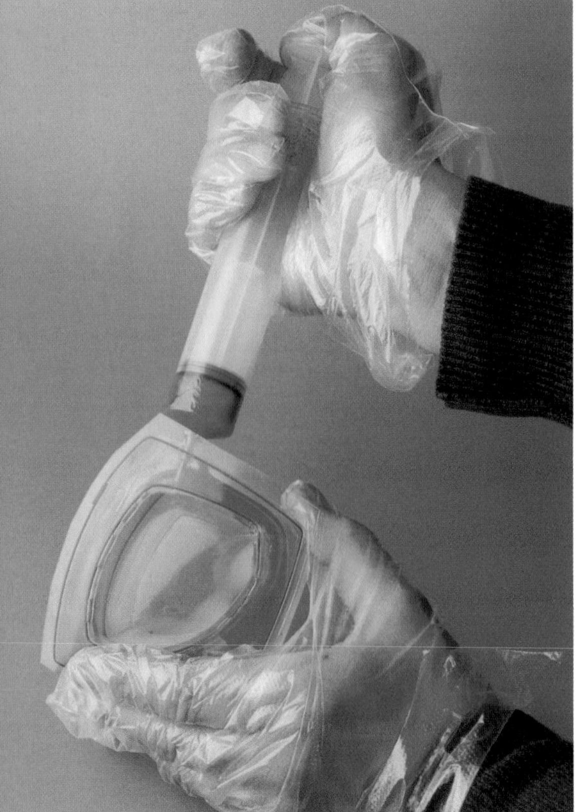

◀ **13.** One way of adding color involves preparing the resin with the desired hue, along with the appropriate amount of catalyst, and injecting it through the triangular hole with a large syringe.

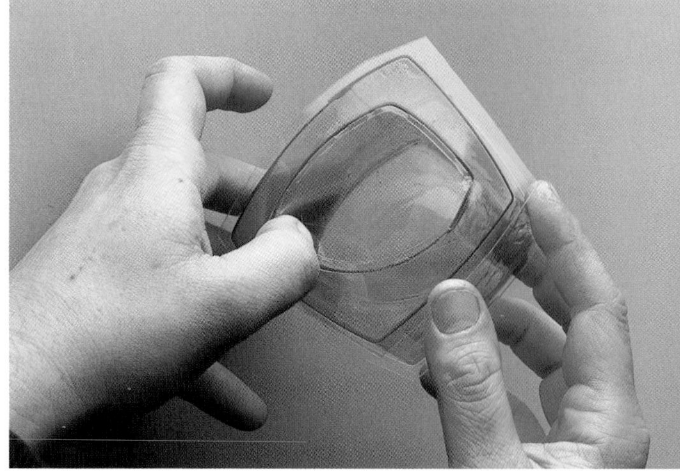

▲ **14.** After a few minutes, when the mixture begins to polymerize, close the opening and spin the mold around a couple of times so that the resin takes on the shape of a teardrop.

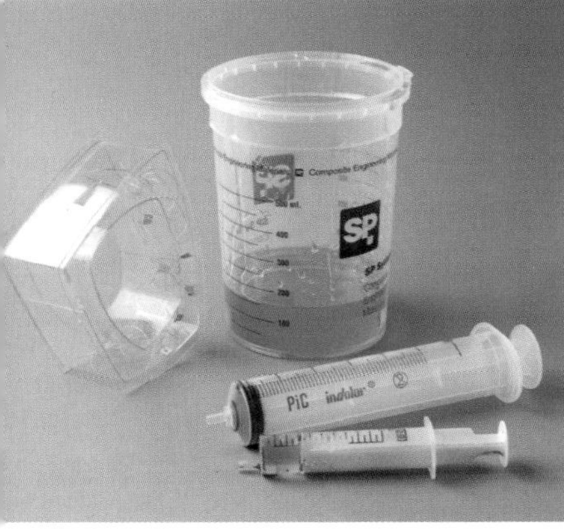


▲ **15.** To fill in the bracelets with clear resin, rst prepare the resin with the precise amount f catalyst. Then, use a syringe to inject the sin through the hole that has been made for at purpose.

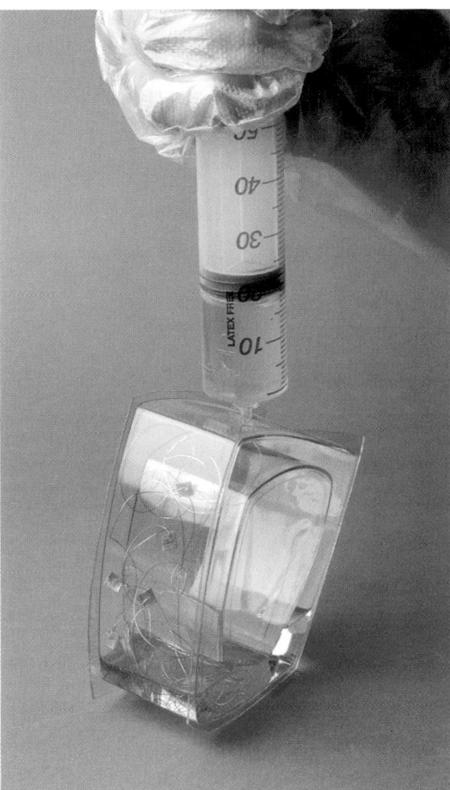

▲ **16.** The resin is injected in successive phases; the piece is jiggled to minimize the amount of air bubbles created, and allow ones that have been created to escape.

▲ **17.** Before the clear resin polymerizes, colored resin is injected through the top and the tab closed with cellophane tape.

▲ **18.** Once the resin has polymerized ompletely, the acetate is removed and the urface is polished with emery paper.

▲ **19.** The successive phases of smoothing vith emery paper, polishing, and buffing are arried out until the finishing is completed, as reviously described in this chapter.

► **20.** Here are the results of the project done by Carles Codina i Armengol.

# Gallery

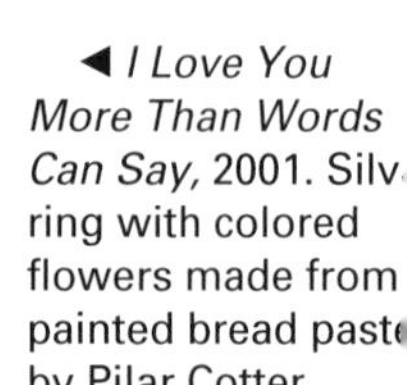

◀ *I Love You More Than Words Can Say,* 2001. Silv ring with colored flowers made from painted bread paste by Pilar Cotter

▶ Bracelet and brooch made from many small, twisted rubber bands (approx. 1 inch [2.5 cm])

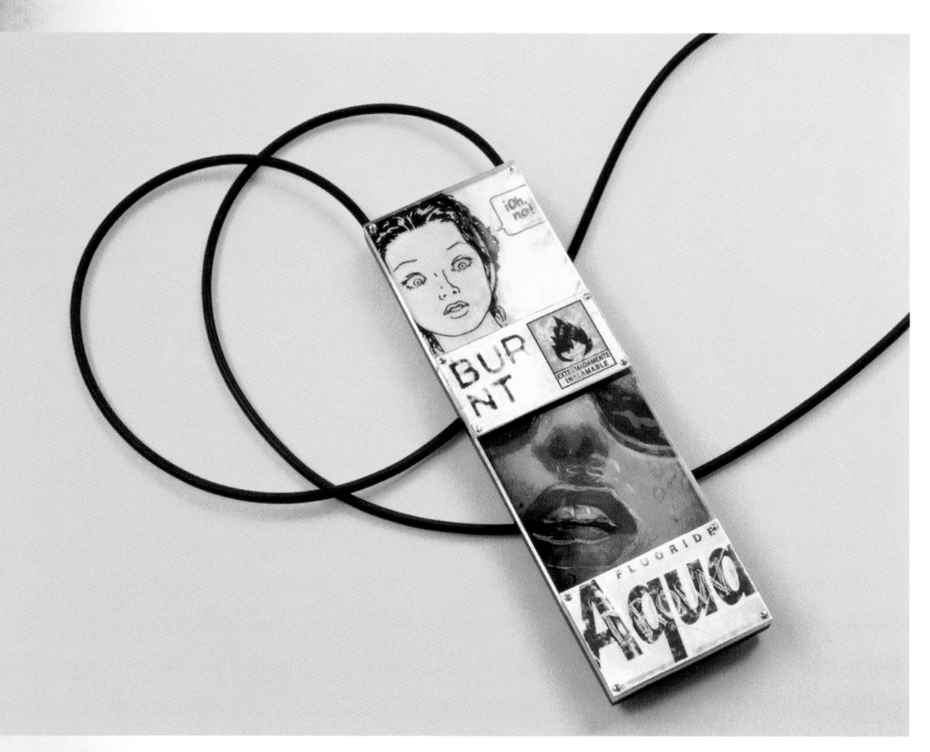


◀ *Burnt Drown,* 1999. Pendant with PVC panel, plastic cutouts and silkscreened metal, paper from a comic strip, and cloth tape Work by Kepa Karmona

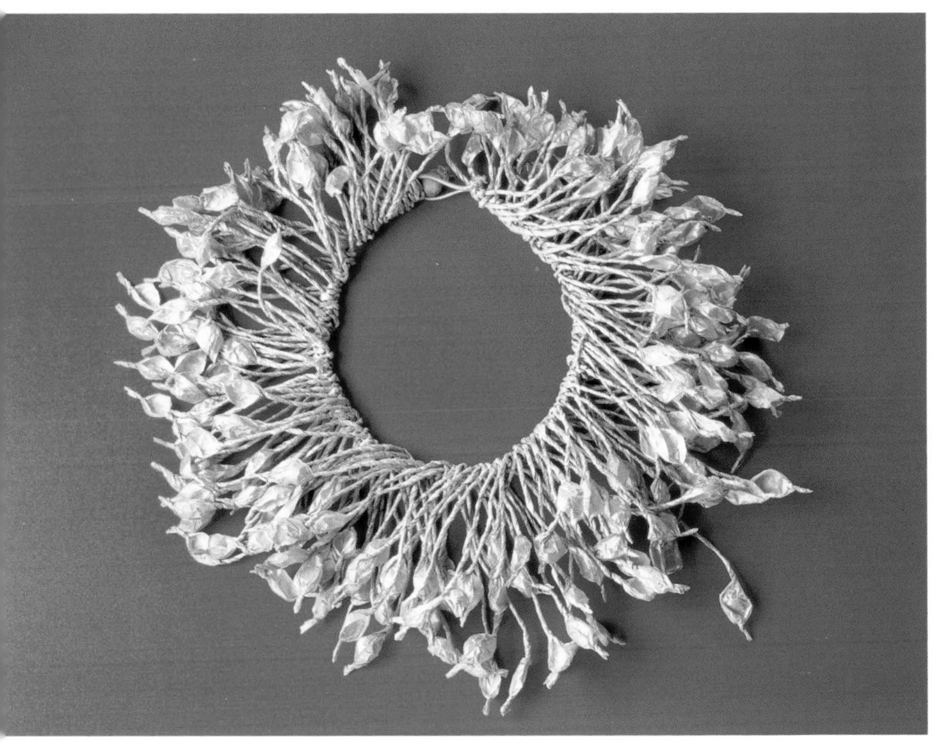

◀ Necklace made from hand-folded silk paper; work by Ana Agopian, 2003

▶ *The Delivery,* 2001. Oxidized silver and printed paper brooch by Pilar Cotter

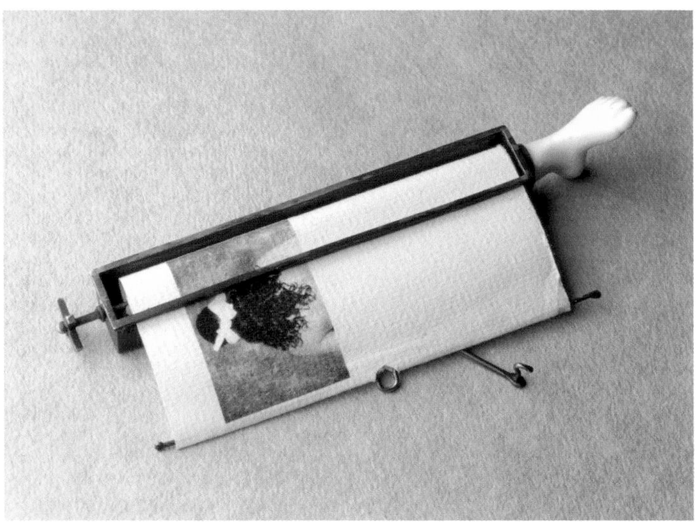

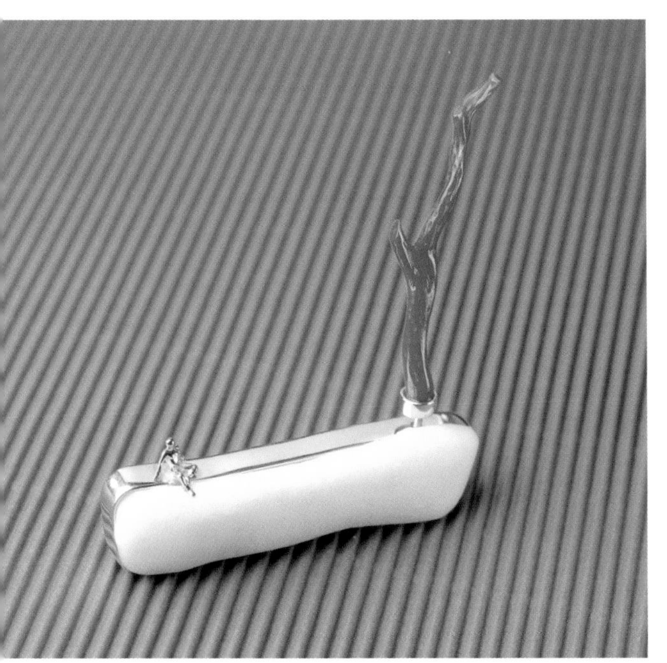

▲ Brooch made of silver with red coral inclusion by Carles Codina i Armengol

▶ *Life Is Long, Baby...* , 2003. Brooch made mainly of silver and bronze; additionally, materials such as plasticized paper and acrylic paint have been used to cover certain metal surfaces. Work by Xavier Ines Monclús.

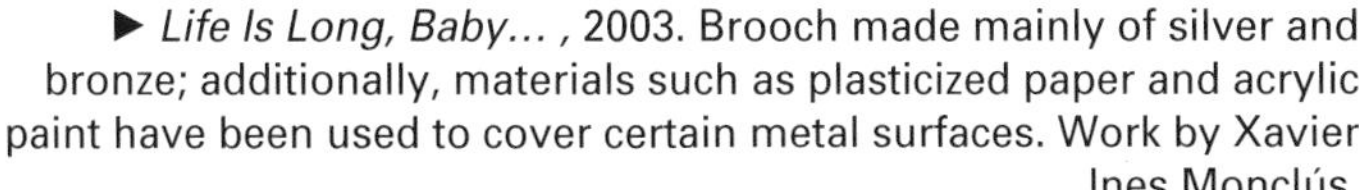

▲ *From Where the Wind Will Be Born,* 2002. Brooch-pendant made of silver, wood, German silver, methacrylate, with acrylic paint and paper; work by Ramon Puig Cuyàs

▼ Silver electroformed brooch by Marc Monzó

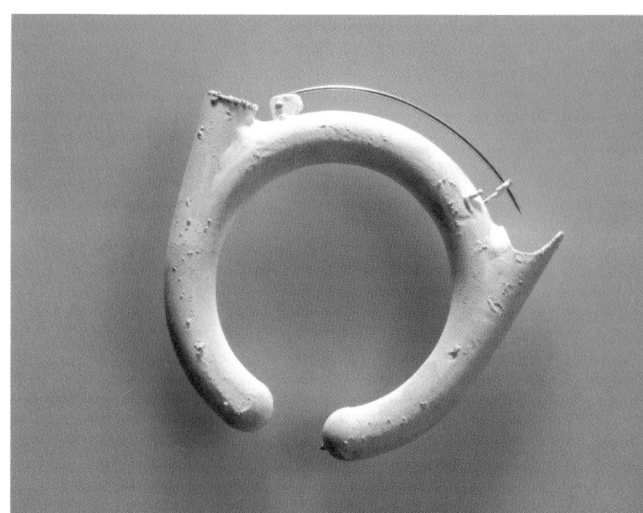

► Paper bracelet with gold and colored rice paper applications, by Walter Chen

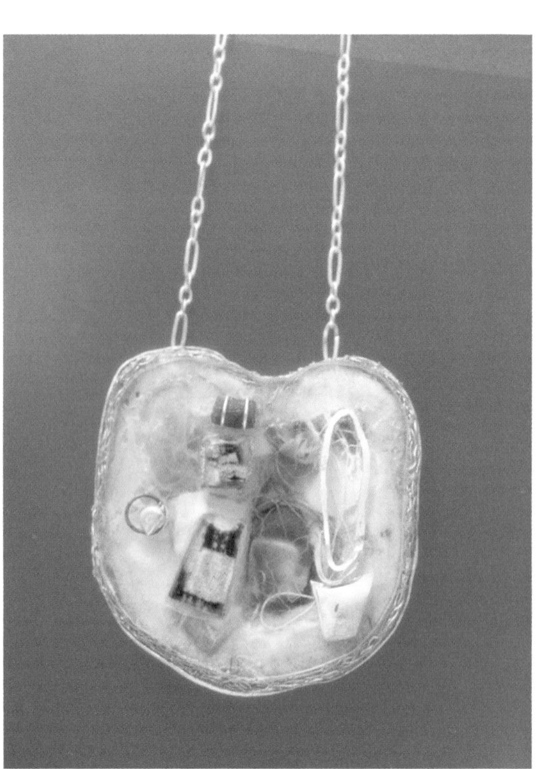

◄ *Vermillion Caputxeta,* 2002. Pendant made of silver and plastic, with printed images, textile, and coral, by Silvia Walz

▲ *Constellation necklace.* Necklace made of glass by Kristina Logan. Photo by Paul Avis

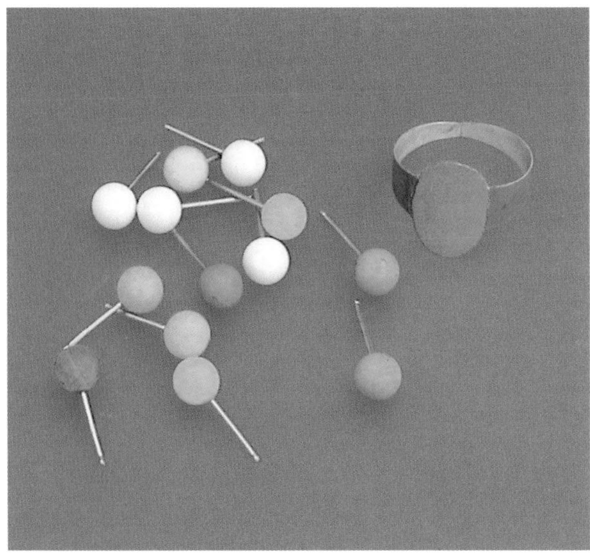

▲ Pendants with gold stem made by Marc Monzó from various plastic pellets

▲ Brooch made of polymer, silver, gold, and ruby by Carles Codina i Armengol

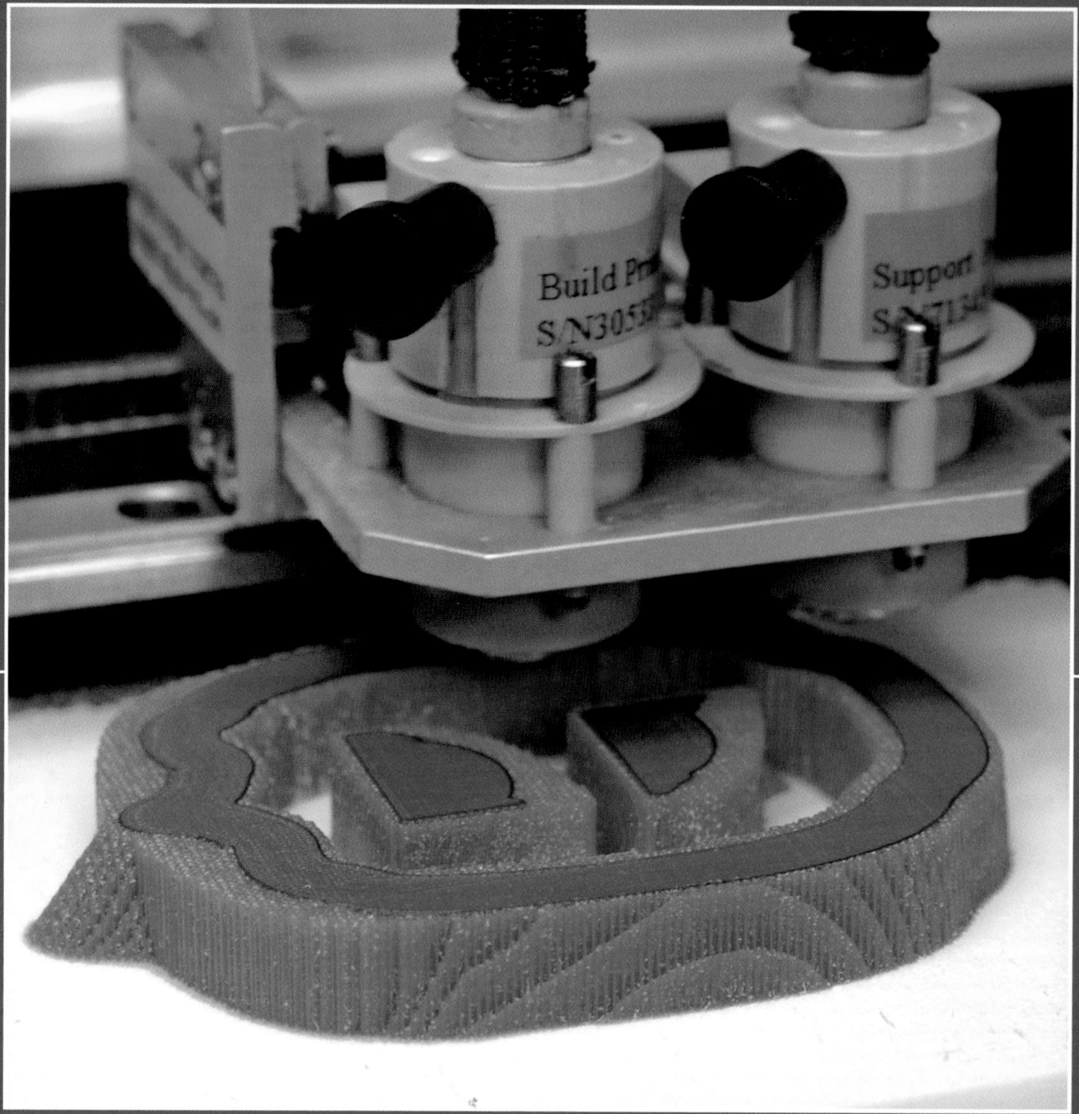

# *Creative* Resources

The next three sections touch briefly on methods for using computer technology in conceptualizing, planning and creating metal jewelry. Using high-tech computerized programs, it's possible to create lots of nontraditional jewelry items.

The first section is on electroforming. Electroforming is a technology that offers amazing possibilities for making objects that sometimes are impossible to create using traditional procedures. The second section explains the techniques used in other futuristic options that are already reality, such as digital input, computer-assisted design, and modeling or printing using computer procedures. These are computer applications that are continually evolving; they also require ways of planning and understanding objects that are different from the traditional ways of working metal, but at the same time they require a thorough knowledge of metalworking techniques. The third section demonstrates further interesting techniques for working with metal.

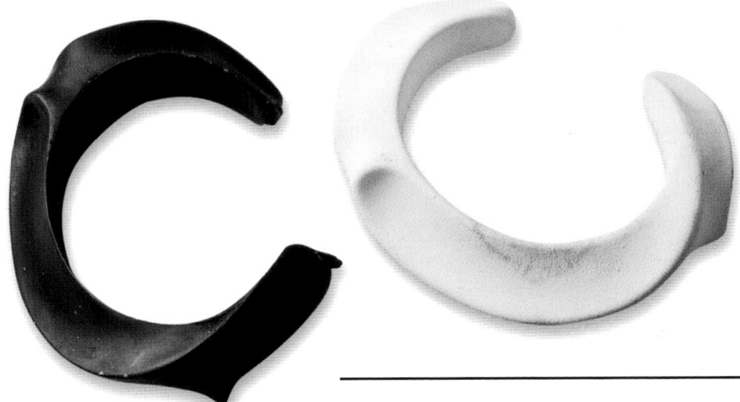

# Electroforming

Galvanization was developed in 1737 by Luigi Galvani. The process involves depositing a layer of metal onto an object or nucleus and gradually covering its surface with metal through an electrochemical process. It's a very versatile technique that makes it possible to deposit such metals as gold, silver, rhodium, copper, nickel, chromium, cadmium, and tin, on top of a broad range of materials. Electroforming also protects surfaces and prevents oxidation, and it can also be used to create certain types of surface finishes.

One of the main advantages of this technique is the possibility of making objects in precious metals based on other preexisting objects made from the most diverse materials that have been modified and transformed.

## The Technique

This chemical process makes it possible to deposit metal onto metallic or nonmetallic surfaces and precisely regulate the thickness of the resulting metal layer. It can be used to produce a sufficiently thick layer for the proper finish and the best possible quality on the resulting surface.

It is used in making sculptures, costume jewelry, jewelry, industrial objects, and decorations. Many everyday items have undergone galvanizing techniques or been manufactured with the process. This technique makes it possible to produce very diverse and intricate shapes from such unlikely materials as polyester resins, waxes, silicones, plastics, ceramics, and clay. It is also possible to decorate objects partially by depositing metal only in the desired locations.

Electroforming is also useful in increasing the thickness of certain shapes previously made of thin copper; this is the case with thin repoussé work, which can be reinforced through electrodeposits of metal right onto the worked metal.

Another option is to make a negative from silicone or some other plastic material based on a certain shape; examples are a metal repoussé item, and a shape sculpted in wax or any other material that can be used to make a mold. Once the mold is made on the basis of the original, preferably in resin or silicone, electrolysis can be used to deposit metal directly onto it. The result is an electroformed copy that's a perfect duplicate of the original.

▲ Gold brooch made from a plastic bracelet by Marc Monzó. First he attached th clasps onto this bracelet, then the bracelet was completely covered in a thick layer of 18-carat gold.

◀ Brooch made by Marc Monzó using various found materials and electroformed in silver; 2003.

▲ Many everyday items, such as little toys, can be electroformed directly in silver. The photo shows some brooches made by Marc Monzó in 2003.

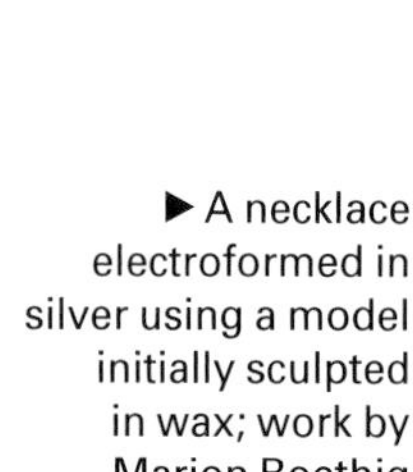

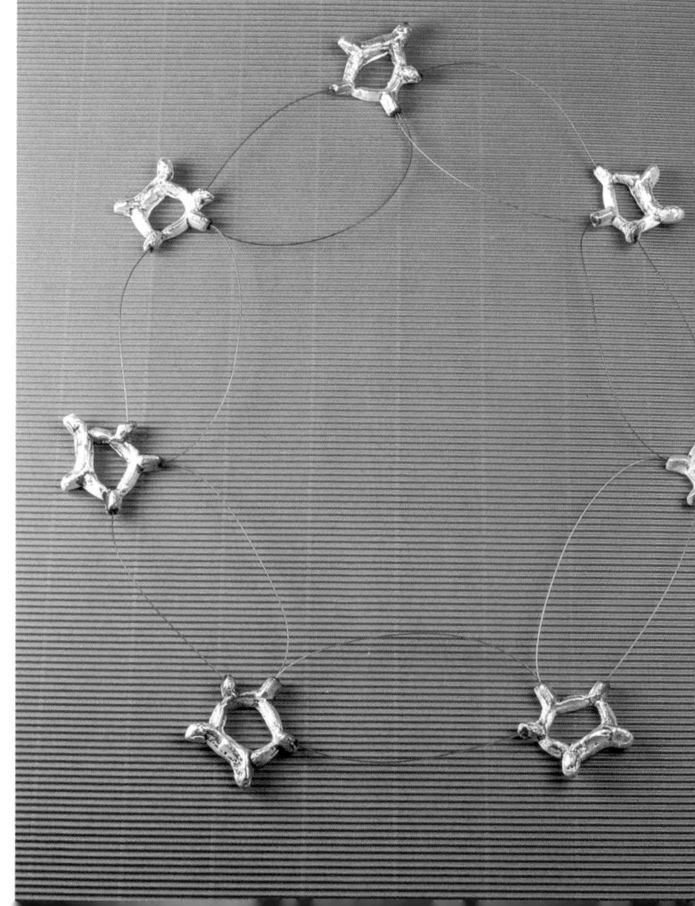

▶ A necklace electroformed in silver using a model initially sculpted in wax; work by Marion Roethig

# ʾreparation and Procedure

When beginning with a nonmetallic model, uch as one made of wax, the surface of the nodel first must be coated with a paint that onducts electricity; only then can the object e put into the galvanic bath for plating. 'arious types of conducting paint are vailable depending on the desired result.

After the model has been coated with the onducting lacquer and allowed to dry horoughly, the model is placed into the alvanic bath if it is to be coated with silver. f the item is to be plated in gold, it's a good dea to apply an initial coat of copper to the urface before putting it into the final bath.

The piece is submerged in the bath and onnected as a negative cathode. The metal or the plating, which in the case of gold is in ne solution in the bath, or in the form of ilver ingots when that metal is being used, is onnected to a positive terminal or anode. ach pole is then given the proper amount of urrent from an external source of electricity.

Electroforming an object requires a ontinuous current; it must vary as a function f the quantity and volume of the pieces ttached to the framework that supports nem. The current travels through the olution and causes the metal atoms that are n the solution or released from the anode to nigrate onto the cathode. The atoms thus over the piece progressively and evenly ntil a desired thickness is reached.

In contrast to a normal electrolytic bath, lectroforming actually increases the nickness of the metal in a uniform, constant ay. Achieving thick, regular coatings is one f the main challenges; the technique equires very precise control of the quantity f current and the temperature of the bath. he amps per square unit received by the athode also must be controlled precisely. In ddition, special compounds are added to ne bath to act as polishers and stabilizers nd improve the object's surface uniformity.

As a general rule, multiple models are nade of wax in advance. Once the metal is eposited on their surface, the wax is emoved from inside by making a small hole n the bottom of the piece, heating the piece n an oven until the wax flows out, and then lugging the hole. In other instances, when ne nucleus is made of polyester resin or arious plastic materials, the way remains insi-e the piece.

◀ **1.** This model was made of wax that was initially injected into a rubber microfusion mold; this is a very common technique in making jewelry. The photo shows the process of painting with copper conducting paint.

▶ **2.** The paint must be thoroughly dry before placing the piece into the bath to act as a cathode.

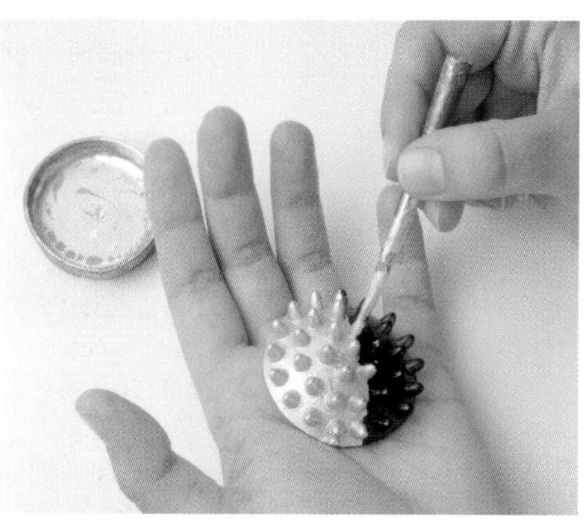

▶ **3.** Silver-colored paint has greater conductivity than copper paint, so it is used on items that require greater precision; the result is a better surface quality.

▼ **4.** The pieces are attached using conducting wire to establish a good contact between the wire and the conducting paint. Next they are secured to the support and put into the electrolyte bath to act as a cathode.

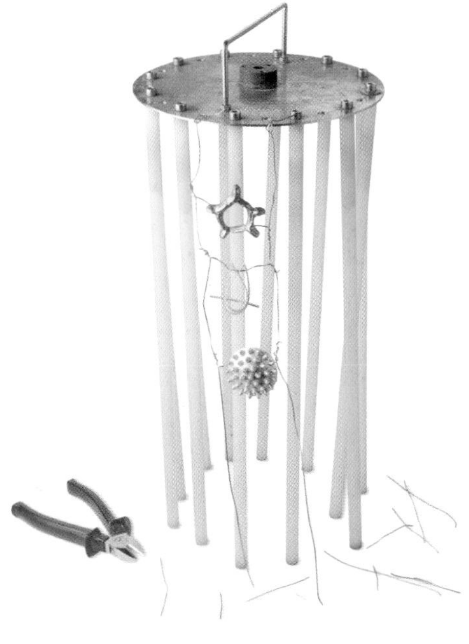

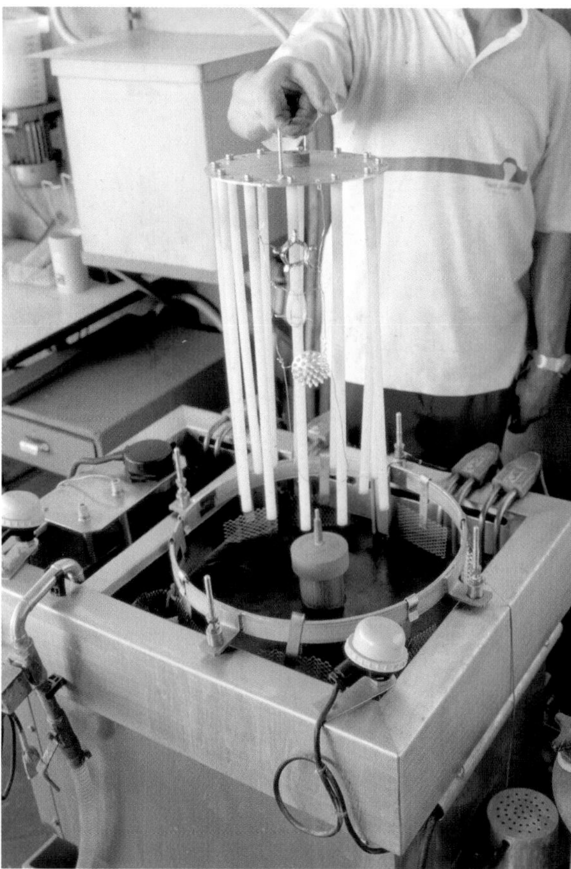

▶ **5.** The metal attached to the support or basket is put into the electrolyte bath.

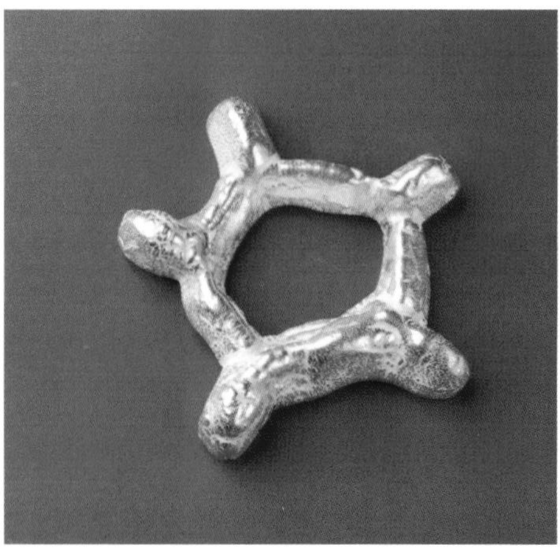

◀ **6.** The metal produced by electroforming techniques can be filed, sanded, and polished. It can also be sawed and soldered in the normal way; this truly is pure gold or silver that can be subjected to any type of manipulation used in the goldsmith's art.

▶ **7.** It's possible to regulate the thickness of the metal precisely to produce uniform thicknesses appropriate for every type of object.

▶ **8.** The copper copies can also subsequently be electroformed in gold or silver, or else copies can be made in any desired material. Here are some completed units made by electroforming.

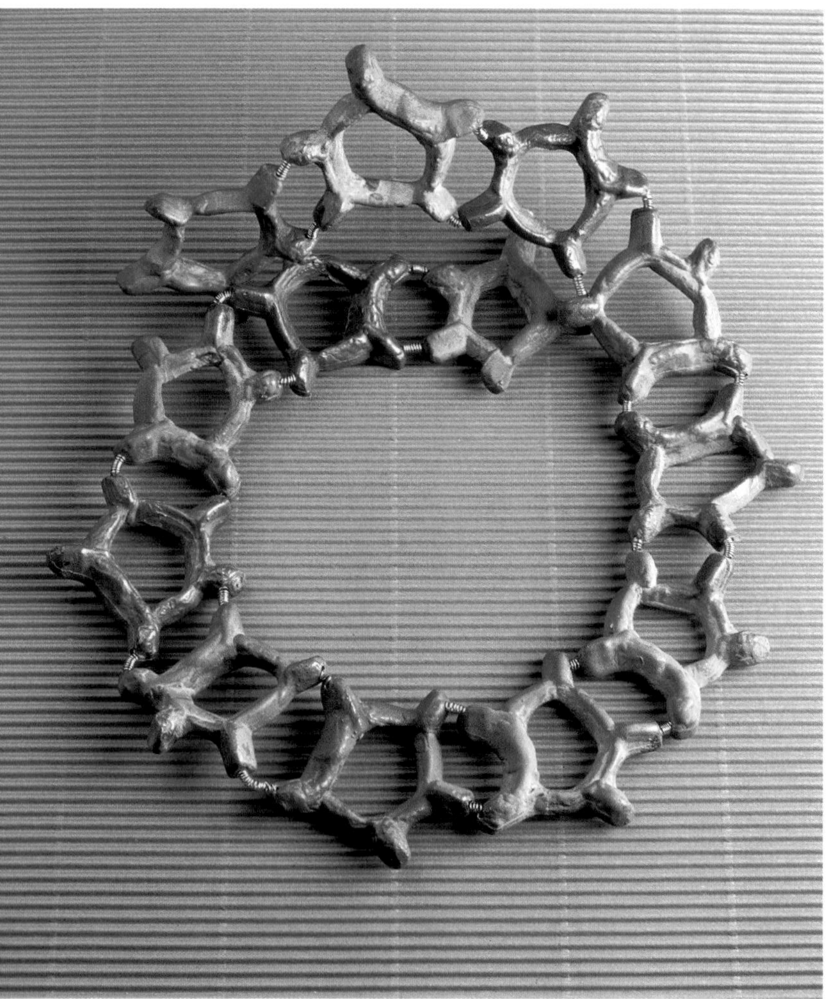

▼ **9.** Copper electroformed necklace made by Marion Roethig

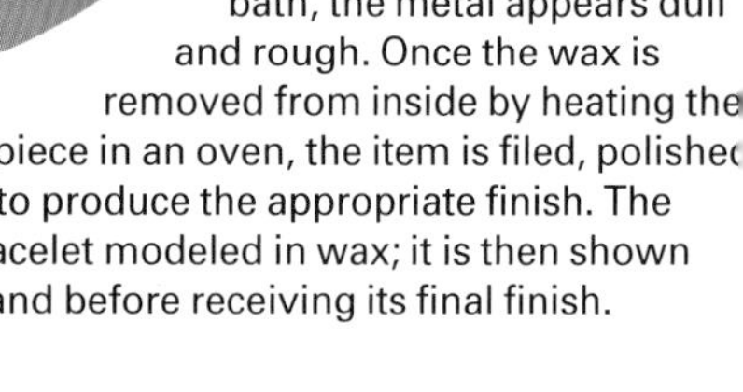

▼ After emerging from the bath, the metal appears dull and rough. Once the wax is removed from inside by heating the piece in an oven, the item is filed, polished with emery cloth, and shined to produce the appropriate finish. The black item shown here is a bracelet modeled in wax; it is then shown after electroforming in silver and before receiving its final finish.

▶ Silver bracelet made by Octavi Sardà by means of silver electroforming on an initial wax model

# Making a Ring, by Marion Roethig

With electroforming it is possible to coat the most unusual materials either totally or partially. The following projects by Marion Roethig show how to make several rings or bracelets using plastic strips partially electroformed in silver. The only tools used are conducting paint, a copper wire, a hobby knife, and a small brush.

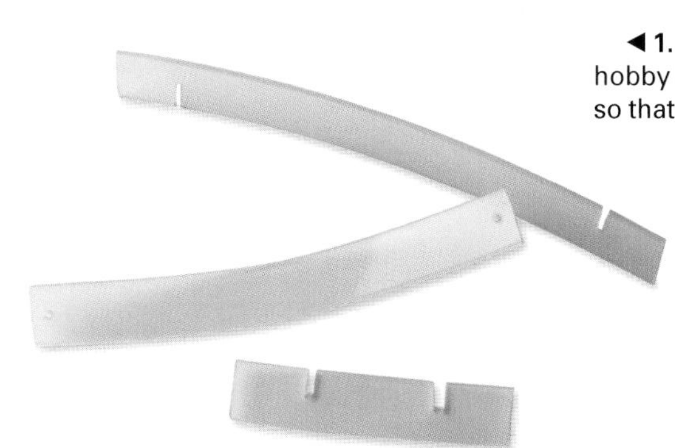

◄ **1.** Thin layers of plastic are cut out with a hobby knife, and the necessary cuts are made so that they will fit together perfectly. It's a good idea to make an initial mock-up from card stock of about the same thickness so you can be sure all the pieces will fit together properly.

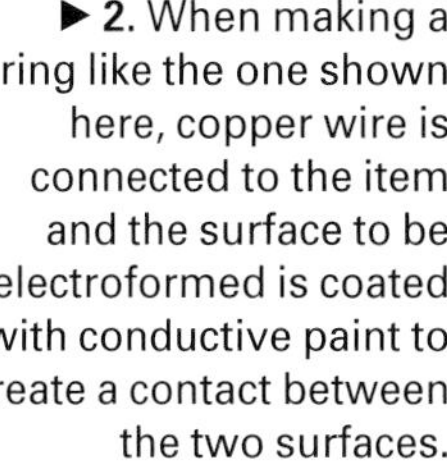

► **2.** When making a ring like the one shown here, copper wire is connected to the item and the surface to be electroformed is coated with conductive paint to create a contact between the two surfaces.

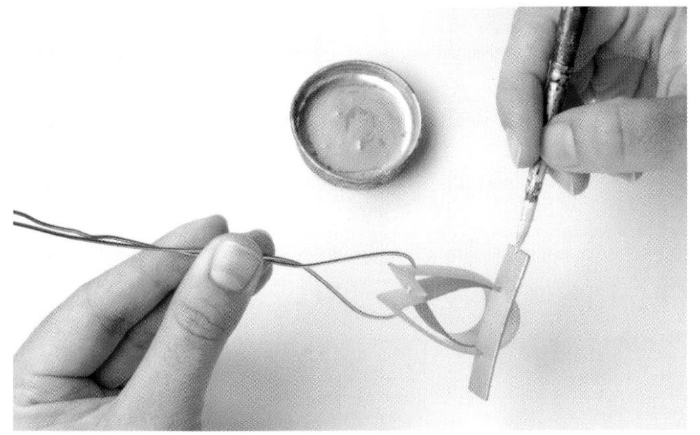

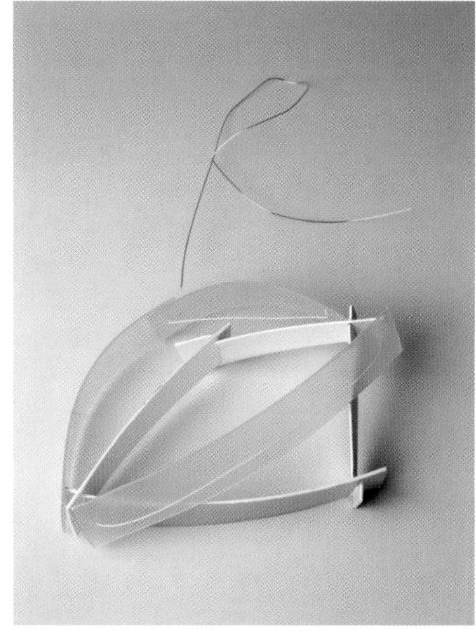

▲ **4.** Here's what the ring looks like after removing it from the bath. Next, the conducting cable is removed and the silver surface is finished.

► **3.** It's important to pass the conducting wire through the entire piece to assure good contact with the surfaces subjected to electroforming.

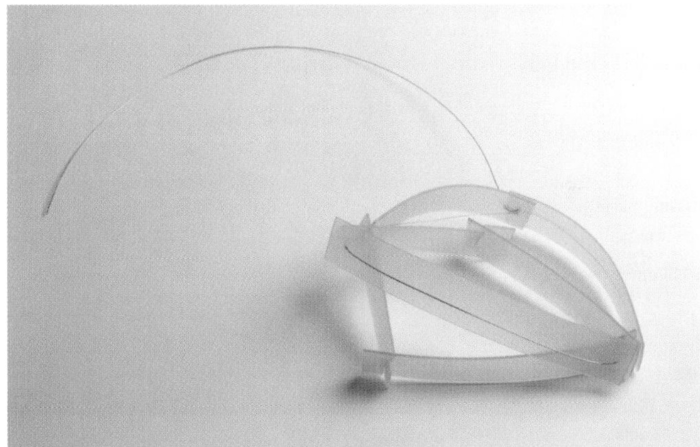

◄ **5.** Silver and plastic ring made by Marion Roethig

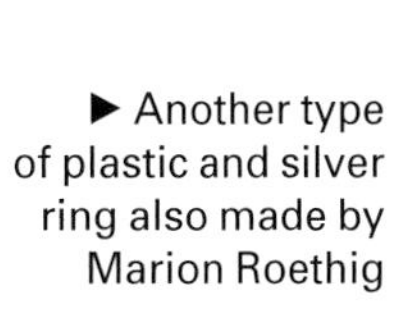

► Another type of plastic and silver ring also made by Marion Roethig

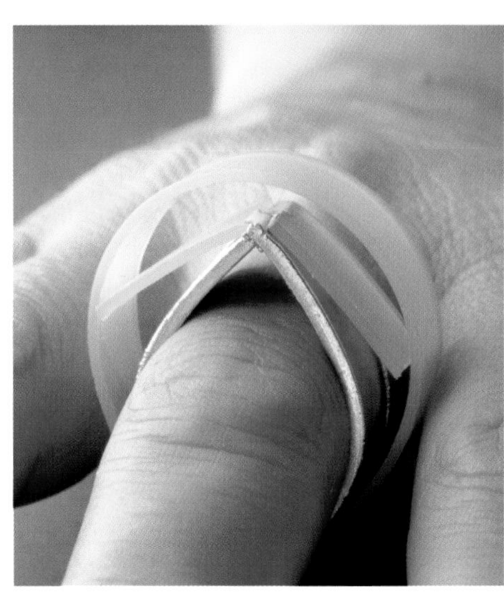

# Creating an Item by Digital Means

Designing essentially involves imagining the future, a process that begins at the workbench with initial readings and the handling of a suggestive material, or with the choice of new elements and materials. Current technology, as well as the technology that surely will exist in the future, is an essential and very useful tool for developing the most complex ideas and turning the most amazing projects into realities. Computerized design programs make it possible to play with imagination, develop ideas, and visualize them so they can later be realized in a digital format that can be used to make a prototype by various means and using different materials.

This section shows how to develop an idea from its abstract creation on paper to its transformation into a solid object. The intent is to show how to develop a project with the aid of current computer tools and make the process totally or partially accessible to any person with a basic knowledge of computers.

▲ Design comes into play from the first moment the hands begin working with a material and the tools at one's disposal. In both handcrafts and industry, design is part of every aspect of creation.

## Triple Optical Measuring Systems

This system, which was developed by th nub3d company, makes it possible to measur precisely a physical object in three dimensior so that the information obtained can later b input and manipulated in a different compute program. This is a technology that has bee introduced into various fields such as se propulsion, industrial design, quality contro and artistic heritage conservation.

The system makes it possible to produce digital model in the form of a computer fil based on a physical object; it can be used t reproduce scale models and make accurat enlargements and reductions without havin to use gradations based on the origina model. It has the advantage of measuring th object without touching it, and it facilitate interactive visualization. The results can b transmitted or edited on the web or with an other computer system.

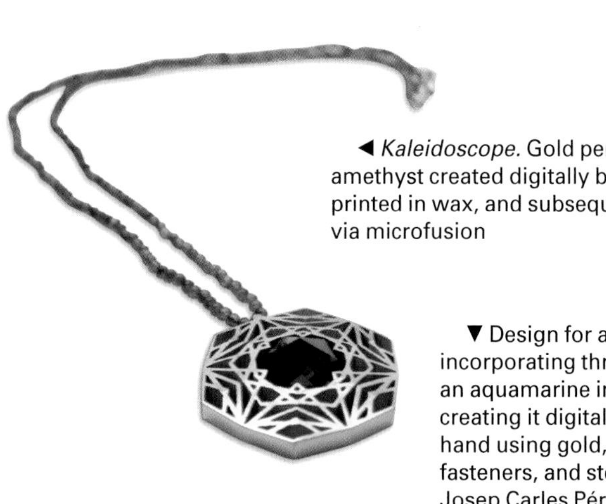

◀ *Kaleidoscope.* Gold pendant with amethyst created digitally by Alex Antich, printed in wax, and subsequently cast in gold via microfusion

▼ Design for a brooch incorporating three amethysts and an aquamarine in a setting. After creating it digitally, it is made by hand using gold, polycarbonate, fasteners, and steel. Work by Josep Carles Pérez

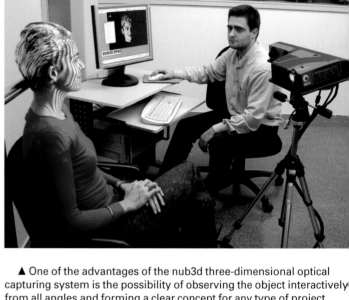

▲ One of the advantages of the nub3d three-dimensional optical capturing system is the possibility of observing the object interactively from all angles and forming a clear concept for any type of project.

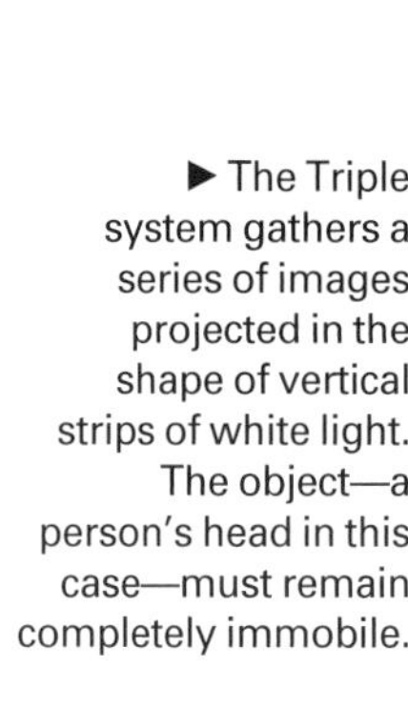

▶ The Triple system gathers a series of images projected in the shape of vertical strips of white light. The object—a person's head in this case—must remain completely immobile.

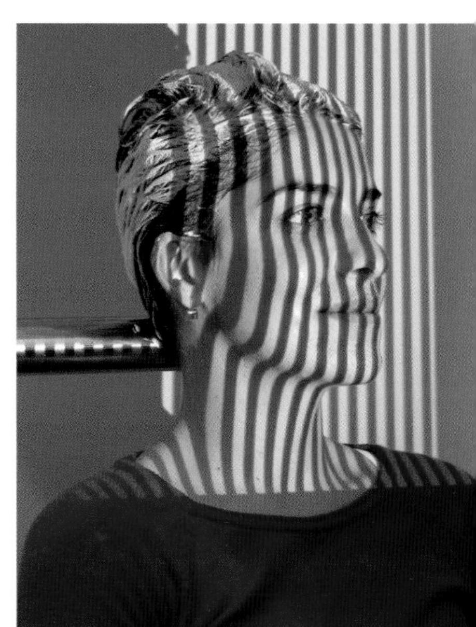

## Modeling Programs: Rhinoceros

Like many other programs, Rhinoceros is a D modeling program for solids, surfaces, nd curves that works in the Windows nvironment. Using this program, it is ossible to model any design intuitively and mply. Rendering the project makes it ossible to visualize the objects so that they an later be printed in wax and then cast in etal to produce items of jewelry, costume welry, or any other object or prototype.

Rhinoceros can read and manipulate files om a broad range of design projects that use ther formats, and it is compatible with most D computer programs. This is a quick odeling tool that connects directly with STL, D language printers, and rapid prototype tools sed for creating costume jewelry and jewelry.

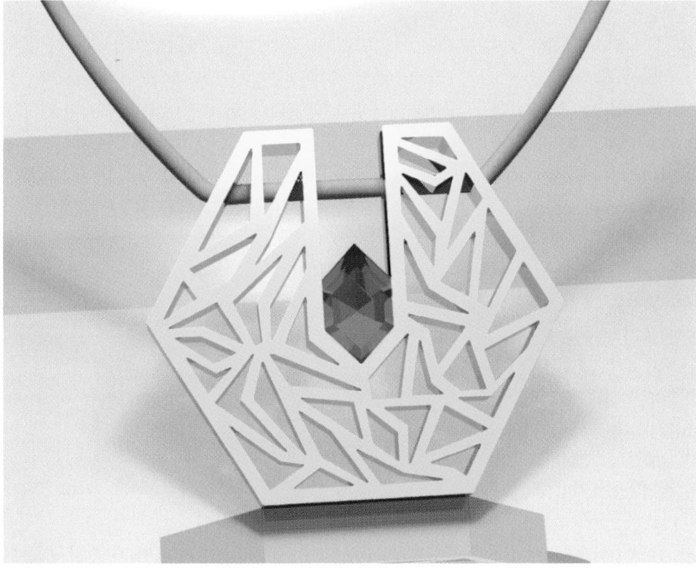

◄ Virtual rendering of a project created in the TechGems program

◄ Pendant designed digitally by Alex Antich, printed in wax, and then cast in gold

## D Imaging Programs

Imaging programs make it possible to sualize designed objects in other 3D pplications, such as Rhinoceros, in a hotographically realistic way. It is thus ossible to evaluate and understand the shape the designed object in all its dimensions.

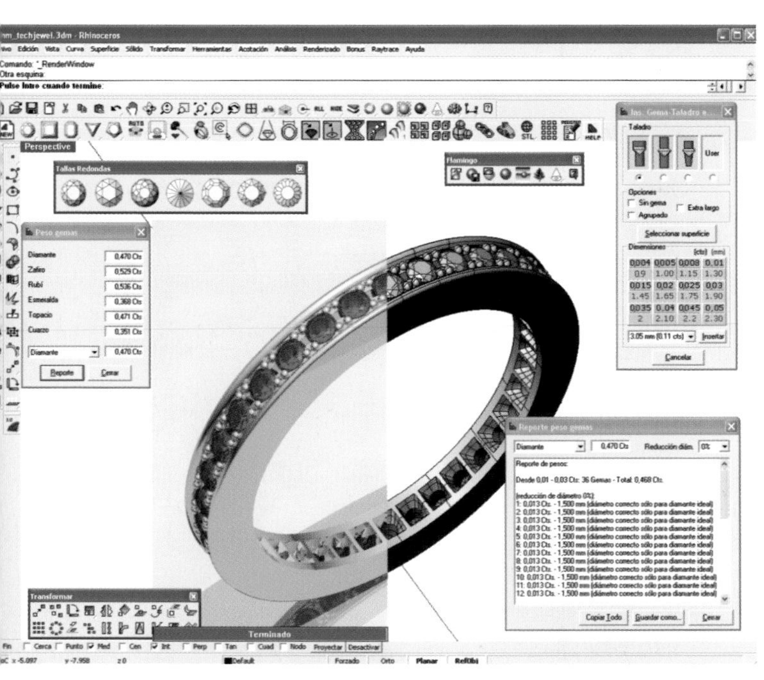


◄ The TechGems *plug-in* contains the tools and other elements necessary for the proper construction of jewelry and costume jewelry projects.

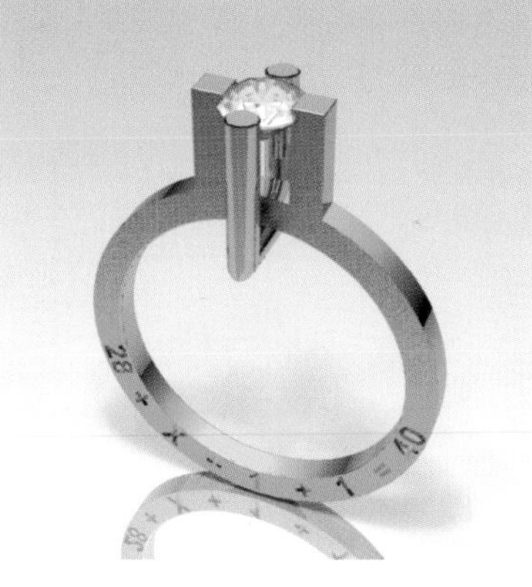

◄ Rendering of a gold ring with a central diamond by Josep Carles Pérez on a project designed by Carles Codina i Armengol. The Rhinoceros program was used, and it was rendered using Flamingo and the *plug-in* from TechGems, which was specifically developed for application in the jewelry field.

## The Process of Making a Project

Every project comes from an idea. The next project, from Josep Carles Pérez, arose from a series of ideas pertaining to a person's gaze, science, and reason. This work aims to explore how the gaze can create a space for self-reflection.

The Triple optical input program from the nub3d company was selected for this project. The representation program was Rhinoceros, which makes it possible to manipulate the information and make a wax prototype using the 3D printer from the SolidScape company, and subsequently cast it in metal.

There are many programs with similar functions and purposes, although some are better for certain tasks or offer higher resolution. The criterion for selecting these computer supports was their ease of use. In the case of Rhinoceros, a selling price within the reach of any professional or student, plus its usefulness in small-format work that requires lots of precision, makes it appropriate for jewelry and costume jewelry projects. If you can't afford the digital input system used here, there are many companies that specialize in this area and charge a reasonable fee.

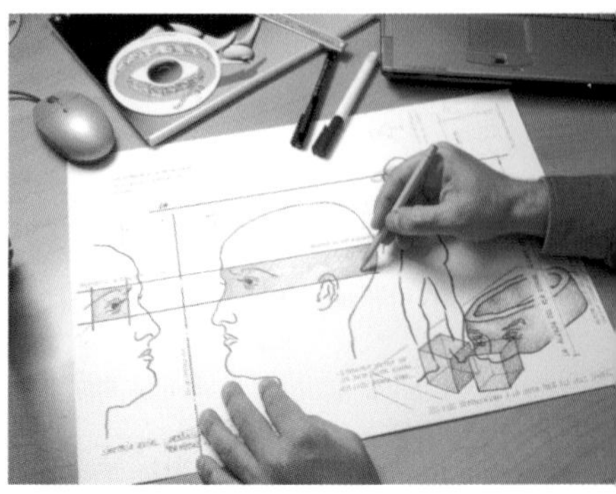

▲ Starting with an idea involving a person's gaze, conceived by the goldsmith Josep Carles Pérez, Alex Antich works it up using the Rhinoceros program and the TechGems *plug-in*.

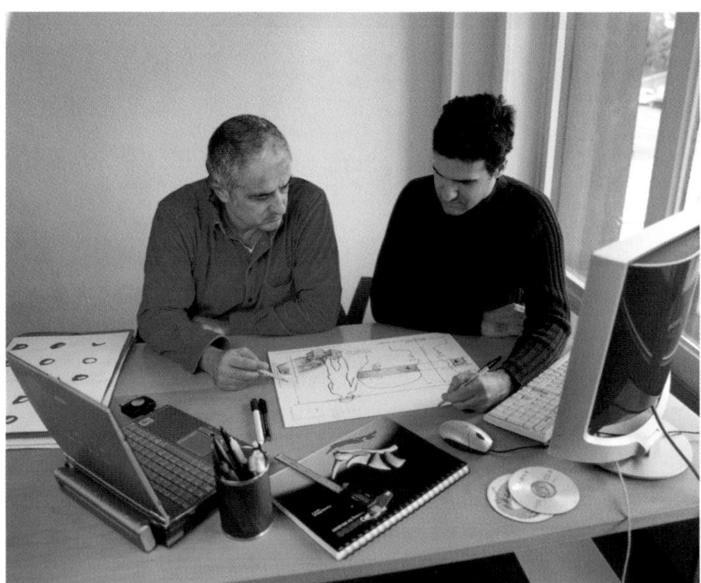

◄ Every design must be understood perfectly and coordinated before beginning to digitalize the project.

## Using the Triple System to Measure an Object in Three Dimensions

The first step in creating the following project involves rendering a human head digitally, using the Triple optical measuring system, which requires no physical contact with the object.

The system takes just a few seconds to measure hundreds of thousands of points on the surface of the object in a density that produces a very real computer description. The measuring is done using the technique referred to as triangulation through structured white light. A series of black and white luminous stripes are projected onto the object, a human head in this case, and the information is gathered by analyzing the distortion of these lines when they reflect on the surface of the object. A measuring scanner captures a series of images in which it observes the piece and its distortion. When these images are processed, the result is a cluster of points on x, y, and z coordinates from the surface of the head.

◄ A special light emitter projects a series of increasingly narrow strips of white light. At the same time, a measuring scanner inputs images and analyzes the progressive distortion in the lines of light.

► The system processes the information and produces a digital file in polygonal format. It is made up of thousands of small triangular facets, polygons generated from the points previously determined by the Triple optical system.

# ɪodeling and ʀendering the Project

The file produced now must be modeled ₛing a program that allows modification and ɪteractive visualization before converting ₑe information into a solid object.

Since the quantity of information captured y the optical system is excessive and ifficult to manipulate, the polygonal grid ill first be converted into NURBS surfaces ₐat are simpler in structure, and thus easier manipulate.

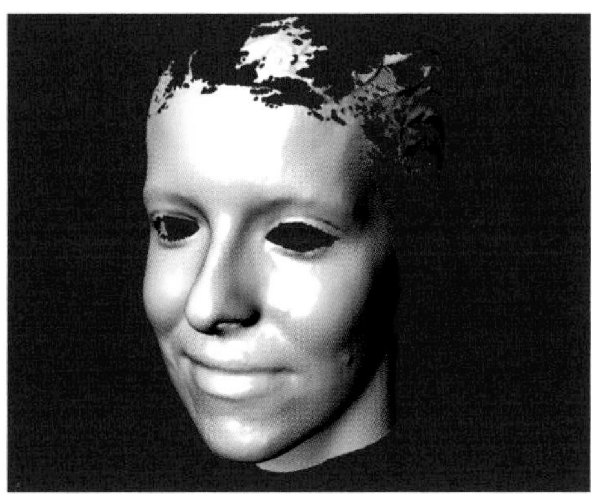

▲ The optical system doesn't correctly capture the information in transparent areas such as the eyes, or in extremely irregular areas like the hair. These areas must be reconstructed as NURBS surfaces by using the Rhinoceros modeling program.

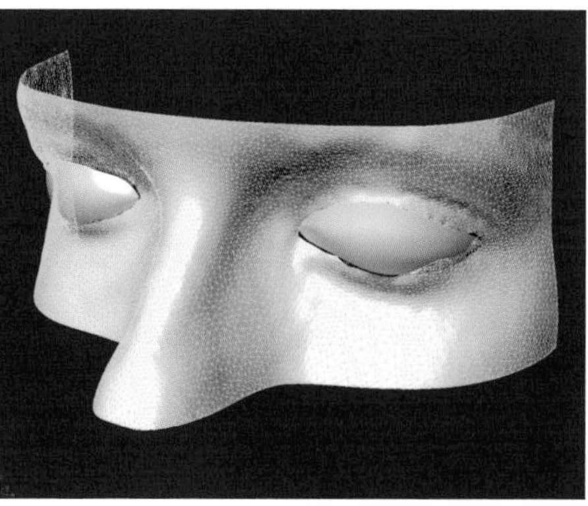

▲ The Rhinoceros program allows cutting, moving, and constructing any kind of object. It has been used to reconstruct the eyes and the hair, and it also has been used to cut through the figure in the area of the eyes.

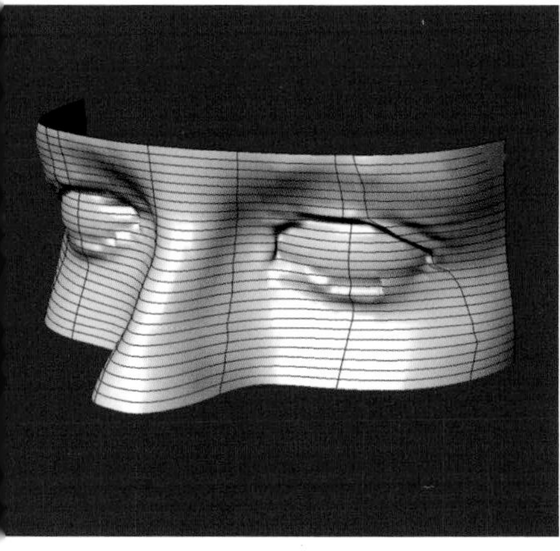

▲ Since the initial polygonal mesh is very ense and contains a vast amount of formation, it's better to simplify it by nverting the triangular polygons into a ngle NURBS surface, which is much easier manipulate with the modeling program.

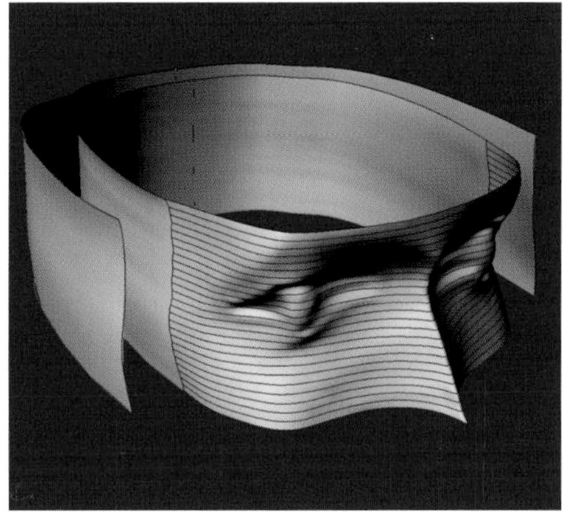

▲ Now all the necessary parts are created much like reflections to produce a certain thickness in the object.

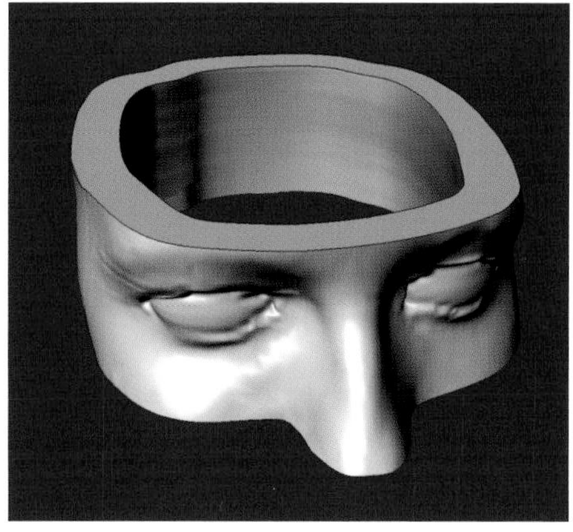

▲ In order to print an object correctly in wax, it's essential to create it as a solid structure. For that purpose the shape has to be closed up.

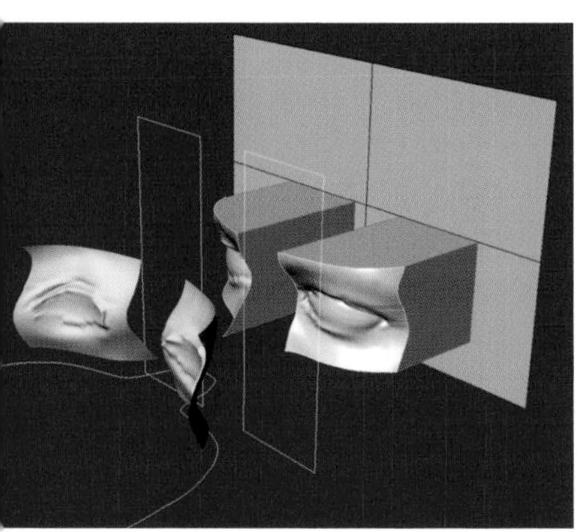

▲ Now an inverted reflection of the eye area produced, and two new solids are generated at will be a reflection of the main body.

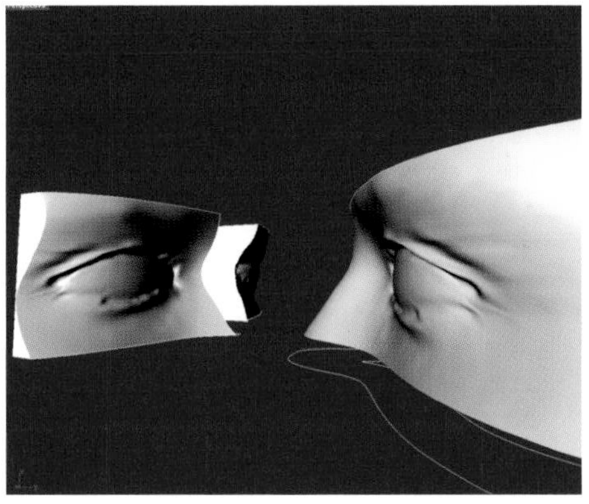

▲ The program makes it possible to visualize and understand the object from any perspective and size. We can see the objects in solidified visualization in real time, or as if we had them in front of us.

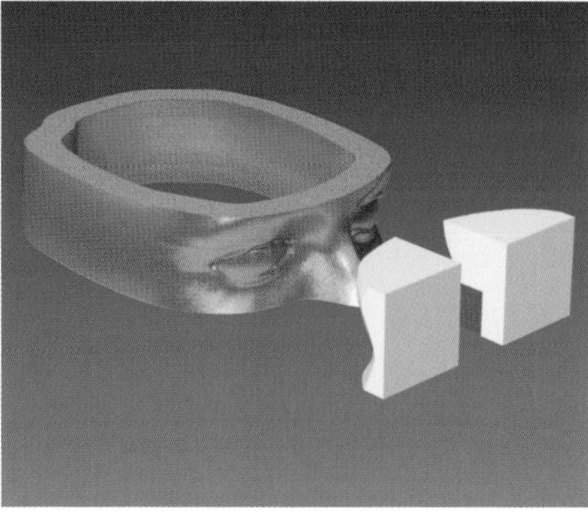

▲ The rendering of the project can be done in any material. Because the program makes it possible to calculate the exact weight and the cost in the desired material, it's possible to know in advance what the project will cost.

## Printing the Model in Wax

The three-dimensional printing is done on a SolidScape printer. Its two heads print two different waxes onto a polystylene surface: a soluble red wax and a blue one that prints the real information from the model in three dimensions. The quality of the surfaces depends on the quantity of polygonal information contained in the STL computer

The procedure for printing a single layer is as follows: First, the outline of the blue wax is formed, as if working with a plotter. That produces a better surface quality than with a printer that uses a linear movement. It fills in the lower part of this outline with a linear movement. Once the printing of the blue wax is completed, the red wax injector begins to work on the outside of the model, likewise creating an outline, and then a square grid structure that will support projections added in further layers.

The printer allows printing with different surface resolutions; thus, in small, delicate projects it can print layers about .0005 inch (0.012 mm) thick, although the most commonly used resolutions vary between .001 and .0015 inch (0.025 and 0.038 mm); the .002 inch and .003 inch (0.050 and 0.076 mm) resolutions are reserved for conceptual projects that need to be constructed quickly.

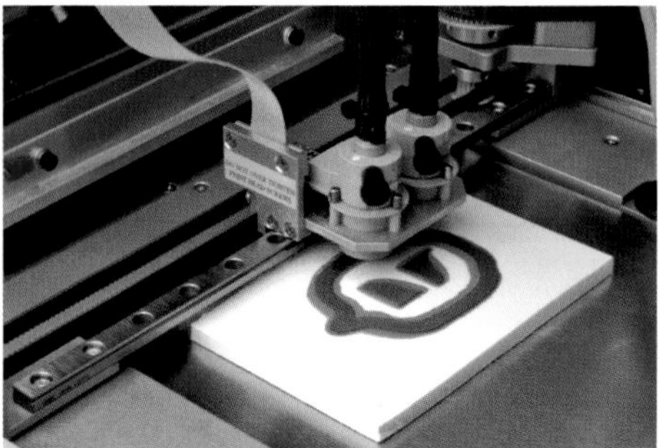

◀ **1.** Before starting to print, the surface of the polystylene base is milled to produce a defined plane, the z-axis. The first layer of bl wax is printed out on this base. A base of red wax is placed around it to act as a support, much like a framework, for the parts of the piece that stick out.

▼ **2.** The printer prints a first layer around .004 inch (0.1 mm) thick, and after letting it cool for couple of minutes, the printing platform goes down to .0015 inch (0.038 mm) and eliminates all excess with a pass of a milling cutter, leaving a totally smooth plane.

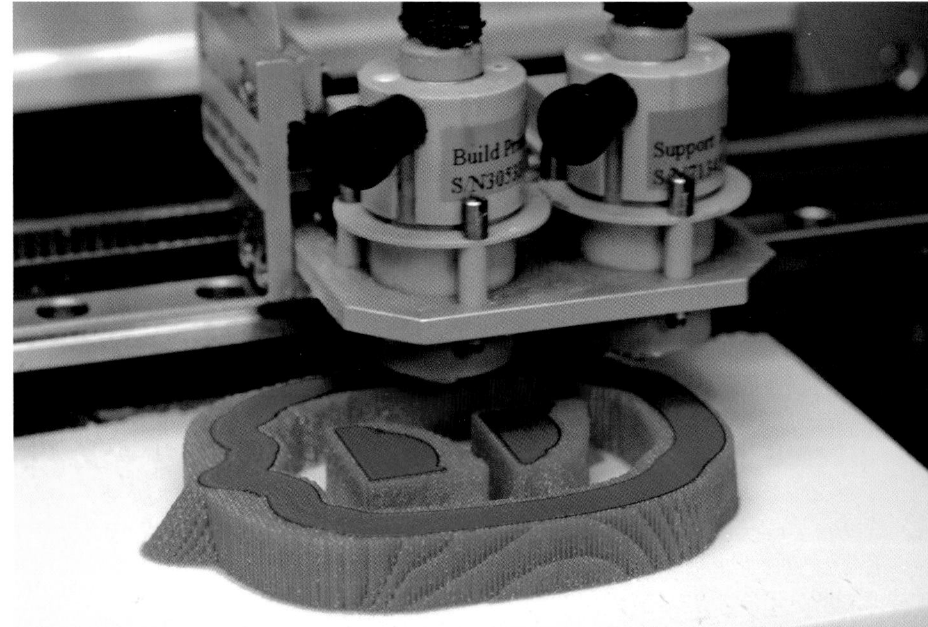

▲ **3.** The red wax is a structure like a framework. The program automatically calculates the required thickness of the wax. In very delicate pieces, the outer thickness can be increased so no breaks result from truing up the surface, and the blue wax inside is supported properly.

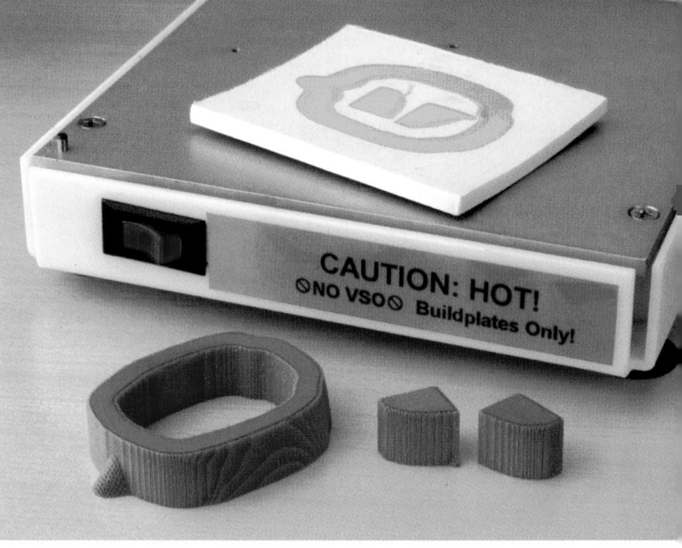


▲ **4.** The first two or three layers are always done in soluble red w so they can be removed without altering the final model made in bl wax. Once the printing is done, it's very easy to separate the mod from the platform by heating it slightly.

▲ **5.** Now a special solvent is used to remove the red wax that has een used as a framework. Since this wax expands more than the blue, slight heat curve is used to soften it gradually and make it easier to emove.

▲ **6.** Here is the result of eliminating the red wax. The definition of the object can be regulated; in this instance, a definition of .015 inch (0.038 mm) per layer. It has taken 26 layers of superimposed wax to create every four-hundredths of an inch (every millimeter) of thickness.

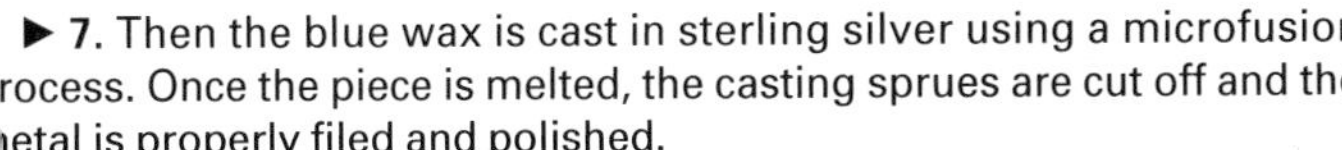

► **7.** Then the blue wax is cast in sterling silver using a microfusion rocess. Once the piece is melted, the casting sprues are cut off and the netal is properly filed and polished.

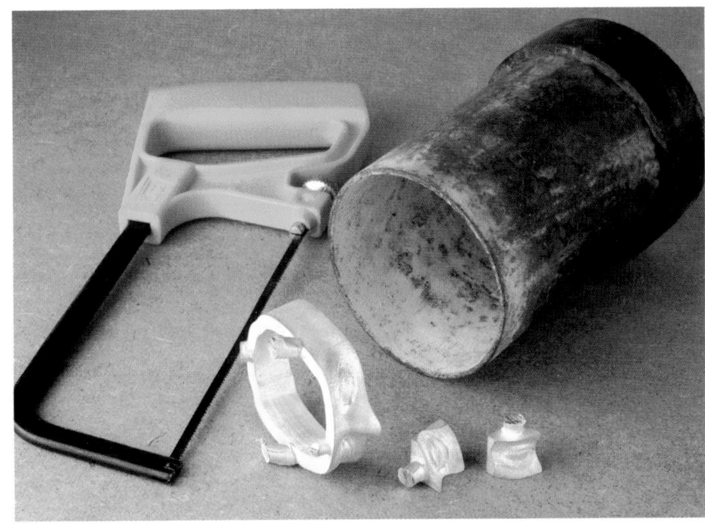

▼ **8.** *Visual Veronica.* The eyes are the opening closest to the inner erson, and the structure is a support for understanding the space that urrounds us. Work conceived by Josep Carles Pérez

▼ Another view of *Visual Veronica,* 2004

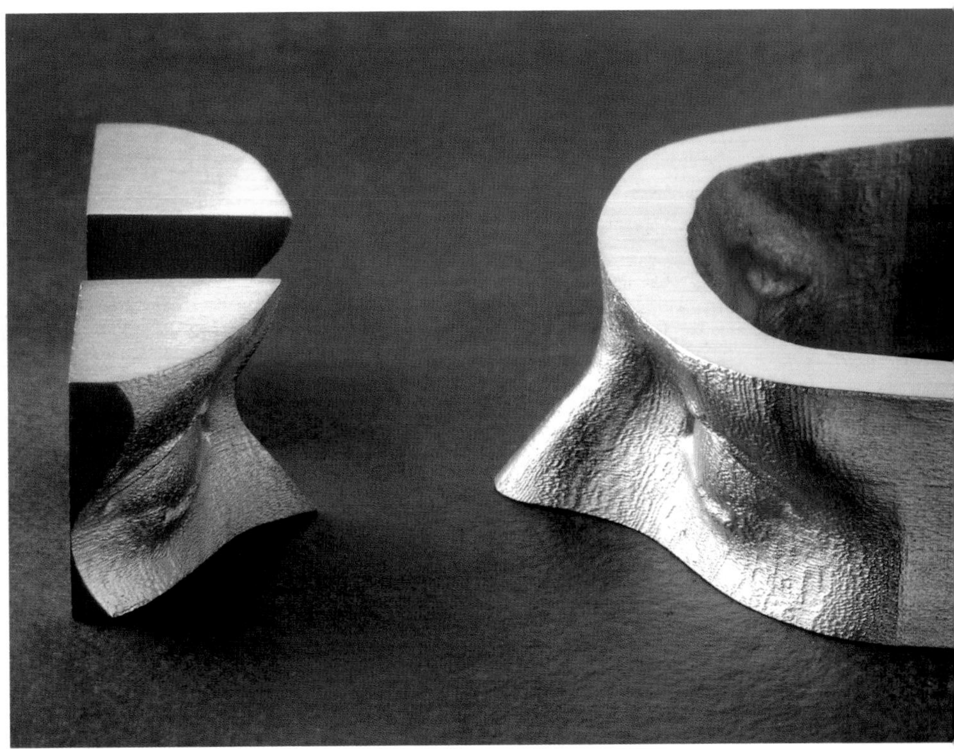

# Techniques with Metal

Most of the techniques shown in previous sections can be used without having to construct items with metal, but it's still useful to be familiar with some basic metal construction methods, especially soldering nonferrous metals such as gold, silver, copper, and brass. By mastering basic metal techniques, you can make simple constructions for the application of diverse materials such as the ones shown in this book, and create new objects from metal such as rings and pendants.

Metal sheets and wires are available from businesses that supply metals, and they are also a source of the solder for joining the various elements made of metal. The metal suppliers can provide any shape or form of gold, silver, or brass wire, plus different thicknesses of sheet metal. There are also businesses that specialize in various metals, including brass, than can supply various shapes and textured sheets.

## Cutting and Sawing Tools

It's necessary to use special shears to cut sheet metal. To cut complicated surfaces or fairly thick sheets, use a jeweler's saw. This consists of a saw frame and various saw blades that are attached to the frame by their ends, with the teeth always oriented toward the bottom of the frame. Once the frame is tensioned, the various sheets are sawed with a vertical motion perpendicular to the sheet.

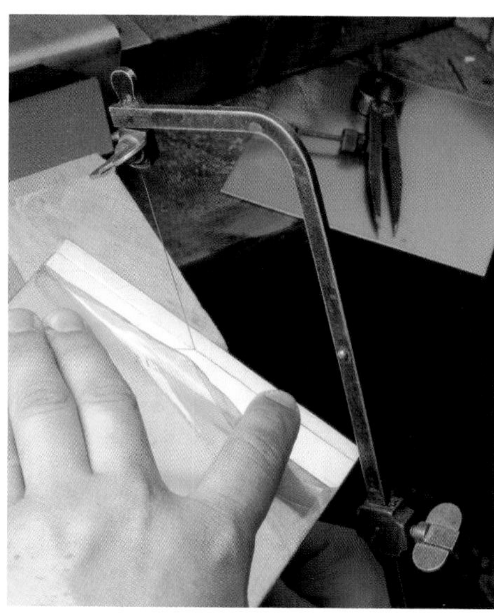

▲ **1.** Special shears are used to cut a thin metal sheet.

◀◀ **2.** After cutting out the metal sheet, lines are marked on it with a pointed compass or a scribe.

◀ **3.** The saw advances by means of vertical strokes. It's important to keep the saw blade very taut; otherwise it's impossible to cut precisely.

▼ **4.** Before soldering, the surfaces are evened out with a file to eliminate any imperfection created by the sawing.

▼ **5.** Wires and thin sheets are bent using pliers, a basic tool found in any workshop.

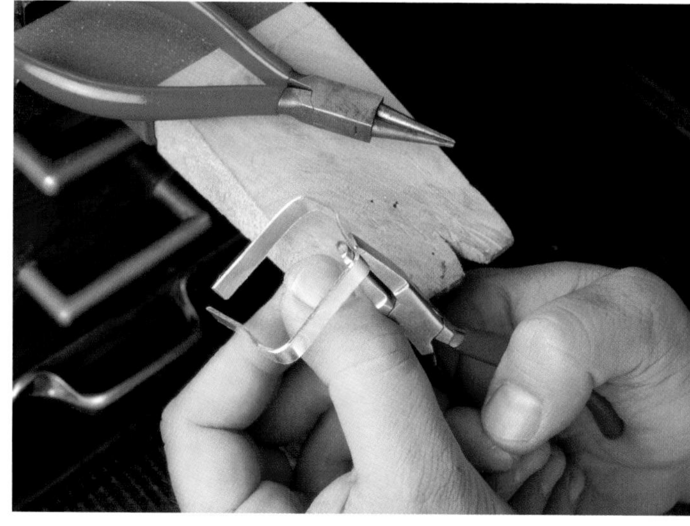

# Solder

Soldering involves the use of a gas torch of the proper type, depending on the size of the objects to be joined, the precision required, and the degree of comfort desired. When gas combusts with the oxygen in the air, it produces the calories necessary to raise the temperature of the project and allow the solder to melt and join the various elements; the solder has a lower melting temperature than the metal being worked.

Some soldering torches use the flame pressure generated by the gas cylinder; others produce the pressure by using outside air, which is supplied by a foot-operated bellows or a small compressor.

Before soldering, the items to be joined must be clean and adjusted to fit together by first roughening the surface with sandpaper or a file.

Once the piece is properly adjusted, a flux such as borax or some soldering liquid is applied to the surfaces to be soldered. Next, solder in the form of little cubes or wire previously moistened with flux is applied. When everything is ready, all the pieces are placed onto a soldering support and the heat is applied with the torch until the solder melts and moves throughout the joint by capillary action.

Once that is done, all the metal will be oxidized, and the surface oxidation will have to be removed with diluted sulfuric acid or some other special product that's available in specialty shops and designed to remove surface oxidation.

▼ **1.** One option for soldering small pieces such as rings and pendants is to use a rechargeable gas torch. A more powerful propane torch is used for larger items.

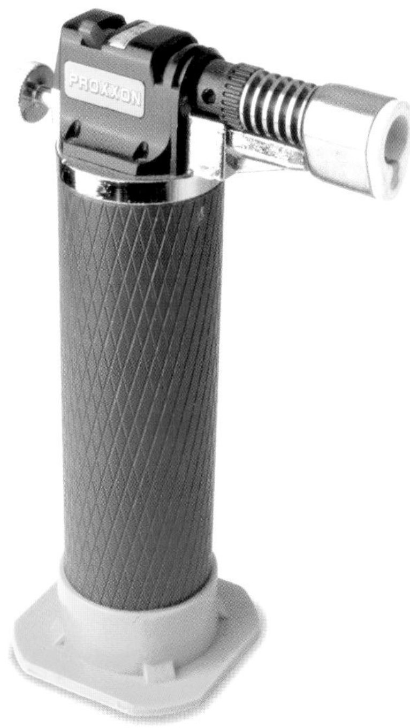

► **2.** Before applying the solder, the surface is cleaned thoroughly with a brush and diluted borax salt, which acts as a flux; this lowers the melting point and prevents the formation of oxidation in the joint. That way the solder will melt properly.

► **3.** Once the joint is ready and the flux has been applied onto the surfaces to be joined, the solder is applied in wire form. The torch flame has to be uniform and must envelop the solder until it melts. Once the solder flows, the heat causes it to run all through the joint surfaces and unite the pieces.

# Filing

Filing is another basic procedure in all metal work. It is done for cutting and evening out metal, removing excess from certain areas, and smoothing the surface. The basic tool is a file, which cuts the metal on the forward stroke. Filing makes it possible to clean up the piece before using emery paper on the surface.

Files come in many sizes and shapes that make it possible to reach into all corners of the piece. They also come in various degrees of coarseness; a coarse file removes much more metal than a fine one, but it also leaves deeper marks on the surface, which are difficult to remove with emery paper.

► **1.** Before filing, all the metal around the solder is sawed off.

► **2.** The file's shape should match the shape of the item being filed, so it's a good idea to have several files of different shapes and coarseness.

# Smoothing

Filing leaves deep scratches on the surface of the metal. To reduce the size and depth of the furrows left by the file, use a progression of increasingly fine emery papers to produce a smooth surface that can subsequently be polished on a buffing wheel.

Emery papers are sheets of carborundum abrasive in various grades that correspond to different numbers.

◄ **1.**Three emery papers in a progression of grits are adequate for providing a smooth, regular finish that can be subjected to polishing and buffing.

▲ **2.** To work more comfortably and accurately, back the sheet of emery paper with a strip of wood; this also avoids unnecessary waste of the abrasive paper.

## 'lasps

There are lots of prefabricated clasps and ırdware ready for soldering to the piece. In ost instances the clasp has to be soldered ıto the surface of the object using solder, ıt there are also closures that are attached the item by means of rivets, or that are tached with glue.

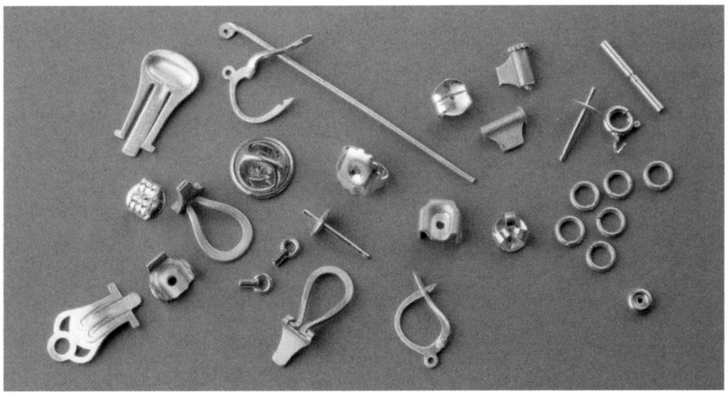

◀ Different types of clasps that are available in specialty stores

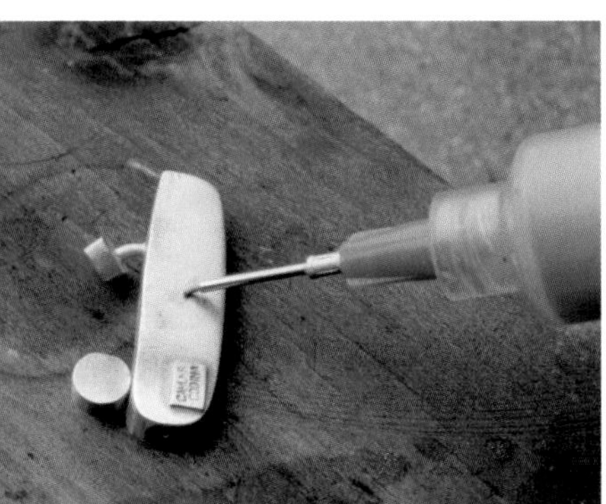

◀ **1.** To solder a clasp, such as this hinge for an omega clasp, begin by applying solder. In this case, silver solder in paste form is applied.

▶ **2.** Heat is applied and the hinge is soldered to the item—in this instance, a silver pendant.

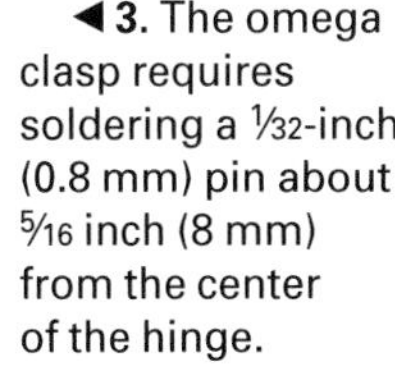

◀ **3.** The omega clasp requires soldering a $\frac{1}{32}$-inch (0.8 mm) pin about $\frac{5}{16}$ inch (8 mm) from the center of the hinge.

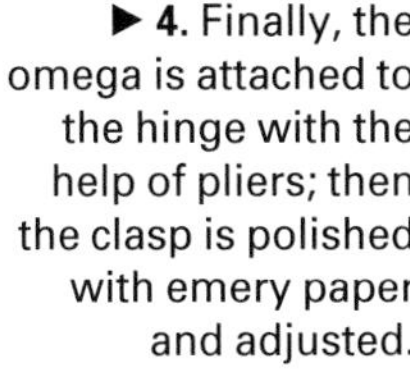

▶ **4.** Finally, the omega is attached to the hinge with the help of pliers; then the clasp is polished with emery paper and adjusted.

## 'olishing

The metal surface can be finished in many fferent ways: the scratches from the emery ıper can be left in place; it can be rubbed ith a scouring pad, scored with a diamond e, and so forth. For a shiny surface, the ece is buffed on a polishing wheel; it is first ıbjected to an abrasive process that moves metal, and then to a second process at polishes it. A small piece can be ılished with a small tabletop polishing heel or an electric polisher.

▶ In the first stage of polishing, a coarse brasive paste is used to remove any scratches emaining from the sanding. Polishing paste is ıplied to a hard polishing brush, and the piece is polished on the buffing wheel.

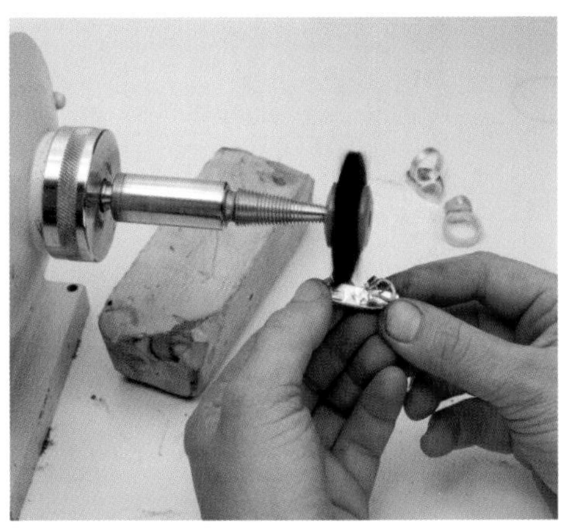

▶ After the piece has been cleaned thoroughly, polishing paste is applied to a softer buffing wheel, generally made of cloth, which will give the piece its final polish.

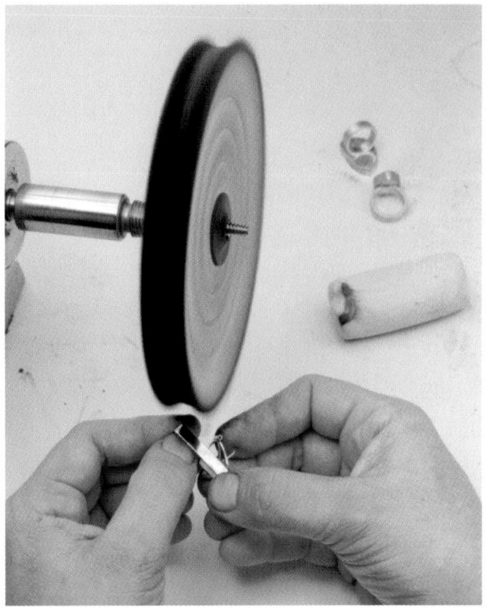

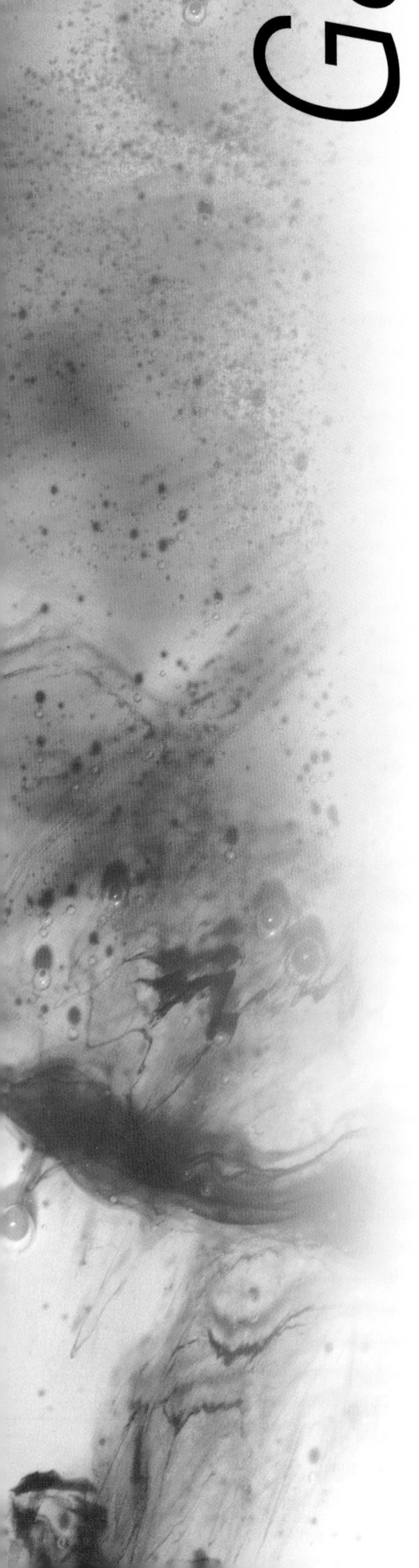

# Gallery

▶ Glass bead with gold applications, by Susana Aparicio Ortiz

▶ Pendants made from recycled bamboo by Walter Chen, 2003

▶ Silver and painted paper necklace, by Sonia Ruiz de Arkaute

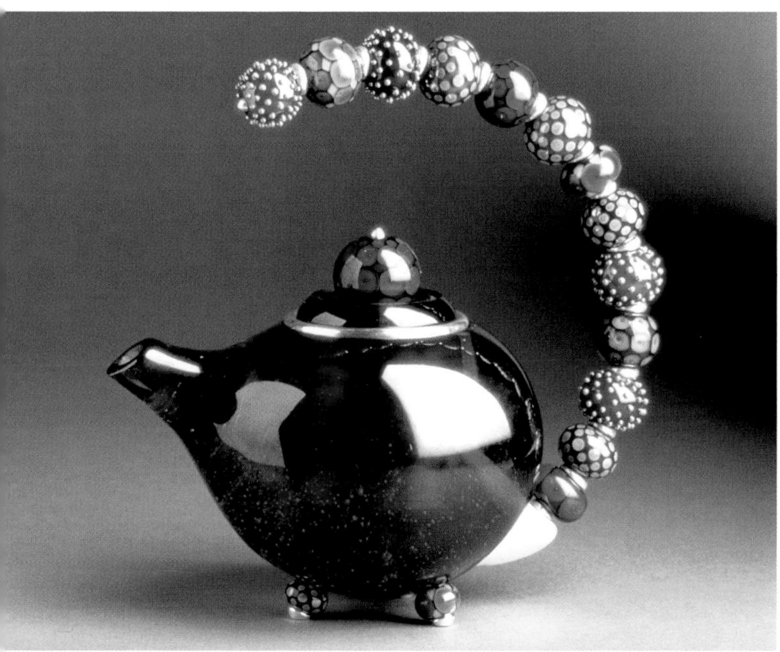

▲ Glass teapot, 2000, by Kristina Logan. Photo by Paul Avis

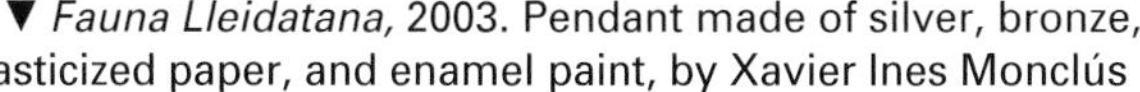

▼ *Fauna Lleidatana,* 2003. Pendant made of silver, bronze, asticized paper, and enamel paint, by Xavier Ines Monclús

▼ Detail of a necklace made of PMC and superheated clay, by Marina Gouromihou

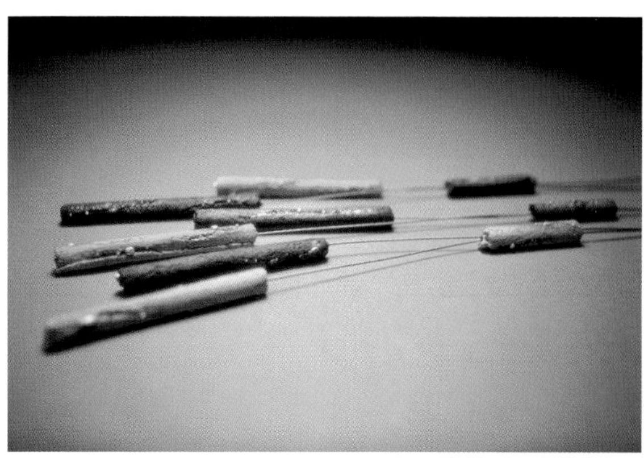

▼ Polyester resin pendant with inclusions, by Carles Codina i Armengol

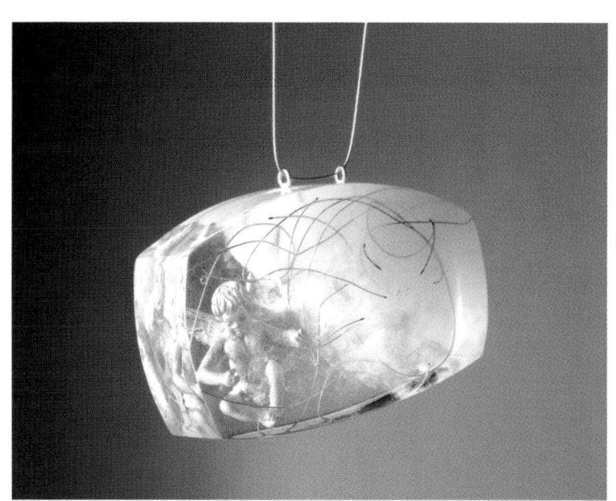

▲ Wooden bracelets constructed from laminations of different woods, by Carlos Pastor

Now that the various techniques, along with the resources and procedures on which they are based, have been explained, it's time to show how some objects and pieces are made. The following step-by-step exercises will show you how to make these items using the techniques explained in the previous chapters. First you will see how Barbaformosa and Pilar Cotter work with ceramics. The next series of photographs show how Sonia Ruiz de Arkaute makes various jewelry pieces from colored cardboard; Walter Chen as he creates a precious object from bamboo; Susana Aparicio Ortiz as she makes handmade glass beads; and Carles Codina as he makes a brooch and a ring from Egyptian paste and glass beads, plus some resin bracelets. These projects were not conceived to encourage imitation, but rather to provide a guideline for gradually getting into the various techniques, with the ultimate purpose of inspiring creativity.

# Step by *Step*

# A Necklace of Earthenware Clay, by Pilar Cotter

*The following project shows how to make a necklace using a basic ceramic material, specifically, earthenware clay. Starting with a single piece, Pilar Cotter will make a personal, unique necklace by stringing ceramic beads. In so doing, she makes a plaster casting mold to accommodate the liquid earthenware or slip used in making a series of the same shape. She applies different decorations, and she bisques and enamels all the ceramic pieces that make up the necklace. This is a small-format, delicate, ceramics project that unites four essential elements—earth, water, air and fire—into a single item.*

► **1.** A ball of earthenware clay or any other type of clay is formed with the hands and placed in the center of a square block made of the same clay. After cutting a thin sheet of plastic that roughly follows the shape of the clay ball, it is put into place over the middle of the sphere.

▲ **2.** Four walls are constructed using the same clay to close up the mold perfectly, making sure that the clay sphere and the plastic sheet remain centered.

◄ **3.** Plaster is prepared by mixing it with water, and it is poured into one side of the mold. Allow the plaster to set for at least 30 minutes before making the second part of the mold.

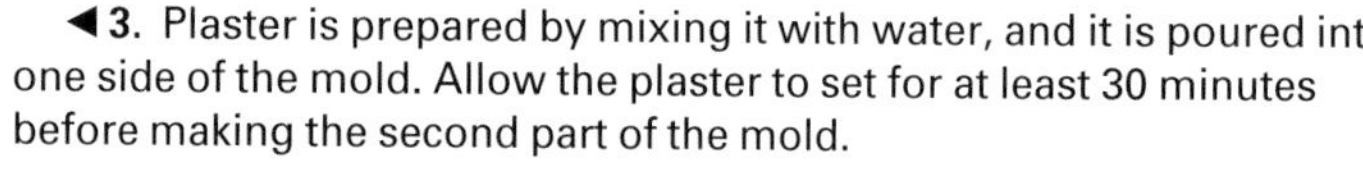

◄ **4.** Once the first part of the mold is dry, the process is repeated in what will be the other half of the mold, and the whole assembly is once again allowed to dry. Once it's completely dry, after several hours, carefully disassemble the clay and take out the plaster mold. The two halves are held together with rubber bands. It's a good idea to repeat the process using clay balls of different sizes in order to have more molds.

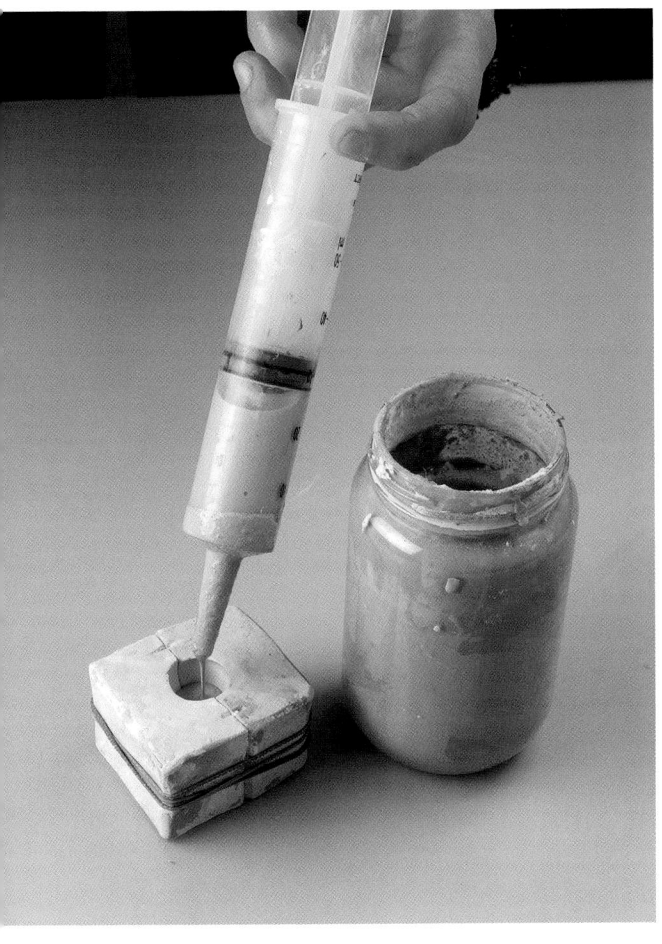

◀ **5.** Now a stoneware slip is prepared using clay or very finely ground ceramic paste diluted in water to create a yogurt-like consistency. In this instance, stoneware dust is mixed with water in an electric blender to assure a good mixture.

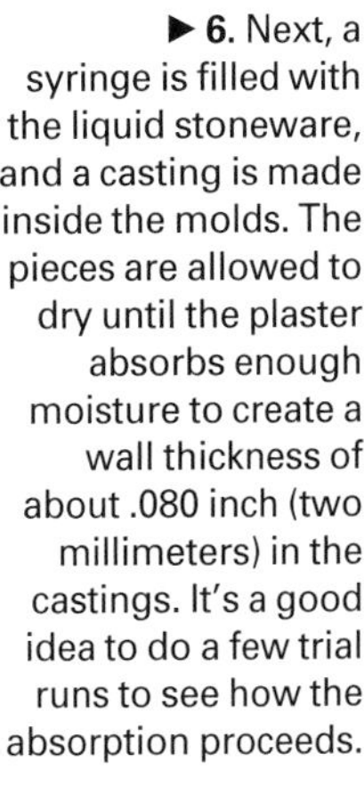

▶ **6.** Next, a syringe is filled with the liquid stoneware, and a casting is made inside the molds. The pieces are allowed to dry until the plaster absorbs enough moisture to create a wall thickness of about .080 inch (two millimeters) in the castings. It's a good idea to do a few trial runs to see how the absorption proceeds.

▼ **7.** The slip is allowed to remain inside until there is a dry layer on the surface that contacts the plaster. After this thickness is achieved, the remaining liquid is poured out from the inside. The result is a hollow piece.

▲ **8.** Once the slip is dry, the mold is opened and the pieces are taken out so they can finish drying.

▲ **9.** The pieces are set aside until they turn whitish in color, a sure sign that the ceramic is dry. Since these are small pieces, the process may take about two or three days.

▶ **10.** The beads produced are smoothed up very carefully by using fine sandpaper or steel wool. An awl is used to very carefully pierce a hole in the bottom of each bead.

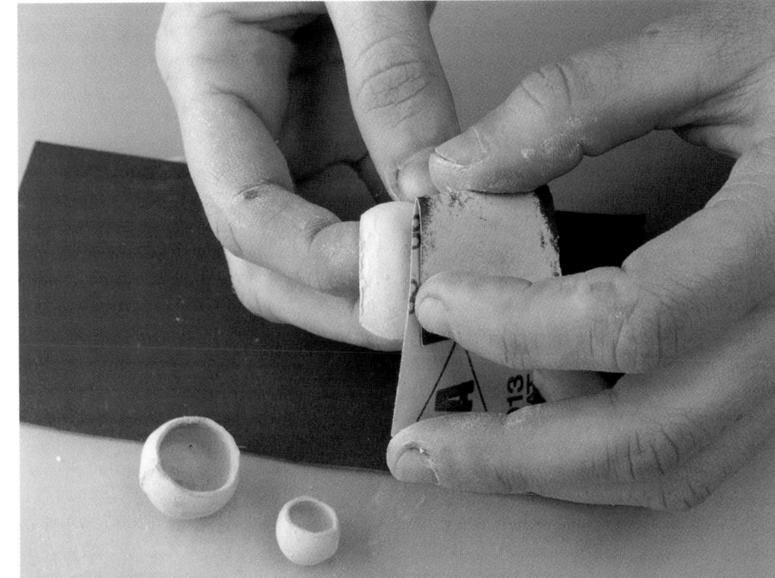

▼ **11.** An awl is used to make the appropriate decorations, and the beads are colored with dye made for ceramics; the excess dye is removed. It has to be allowed to dry before firing the earthenware, the component that makes up all the beads.

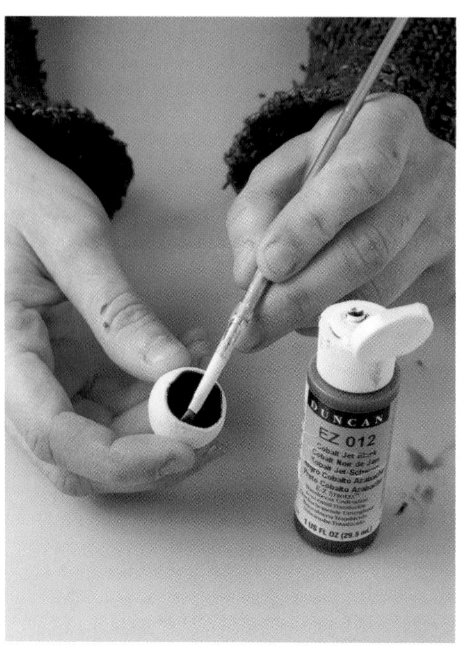


▶ **12.** The firing is done by raising the temperature slowly, producing a bisquing as described in the chapter on ceramics.

◀ **13.** Next, liquid ceramic enamel is prepared and poured inside each bead; then the excess is poured off.

▼ **14.** Using a support like the one shown here, enamel is poured over the outer surface of each bead and allowed to dry.

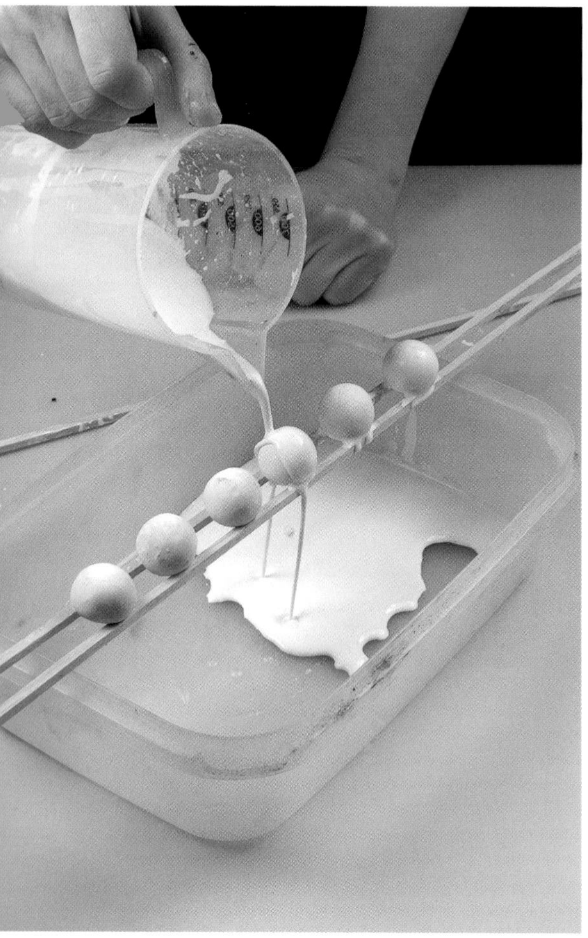

▲ **15.** Once again, enamel is applied to the most delicate areas, such as the edges and wherever a little reinforcement is needed. Next, the pieces are fired a second time, progressively increasing the temperature to 2282°F (1250°C) and holding it for 15 minutes. Then the pieces cool down to room temperature.

▶ **16.** A cutting burr is used to enlarge the hole made previously, while the clay was still in an unfired state.

◀ **17.** Finally, some small pieces are made of silver that act like clothespins to hold the beads in place, making it possible to string them on a cord.

▲ Ceramic rings made using the same technique, but decorated on the outside, by Pilar Cotter

▼ **18.** The finished necklace by Pilar Cotter

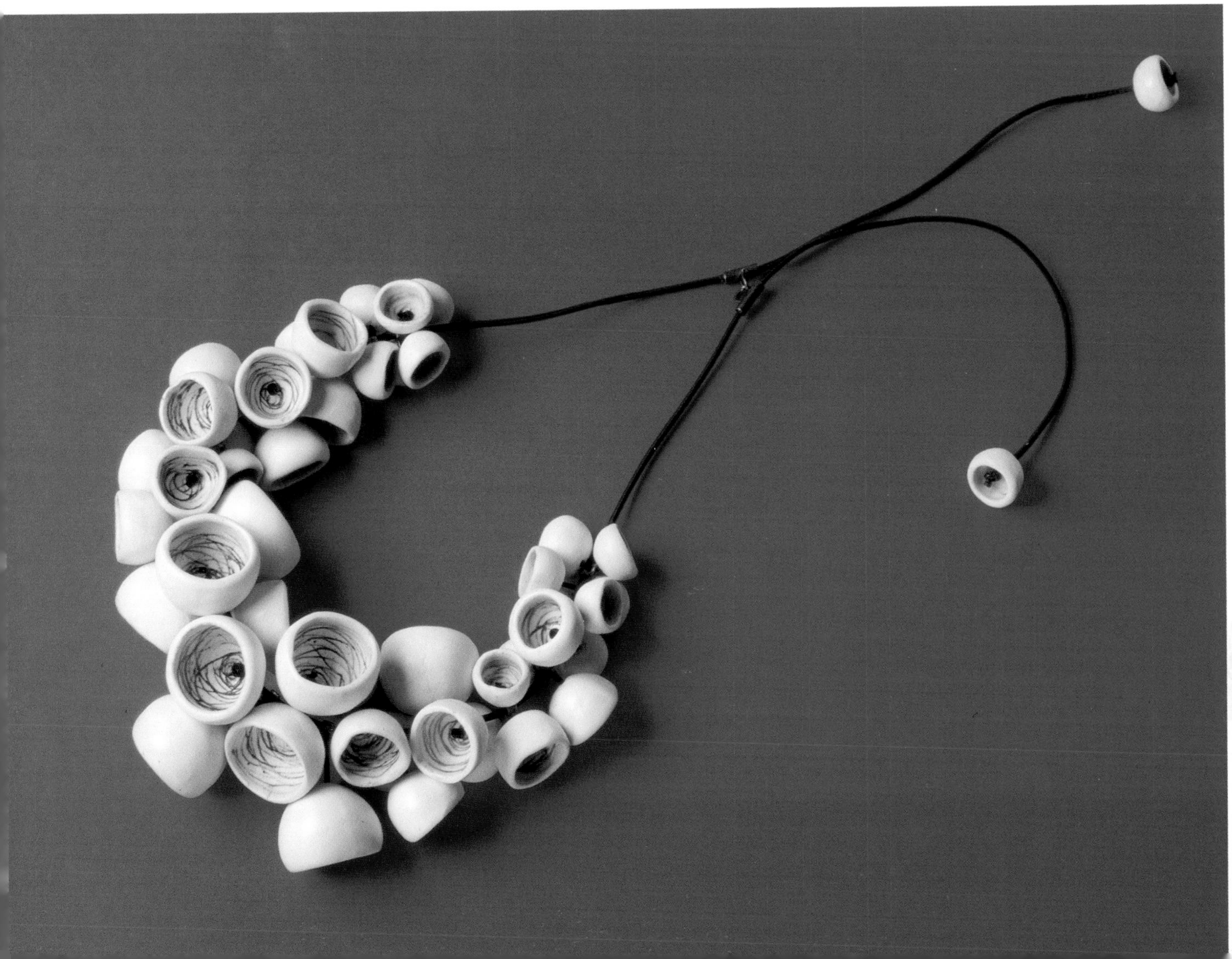

# Pieces of Colored Cardboard, by Sonia Ruiz de Arkaute

*Next, Sonia Ruiz de Arkaute shows how to make various jewelry pieces. For this project, she uses thin cardboard matting of the type commonly used in framing paintings and photographs; this material is easy to cut, and it takes color perfectly.*
*The artist uses this material as a means of expression with children's themes and purely expressionistic shapes to produce several ingenuous pieces that take on a life of their own when they are worn.*

▲ **1.** First, the drawing is made in pencil on the matting.

▲ **2.** A total of four irregular pieces are cut out. The edges and the inside are smoothed with very fine sandpaper to eliminate all roughness.

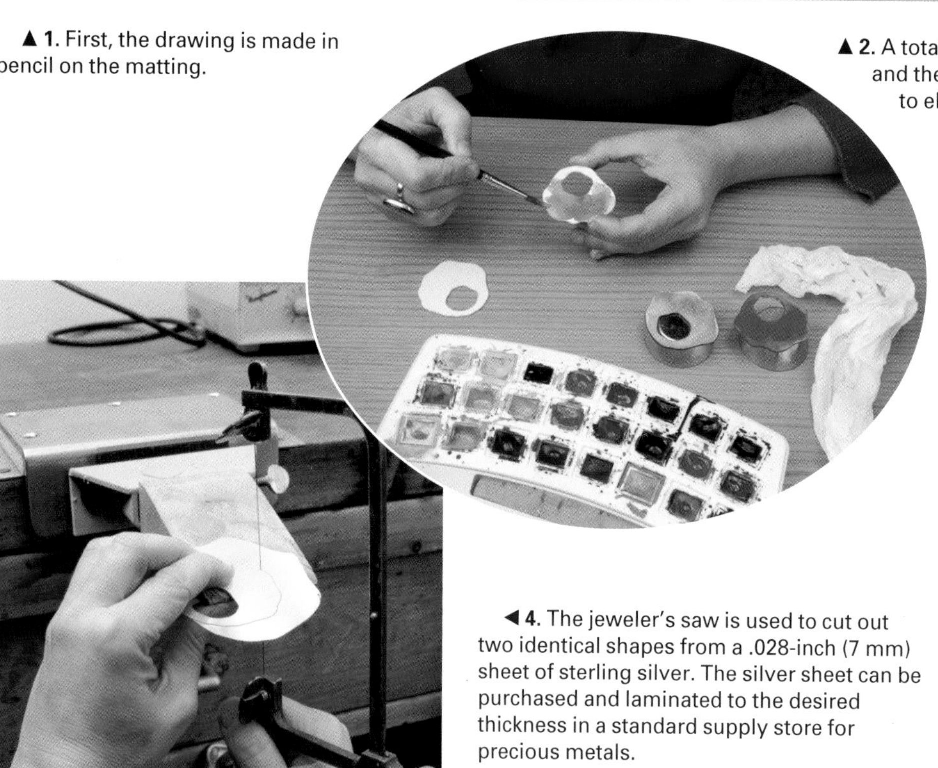

◀ **3.** This material takes color very well. Here, Sonia Ruiz de Arkaute chooses watercolors for coloring the various pieces.

◀ **4.** The jeweler's saw is used to cut out two identical shapes from a .028-inch (7 mm) sheet of sterling silver. The silver sheet can be purchased and laminated to the desired thickness in a standard supply store for precious metals.

▶ **5.** A few holes are made through the two silver sheets and the pieces between them, then all the pieces are assembled together.

▼ **6.** An annealed, round silver wire is passed through the holes and iveted at the top and bottom. The end of the wire is beaten lightly on ɔoth sides to close up the assembly.

► **7.** *Landscape,* 2002 by Sonia Ruiz de Arkaute

▲ *The Orange House,* 2002, by Sonia Ruiz de Arkaute

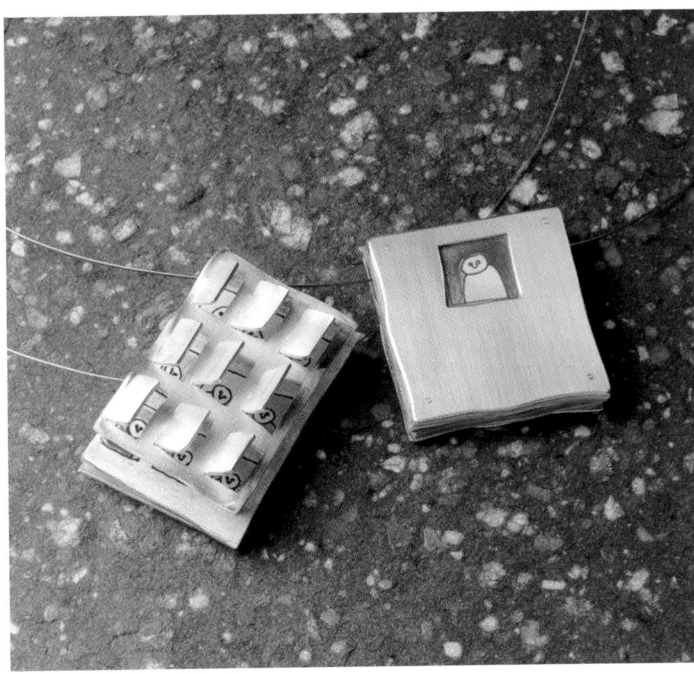

▲ *Neighbors in the Windows* and *Looking Out 2,* 2002. Two pendants by Sonia Ruiz de Arkaute

# A Hair Ornament, by Walter Chen

*Because of its strength and flexibility, bamboo has been used since ancient times as a raw material for many purposes: hunting and fishing implements, musical instruments, kitchen tools, floors, decorative objects, and even in the construction of houses. However, not all bamboo canes are the same or appropriate for certain uses. There are more than 1200 varieties of this plant, and each one has different characteristics. For the following project Walter Chen has selected a type of bamboo with the appropriate flexibility for this work. Beginning with an old, discarded bamboo breadbasket he transforms it into a delicate and subtle hair ornament Using a precise and delicate work rhythm.*

▲ **1.** Bamboo is found in many manufactured items; to choose the best strips of bamboo, simply take note of its quality and do a couple of initial flexibility tests before starting the project.

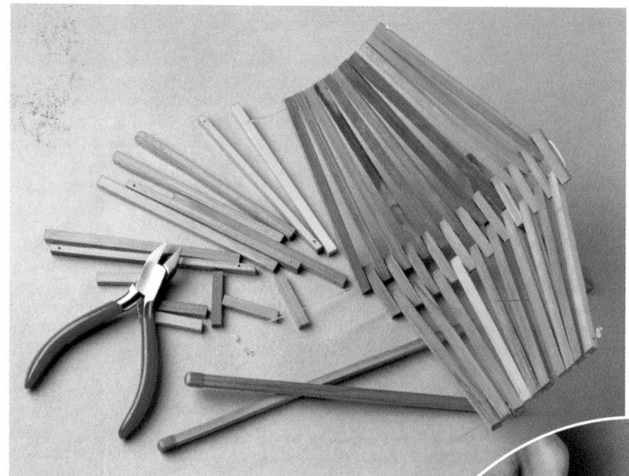

▲ **2.** The bread basket is disassembled by cutting the nylon threads that hold it together. The best strips are chosen based on their longitudinal grain distribution and their straightness.

▼ **3.** First, the varnish is removed from the surface of the bamboo by scraping it with a hobby knife to completely eliminate the varnish and expose the bamboo's natural texture.

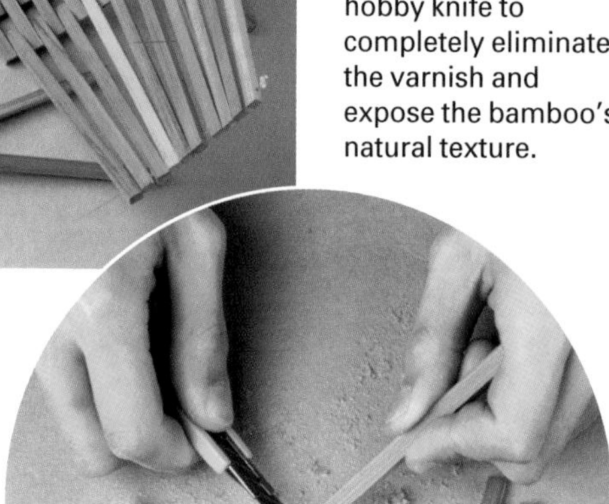

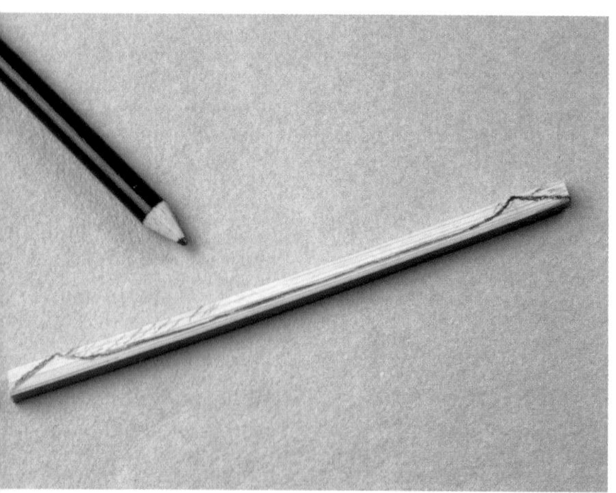

◀ **4.** A pencil is used to mark the cut along the length of the bamboo strip, and the ends are cut.

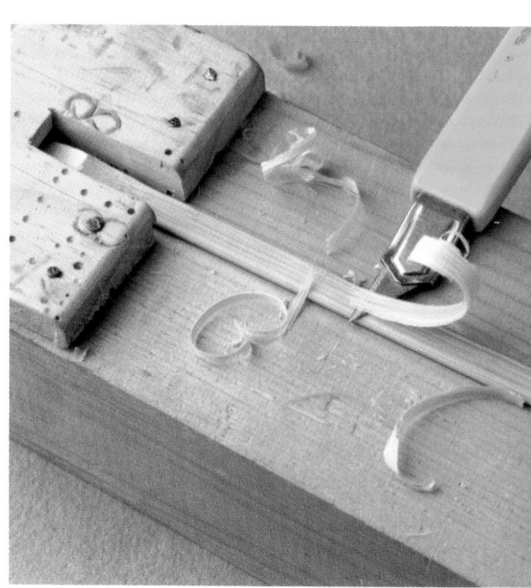

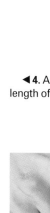

▶ **5.** The inside of the strip is planed down using a special tool made expressly for the purpose.

▶▶ **6.** The interior is now shaved down and smoothed following the direction of the fibers, until the strip is as thin as it needs to be for maximum flexibility.

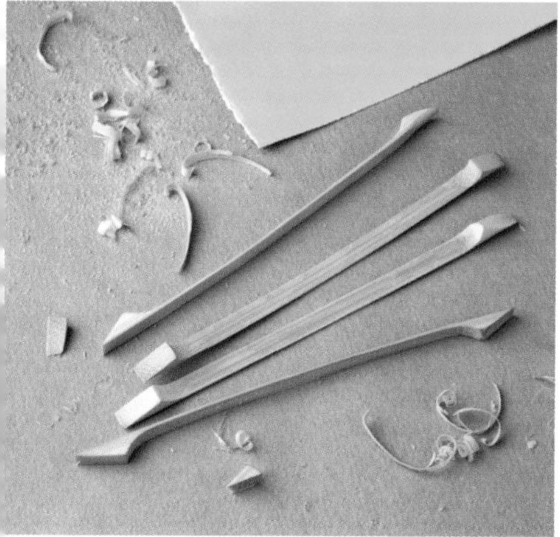

▲ **7.** The four pieces necessary for making this hair clasp are thinned down with sandpaper.

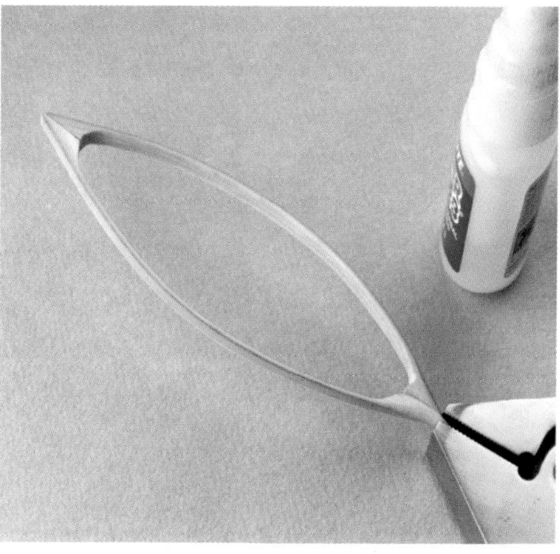

▲ **8.** The ends are glued and held together with a clamp while the glue dries.

► **9.** The other bamboo pieces are glued in the same manner.

◄ **10.** A couple of slots are made in the end of the piece using the point of a hobby knife so the thread that ties the ends of the bamboo together can be knotted and will stay in place.

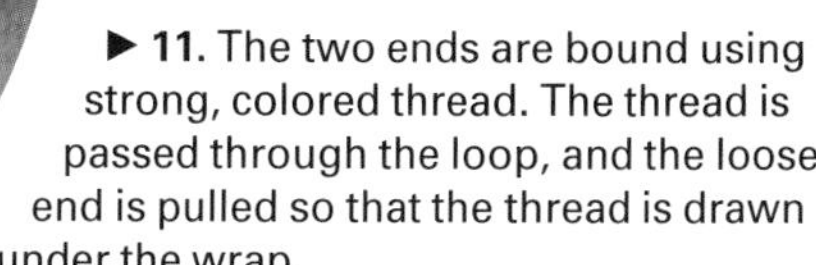

► **11.** The two ends are bound using strong, colored thread. The thread is passed through the loop, and the loose end is pulled so that the thread is drawn under the wrap.

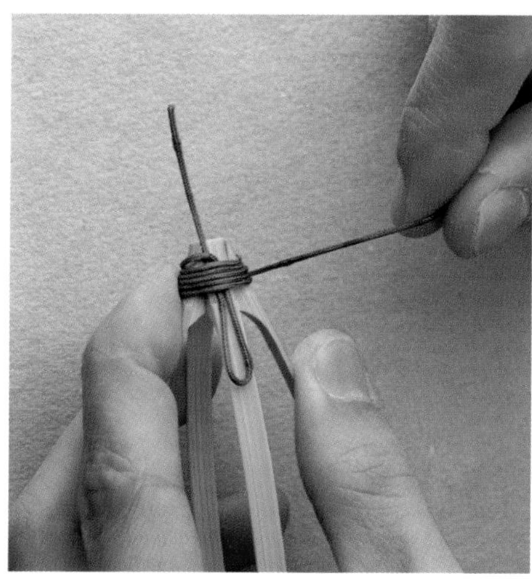

▼ **12.** The bamboo has been left unvarnished. The resulting surface quality is better and more natural when it's left free of varnish. Piece made by Walter Chen

▼ The hair ornament in place. Work by Walter Chen 陳 文 峰, 2004

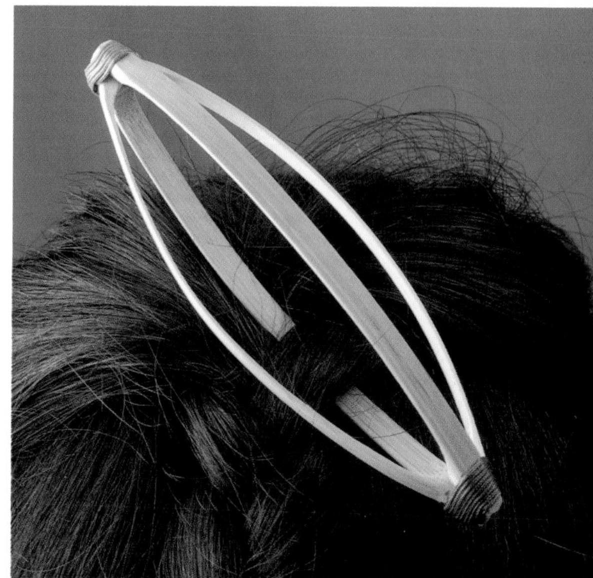

# Glass Beads Using the *Murrina* Technique, by Susana Aparicio Ortiz

*The* murrina *technique originated in northeastern Iran. It dates from A.D.1000, and was practiced by Egyptians, Phoenicians, and Romans until it was abandoned with the advent of blown glass. In the second half of the 15th century, it was revived in Murano, near Venice. In the 19th century, Domenico Bussolin created millefiori rods, and Vicenzo Moretti and his descendents revolutionized this technique with many effects and made very typically Venetian glass objects with murrinas.*
*In the following pages you will learn how to prepare these multicolored cut threads, referred to as murrinas, which commonly are made up of several concentric layers of colored glass. They may include the shapes of braids, layers, or any number of designs such as faces, hearts, and flowers, depending on the skill and the creativity of the artisan. This is a very interesting technique that makes it possible to produce many different results.*

▲ **1.** A rod of white glass is held in one hand, and a red one in the other; the red glass is melted until it forms a ball at the end. At the same time, the white rod is tempered by lining it up with the flame behind the red rod, keeping it in continuous rotation.

▲ **2.** Various stripes of red glass are very carefully added to the white rod by creating longitudinal stripes beside one another until the white rod is completely covered. Throughout the process, the shape of the glass is kept uniform.

▶ **3.** While the red glass is melted onto the white, a green rod is tempered just beyond the heat source.

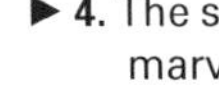

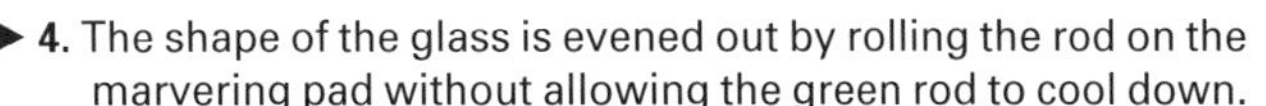

▶ **4.** The shape of the glass is evened out by rolling the rod on the marvering pad without allowing the green rod to cool down.

◀ **5.** The end of the green rod is melted into a ball. At the same time, the other hand continues to rotate the white rod to maintain the temperature.

▼ **6.** Successive stripes of green glass are likewise applied one beside the other. It's important to remember that the hand that supports the white rod has to continue the constant rotation and achieve a balance that keeps the glass melted at the end.

◀ **7.** The red color must entirely cover the green glass.

▶ **8.** Now the entire piece is melted while a green rod is kept hot.

▼ **9.** The end of the green rod is melted to form a ball, which is flattened vertically on the end by pressing against the marvering pad. In the meantime, the white rod is kept hot in the flame.

▼ **10.** Next, the end of the green rod is joined to the end of the melted material by exposing the joint to the flame so that the two pieces fuse.

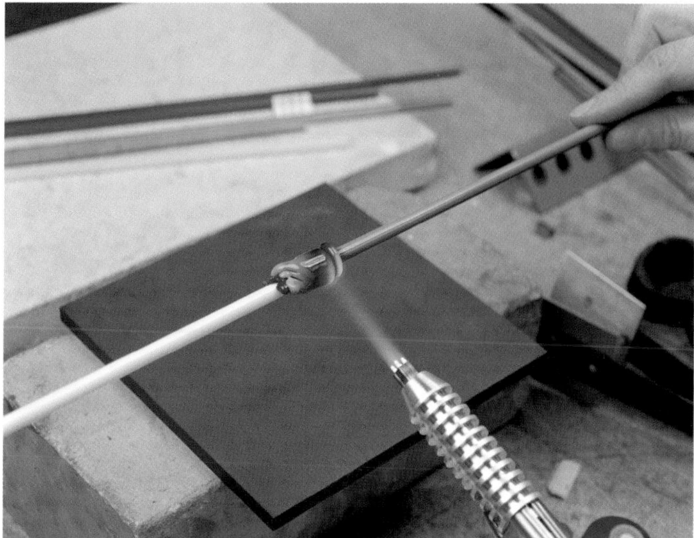

▶ **11.** At this point the force of the flame is reduced.

▼ **12.** It's important to heat just the center of the glass block so that it can be stretched out.

◀ **13.** Now the two rods are pulled outward using a smooth, gentle motion toward the ends.

◀ **14.** The thread is stretched out to the desired length and cut off by applying the flame at a specific point.

◀ **15.** A cutter is used to cut the thread into pieces a couple of millimeters long. They are placed vertically on the marvering pad so they can be grasped with the tweezers.

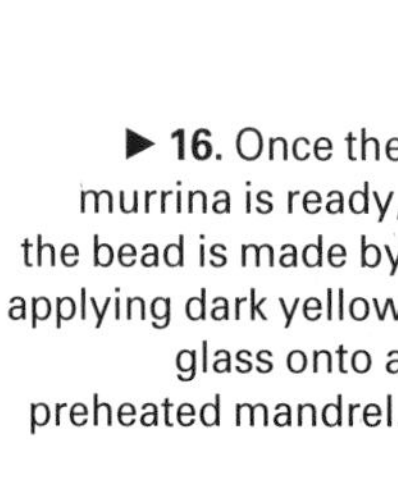

▶ **16.** Once the murrina is ready, the bead is made by applying dark yellow glass onto a preheated mandrel.

▲ **17.** Successive layers of yellow are applied to create the desired volume of glass.

▲ **18.** Then it's remelted to even out the bead.

◀ **19.** Now more yellow glass is added to what's already there to produce a slightly cylindrical bead.

◀ **20.** The bead is rolled on the marvering pad to even out its shape.

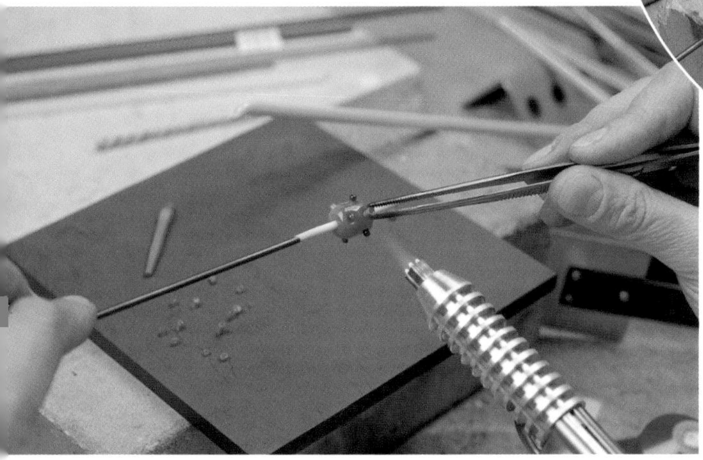

▲ **21.** A specific point on the bead is heated red, and tweezers are used to insert a piece of *murrina* by pressing it into the surface of the melted glass; the process is repeated as many times as the design calls for.

▶ **22.** Paddles are used to press pieces of murrina into the bead, and the bead is melted again to integrate the murrinas into the bead.

▲ **23.** The flat part of the paddle is used to even out the murrina with the surface of the bead.

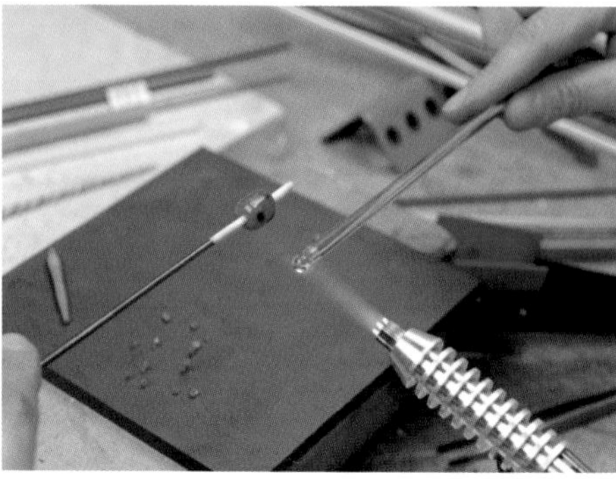

▲ **24.** A rod of clear glass is melted while keeping the temperature of the bead up.

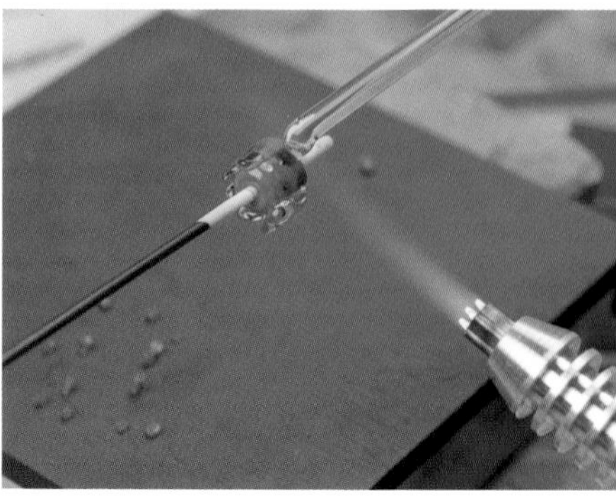

▲ **25.** Next, successive stripes of clear glass are applied onto the bead until it is completely covered.

▶ **26.** The transparent glass on the bead is melted completely.

▶ **27.** Once again the clear rod is melted to create a significant thickness of glass to cover the bead.

▼ **28.** A considerable thickness of clear glass is applied to each side of the bead and melted once again.

▼ **29.** Finally, a thickness of clear glass is applied to the middle of the bead; it is then melted and marvered to produce a uniform shape.

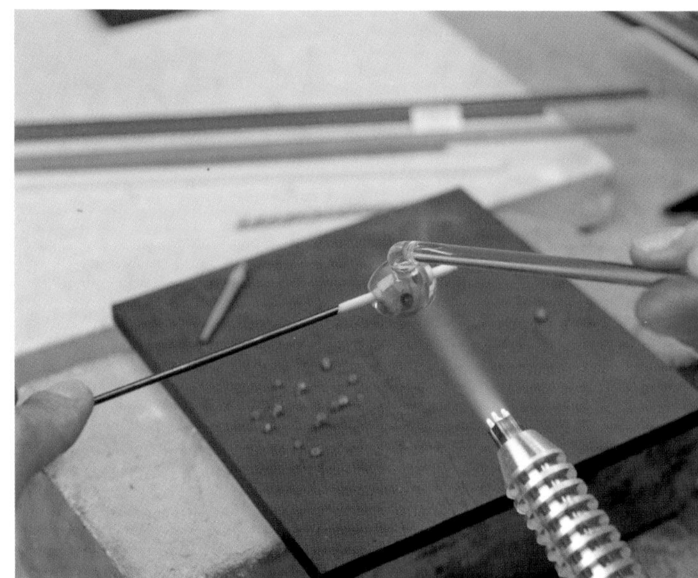

▲ **30.** The bead is placed between the squashing pliers and held there a couple of seconds until it reaches the right temperature.

▲ **31.** The pliers are squeezed together to flatten out the bead.

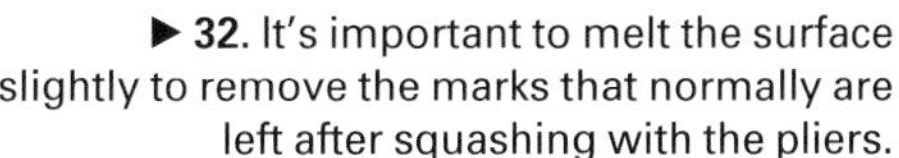

▶ **32.** It's important to melt the surface slightly to remove the marks that normally are left after squashing with the pliers.

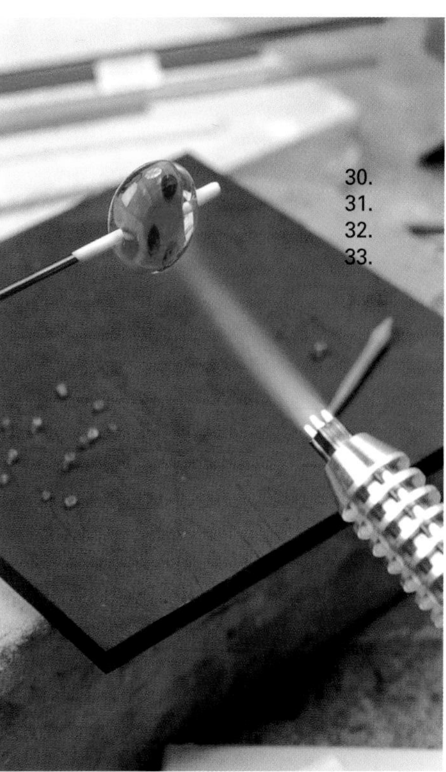

▲ **33.** The bead is quickly transferred to the annealing kiln, which has been preheated to 878˚F (470˚C), where it will remain for at least two hours. After that, the kiln is turned off and kept closed until it cools to room temperature.

▶ The finished bead, by Susana Aparicio Ortiz

# Resin Bracelets

*This section provides a step-by-step explanation of how to make bracelets from colored polyester resin using a prototype made of polyurethane foam reinforced with mastic. This process is commonly used in modeling industrial objects, but it can also be applied to the creation of jewelry.*
*This step-by-step procedure includes everything from making and preparing the polyurethane foam model up to the final finish of the polyester resin.*

► **1.** Beginning with a block of polyurethane foam, a very soft material that is easy to cut and manipulate, pencil a drawing on one side, then cut it out with a hobby knife.

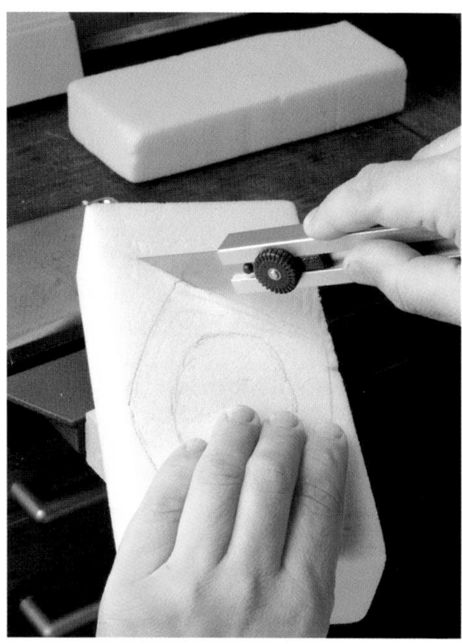

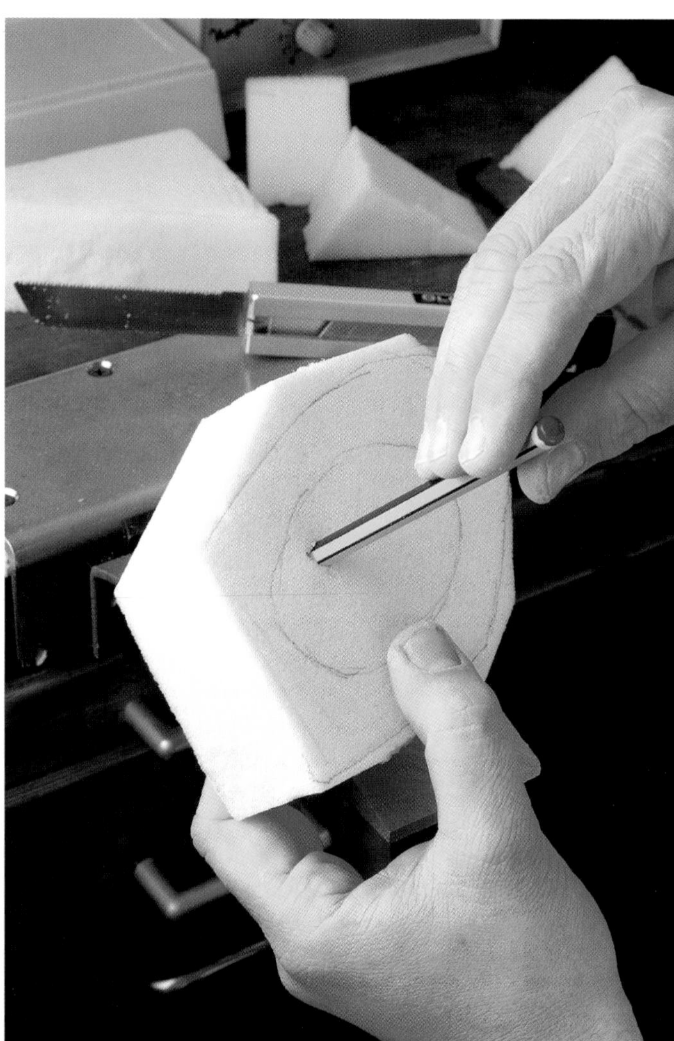

▲ **2.** Because the foam is so soft, it's easy to make a hole in it by simply pushing with a pencil or an awl. This hole is used for inserting the coping saw blade.

◄ **3.** A coping saw is used to cut out the inner shape, keeping the cut as vertical and uniform as possible.

▲ **4.** A coarse file is used to gently smooth nd round the entire inner part to create the esired shape.

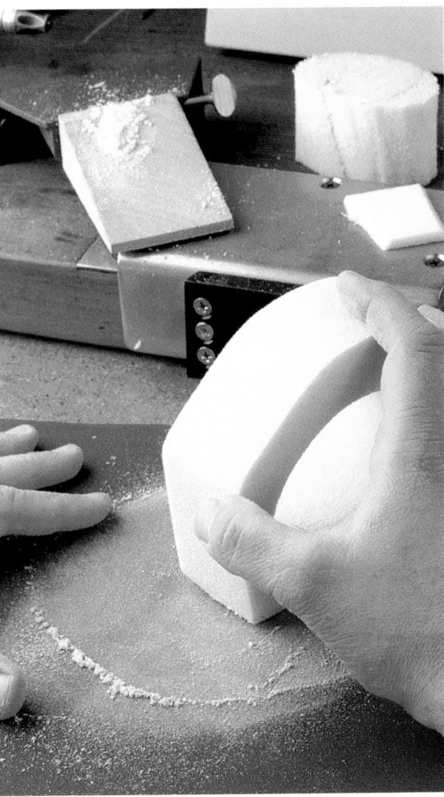

▶ **5.** To shape the bracelet, sand the foam with coarse emery paper. The polyurethane foam is easily removed, but also becomes more fragile as the walls become thinner.

▲ **6.** The surface of the polyurethane foam must be very smooth to the touch, so the emery paper has to be used in a progression of increasingly fine grits up to 800 or 1000.

▲ **7.** To close up the pores, coat the polyurethane foam with inegrained mastic.

▶ **8.** The mastic is mixed with water to give it a yogurt-like texture. It is set aside for a couple of minutes before applying the first coat to the polyurethane foam.

▲ **9.** A brush with soft bristles is used to apply the first coat of mastic.

► **10.** Because several layers of mastic will be applied, and each layer must be thoroughly dry before applying the next layer, the drying process can be speeded up by using a hair dryer.

▼ **11.** Successive layers of mastic are applied until the desired result is achieved. For this project, a total of seven layers of mastic has been applied.

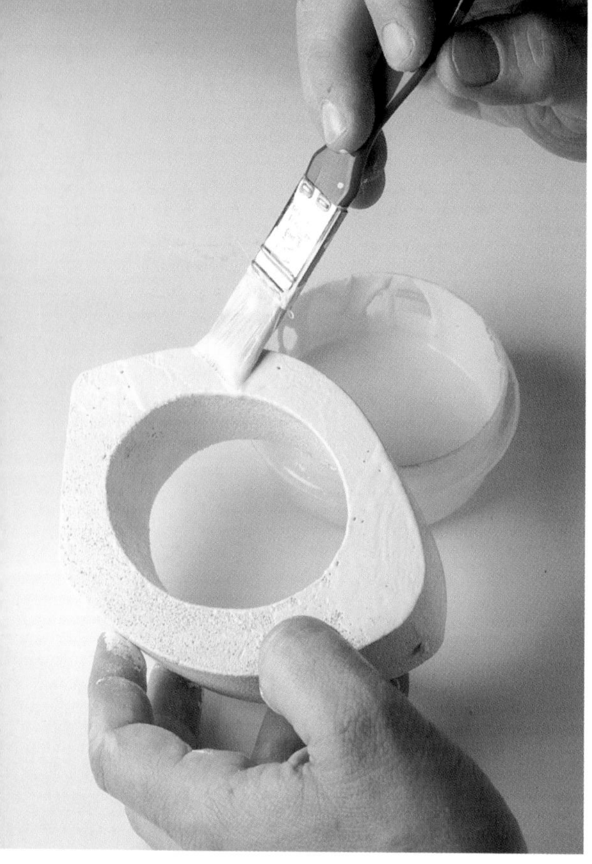

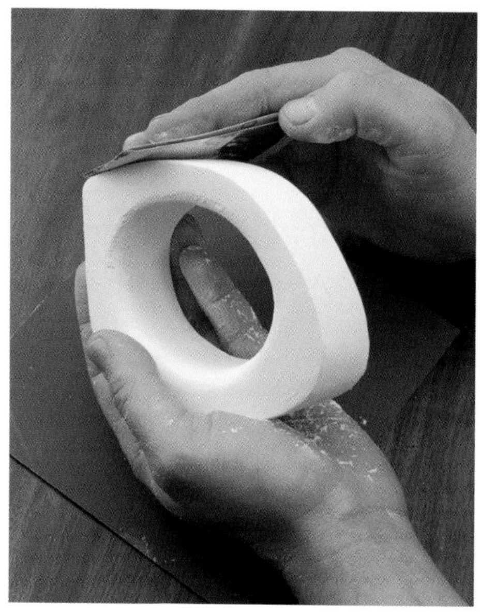

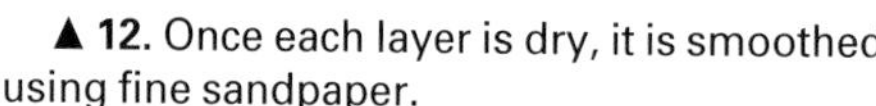

▲ **12.** Once each layer is dry, it is smoothed using fine sandpaper.

▲ **13.** The last layer is the most important one. It must be sanded with very fine sandpaper, dried, and finished perfectly. The extremely smooth final finish on this model has been achieved by using a very fine scouring pad.

◄ **14.** The silicone mold needs pouring holes for the resin and escape routes for the air that will be produced as the resin is prepared and poured. These holes also act as supports inside the mold; they are made from the stems of cotton swabs cut on an angle to about 1 inch (2.5 cm) long.

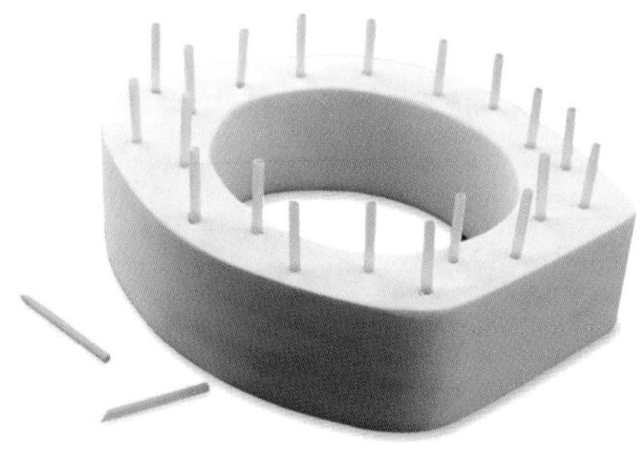

◄ **15.** The plastic tube are stuck onto one side of the bracelet about 1 inch (2.5 cm) apart in order to vent the air trapped inside the resin.

► **16.** To build the silicone mold, cut out a base from ¼-inch (6 mm) featherweight board that is roughly ½ inch (1.3cm) greater than the width of the bracelet.

► **17.** Use ordinary glue to attach the tubes to the base of the mold.

◄ **18.** The sidewalls of the mold are cut out in the same way and glued together with a glue gun; this adhesive assures a strong joint and a perfect seal of the mold walls, which is necessary to keep the silicone from bleeding through the joints in the walls after the pour. To keep the silicone from sticking to the mastic on the bracelet, apply a layer of specific releasing compound to the entire surface of the model.

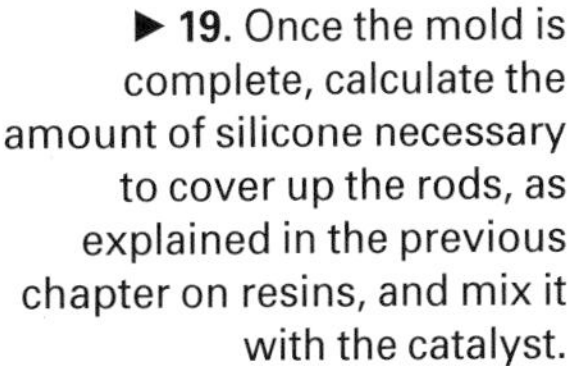

► **19.** Once the mold is complete, calculate the amount of silicone necessary to cover up the rods, as explained in the previous chapter on resins, and mix it with the catalyst.

▼ **20.** The silicone is poured into the mold slowly and steadily until it comes up to the base of the mold and just covers the rods. Then it is set aside for 36 hours to solidify.

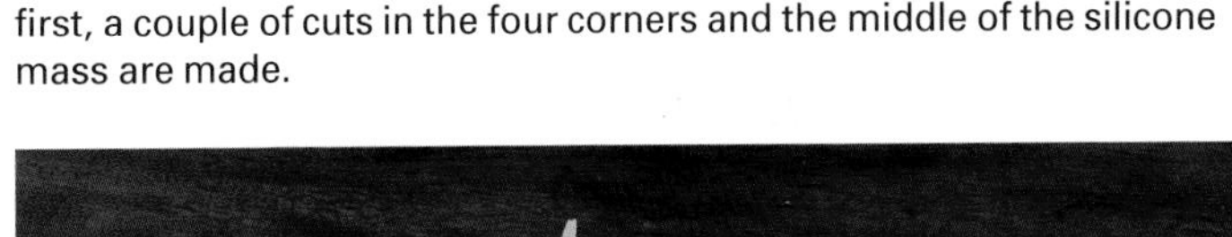

▼ **21.** To ensure the second half of the mold fits perfectly with the first, a couple of cuts in the four corners and the middle of the silicone mass are made.

◀ **22.** Another layer of releasing agent is applied prior to pouring the silicone into the second part of the mold.

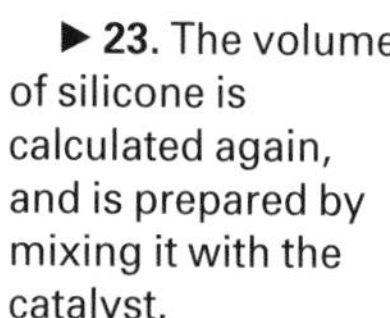

▶ **23.** The volume of silicone is calculated again, and is prepared by mixing it with the catalyst.

▼ **24.** Now the silicone is poured in to completely cover the bracelet; the silicone should be no less than ¼ to 5⁄16 inch (6 to 8 mm) thick on the top.

▲ **25.** Once the second pour of silicone has solidified, the mold is opened up by removing the featherweight board, taking out the foam model, and separating the two halves. Now the mold is ready to accept the pour of polyester resin.

◀ **26.** If necessary, reapply separator to the silicone mold. Because it's usually very easy to get the polyester out of the silicone mold, this step can sometimes be skipped.

▶ **27.** After preparing the polyester resin and catalyst, the material is poured into the open mold.

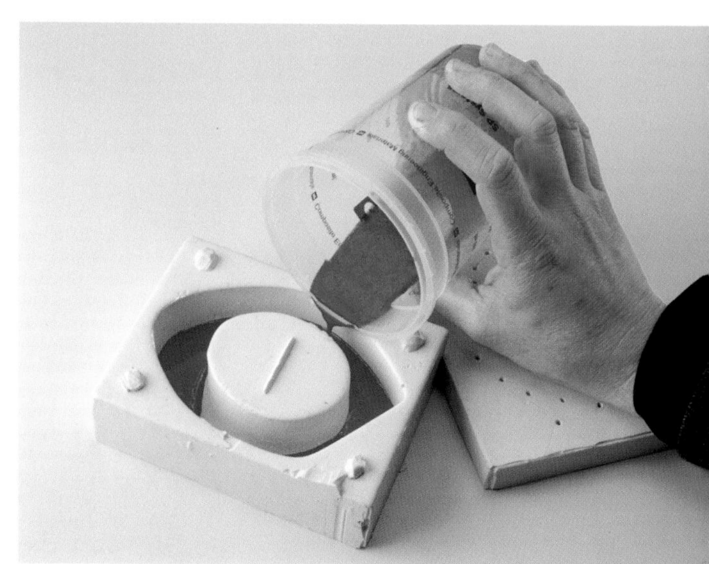

▶ **28.** Several colors are poured for this bracelet project.

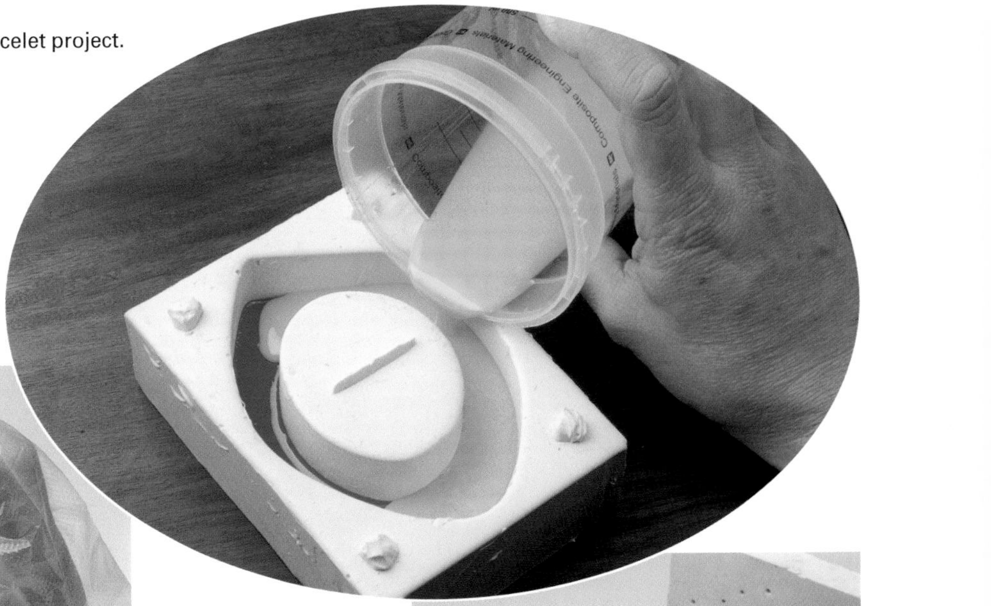

▼ **29.** The two halves of the mold are put together, and small staples are put into the corners to keep the two halves firmly in place. To finish filling the mold, a large syringe is filled with resin and injected under pressure through one or several of the holes in the top. The air contained in the mold will escape through the remaining holes.

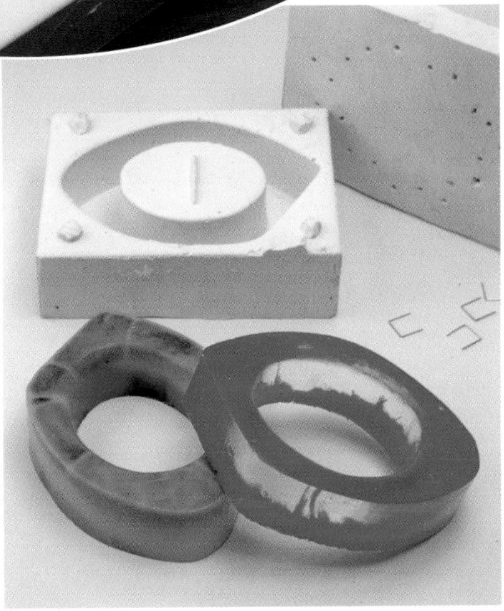

▶ **30.** The resin is easily removed from the silicone after about 36 hours.

▼ **31.** The first phase of the polishing can be done on a belt sander. This tool facilitates truing up the surface and reduces the sanding time; it also produces a smooth, uniform surface.

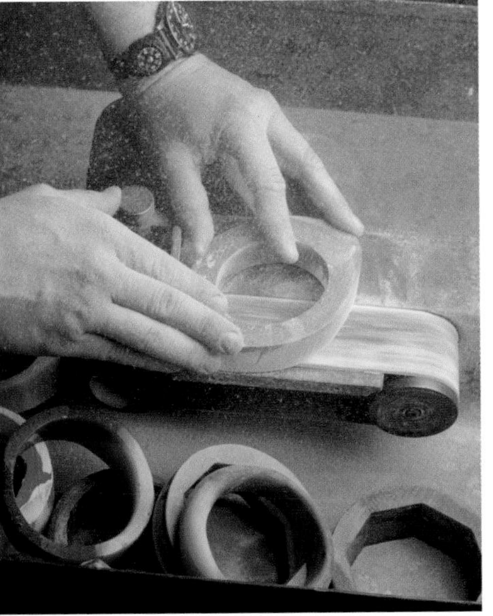

▼ **32.** Now the sides are smoothed. As in previous instructions, change the direction of the sanding constantly to produce a fine, uniform abrasion of the surface.

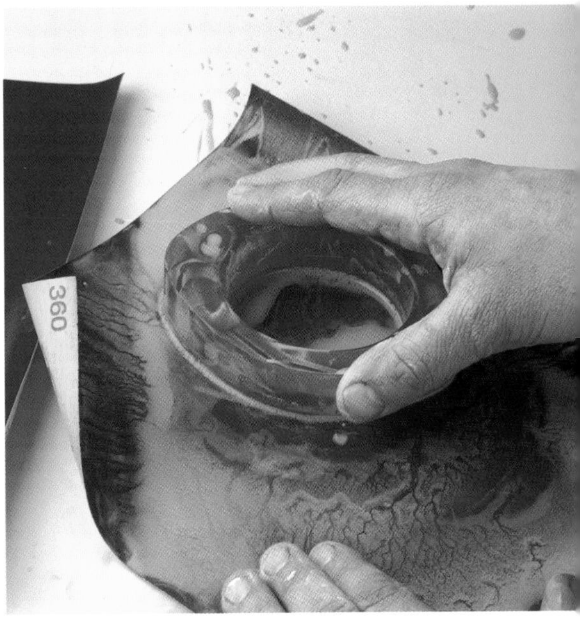

▲ **33.** To achieve a very smooth surface, various grits of wet emery paper are used, up to a grit of around 1200.

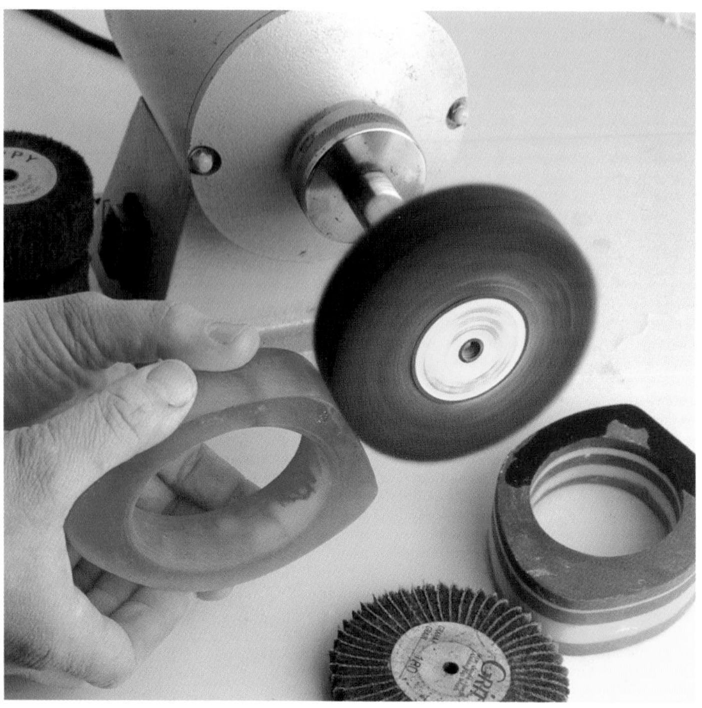

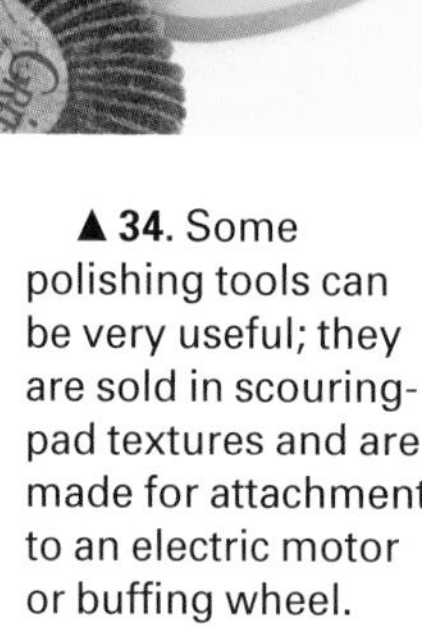

▲ **34.** Some polishing tools can be very useful; they are sold in scouring-pad textures and are made for attachment to an electric motor or buffing wheel.

▲ **35.** The bracelet is first smoothed on the buffing wheel by applying an aggressive polishing paste and using a stitched cloth wheel. Change the direction of the polishing continuously to avoid heating up the resin excessively.

▲ **36.** A small, dense, fleece polishing attachment is used to smooth and polish the inside of the bracelet.

▲ **37.** Once the bracelet is polished perfectly, polishing paste is applied to a new stitched cotton wheel that will be used only for buffing.

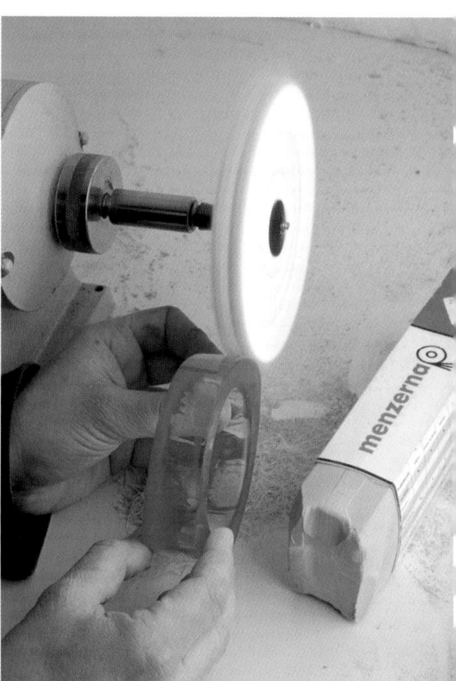


▲ **38.** The bracelet is buffed, making sure to avoid heating up the surface of the resin too much, and continually changing the direction of the polishing.

▲ **39.** Finally, with a very light, unstitched cotton buffing wheel, a final layer of polishing paste is applied. The compound's very high wax content gives the bracelet its final sheen.

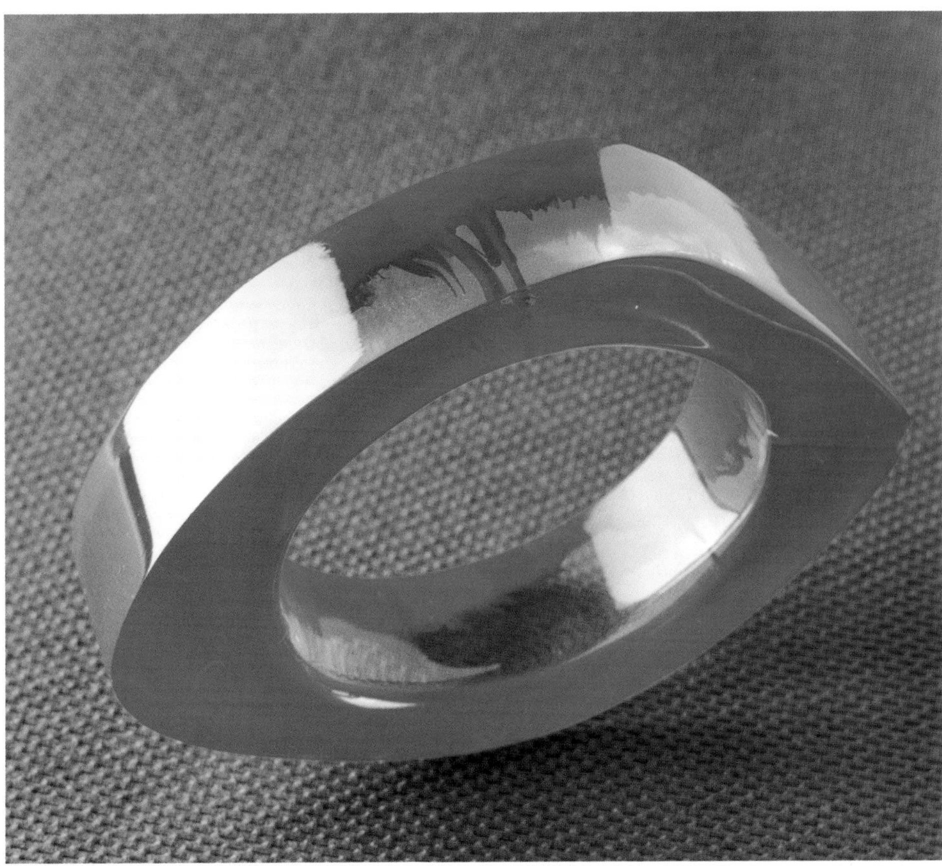

► **40.** Here is one of the results of the casting of clear and red resins. Project by Carles Codina i Armengol

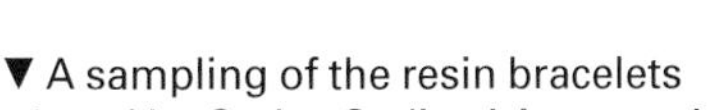

▼ A sampling of the resin bracelets produced by Carles Codina i Armengol

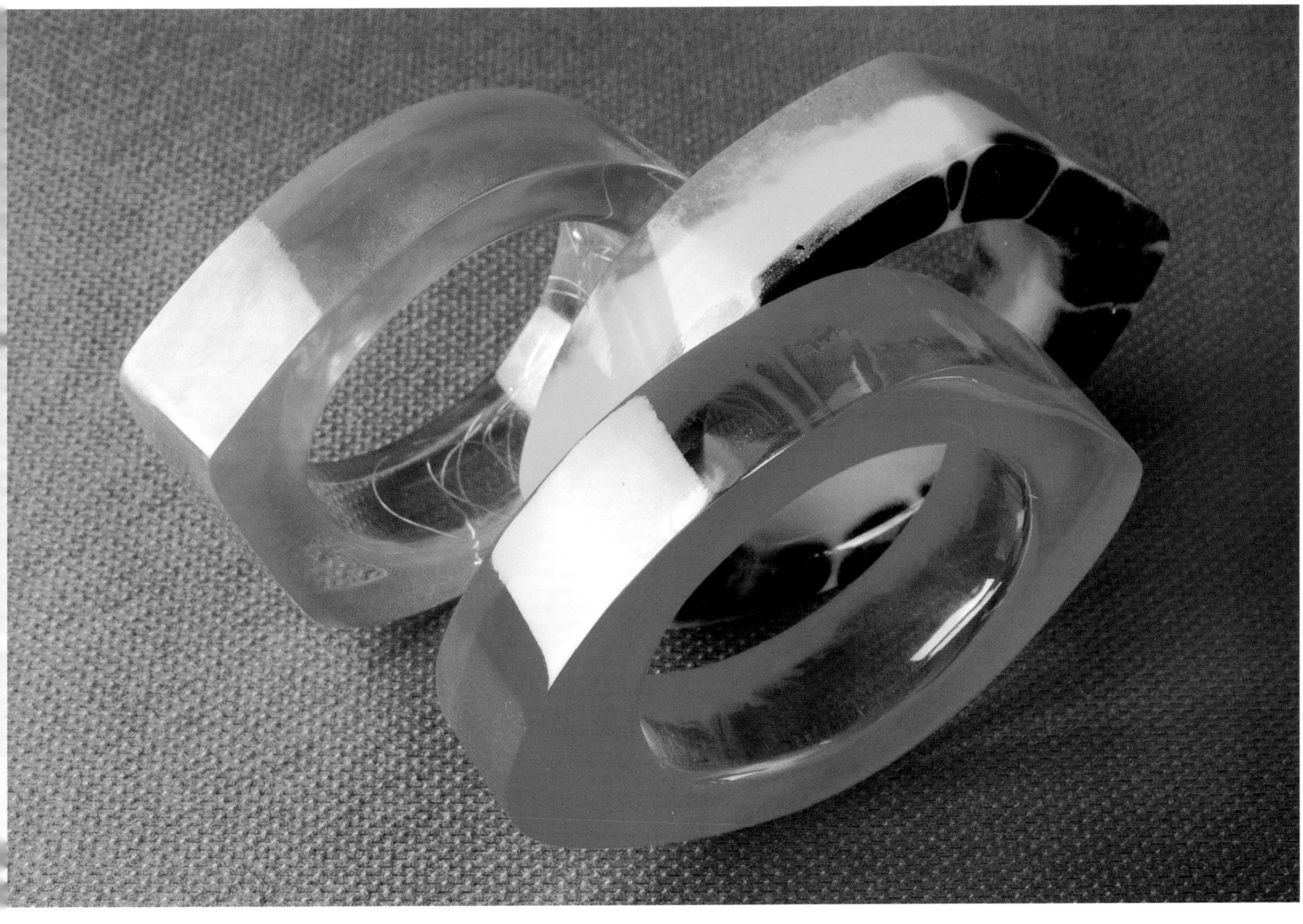

# Brooch Made of Egyptian Paste and Glass

*The following project demonstrates the step-by-step process of making this metal brooch. This project brings together the two techniques demonstrated in previous chapters of this book on creating and using Moretti glass beads and ceramic disks made of Egyptian paste by Barbaformosa.*

▲ **1.** The entire structure of the piece can be made from two sheets of silver, one about .050 inch (1.2 mm) thick, and a thicker one measuring about .070 inch (1.7 mm). This item can be made in silver or other metals, preferably brass or German silver, both of which can be bought in sheets of different thicknesses from any supplier.

▲ **2.** To begin, a divider is used to mark off a parallel-sided strip about ¼ inch (6 mm) wide on the thicker sheet. Next, the strip is cut out using a jeweler's saw. Five more strips are cut in the same way. Before manipulating the metal, it is annealed to make it more ductile; then it is pickled to remove surface oxidation by immersing the piece in a specific pickling solution.

► **3.** Using a file with one round and one flat side, each of the six strips are bent into a hoop shape, adjusting the joint properly for the subsequent soldering.

► **4.** In order to make the ring completely cylindrical, it is shaped using a nylon hammer and a steel mandrel.

▶ **5.** The flat face of the metal file is used to even up both sides of the rings.

◀ **6.** A ½-inch (1.3 cm) cylindrical cutting burr is used to make a vertical cut in each side halfway through the rings as well as the bar that will connect them.

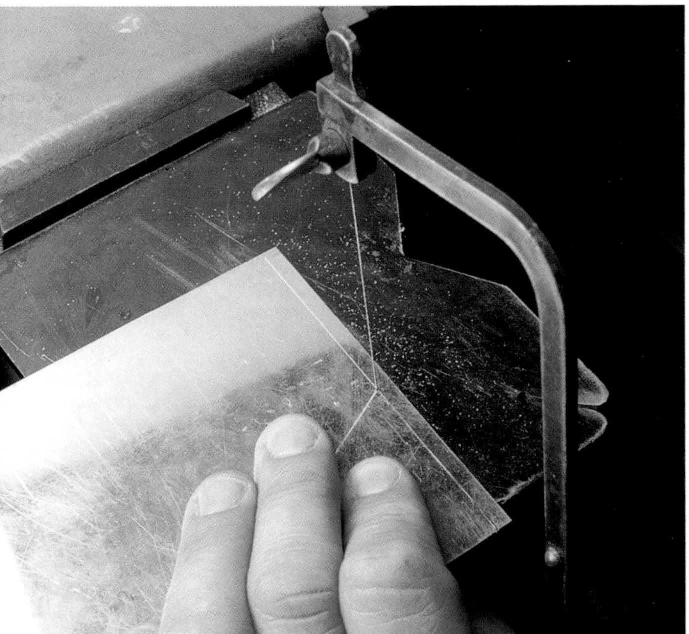

◀ **7.** Now the piece that will be used to connect the six rings is cut.

▲ **8.** Again, after cutting the metal with the jeweler's saw, the surfaces are filed.

◀ **9.** Once the sides have been trued up, a series of notches spaced according to the outside diameter of the rings are made.

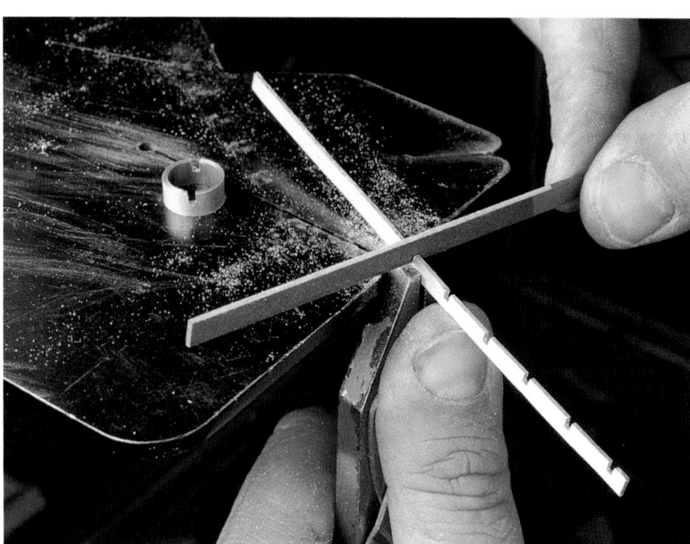

◀ **10.** Because the notches made with the grinding burr may be uneven, they must be cleaned up using a flat file slightly thinner than the stock to be fitted together.

◀ **11.** Once the pieces have been pickled and cleaned, they are fitted together by assembling the structure on top of the soldering brick and preparing the piece for soldering.

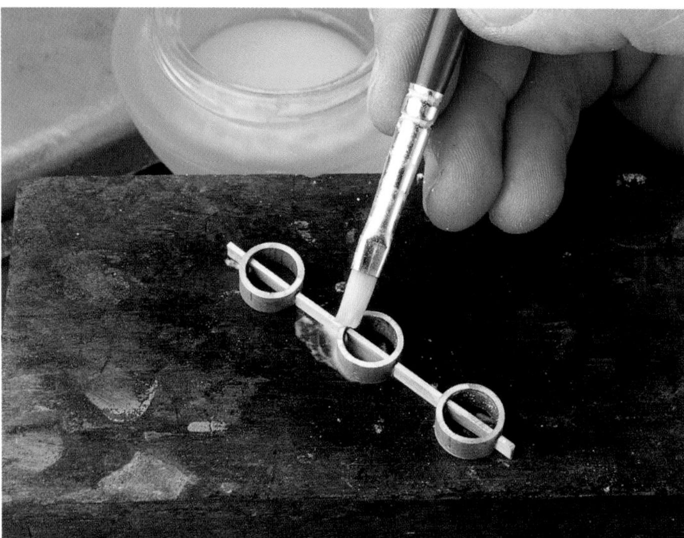

◀ **12.** Liquid soldering flux is applied to the surfaces to be joined. This product, which is made from borax, prevents oxidation in the area of the joint and allows the solder to flow freely.

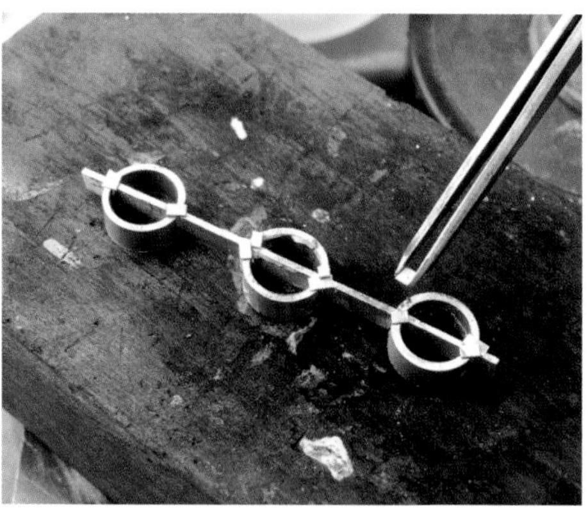

◀ **13.** The solder, cut into small metal cubes, is placed onto each of the joints.

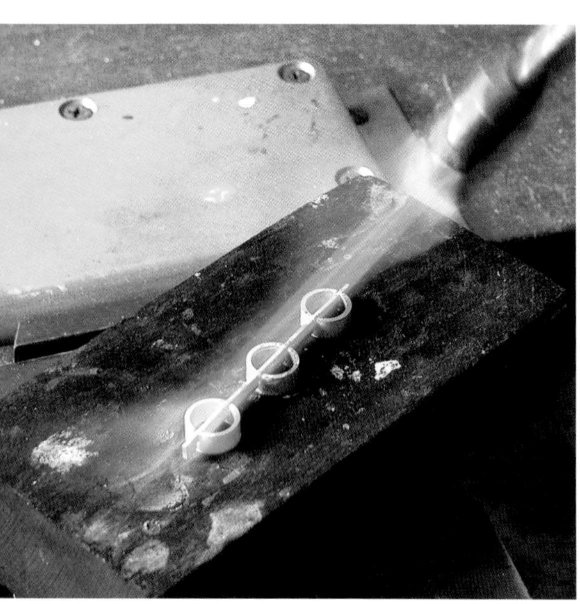

◀ **14.** Heat is applied with an oxy-propane torch to melt the solder. Because solder always has a lower melting point than the metal being worked, once liquefied, it flows all through the joint. When cooled, it forms a strong joint.

▶ **15.** After pickling the metal once again to eliminate any surface oxidation, the inside of each ring is cut out, and the remnants of the metal are removed from the inside with a round file.

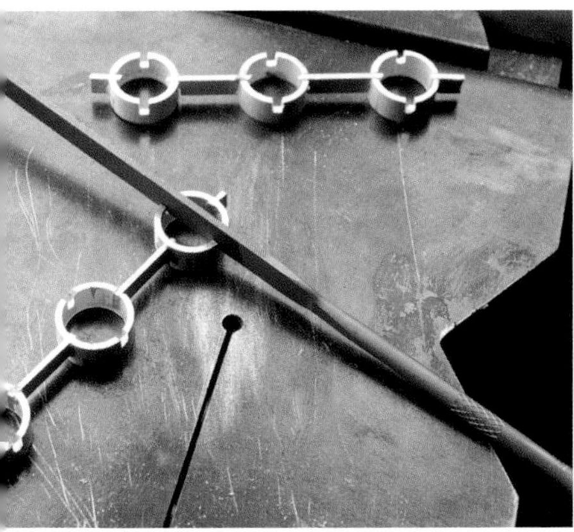

▲ **16.** The same structure is made twice more, and transverse notches are likewise cut so that the two structures can be connected in parallel.

▲ **17.** The structure is once again readied for soldering, and the two elements are soldered together.

► **18.** The insides and the excess outer projections are cut off using the jeweler's saw.

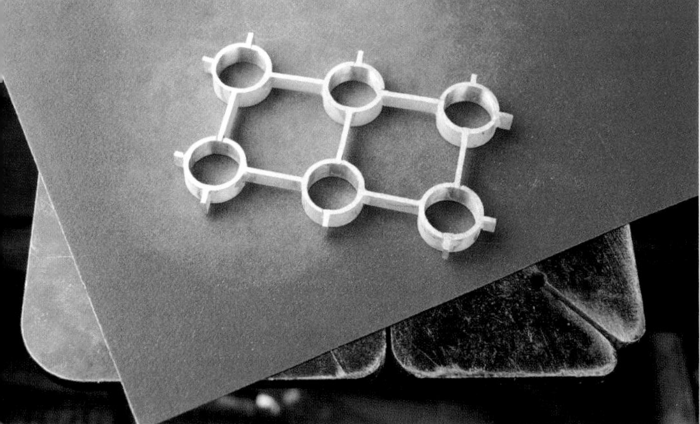

▲ **19.** The insides of the rings are finished off using a round file and emery paper.

► **20.** To cut out the small metal disks the same diameter as the ring, either a jeweler's saw or a metal punch, such as the one shown in the photograph, can be used.

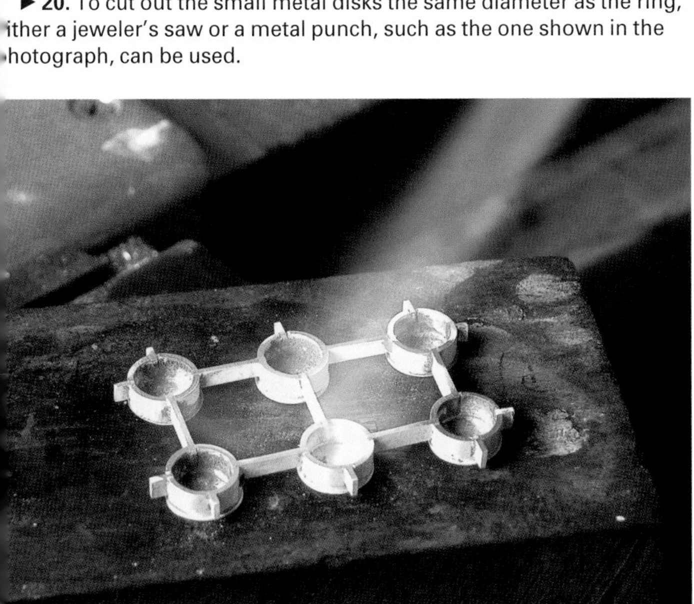

◄ **21.** The flame must be gentle; rexcessive air pressure would oxidize the piece unnecessarily.

► **22.** This is how the framework looks once the disks have been soldered onto each of the rings and the surface has been trued up with a file and emery paper.

▲ **23.** A hole is made in the center of each module, and little metal tubes are soldered into place; they will serve to attach the various elements that make up the brooch. The little tubes can be cut from one made to dimensions or fashioned from .020-inch (.5 mm) sheet stock. In either case, the inner diameter of the tubes has to be slightly smaller than the screw that will later be used for attaching the glass and the ceramic.

▲ **24.** A clasp for the brooch is made from a piece of thin tubing about ⅜ inch (10 mm) in diameter and then soldered onto a small piece that has been bent into an L shape.

◀ **25.** The entire piece is now soldered onto one end of the back of the structure. To keep everything from coming apart, a special solder protector is applied.

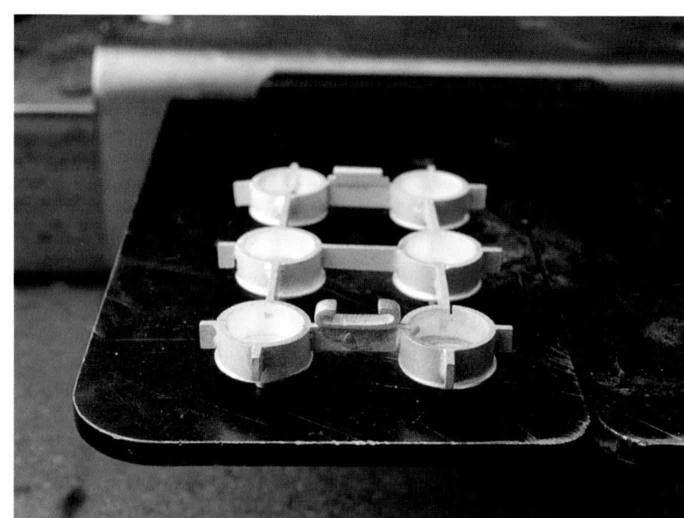

▲ **26.** The other end of the clasp is made by using pliers to bend a piece of .050-inch (1.2 mm) sheet metal into an elongated C shape as shown in the photo.

▶ **27.** Since the item is made from silver sheet, it can be oxidized by immersing the entire piece in silver oxide to darken it.

▶ **28.** The other part of the clasp is made by bending a steel wire with pliers at the point where it is threaded through the tubing into the shape shown here.

▲ **29.** The elements selected to make up this brooch include some disks made of Egyptian paste by Barbaformosa, and various glass beads made by Carles Codina.

▲ **30.** These elements are added to the structure using precision attachments for eyewear. Each screw goes through a glass bead and the ceramic piece and screws into the little silver tube previously soldered into place.

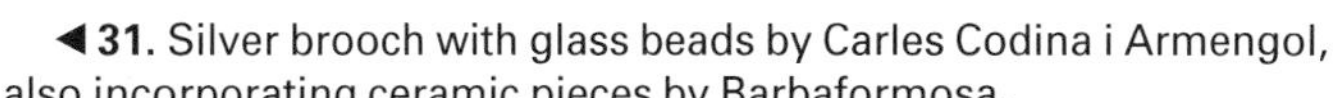

◀ **31.** Silver brooch with glass beads by Carles Codina i Armengol, also incorporating ceramic pieces by Barbaformosa.

▼ Rotating ring incorporating ceramics by Barbaformosa and glass beads by Carles Codina i Armengol, made using a similar technique

# Glossary

a

**Alloy:** A term applied to a metal that results from the combination of two other metals
**Annealing a metal:** The action of heating a metal to red and then allowing it to cool in order to soften it and make it easier to work
**Annealing glass:** In glasswork, annealing refers to the process of stabilizing the material at a constant temperature in a kiln to keep it from breaking.

b

**Bisqueing:** A preliminary firing to harden a piece before enameling it

c

**Casting:** A system of reproducing ceramic pieces in which liquid ceramic is poured into plaster molds
**Clay:** A material comprised mainly of aluminum silicate with impurities. It is plastic in a moist state, and it becomes hard when it's fired in a kiln.
**COE:** Coefficient of Expansion; a value that characterizes each type of glass and quantifies the expansion it experiences during the melting process. When glass melts, it passes from a solid to a pasty state in a gradual, progressive sequence, and back to a solid state as it cools. Expansion results from heating the glass; the glass undergoes a contraction in the cooling process.
**Compatibility:** The property by which one type of glass may be melted with another. In such cases both Coefficients of Expansion (COE) must be the same.
**Curing:** In work involving plastic resins, the term applied to the period of time it takes for a resin to polymerize

**Deflocculant:** A substance that acts chemically on casting pastes to keep the cla particles separate and in suspension. This makes it possible for the casting pastes to remain in a liquid state with very little water, and it reduces shrinkage.

**Earthenware clay:** A type of hard, compac waterproof ceramic of variable composition
**Enamel:** A vitreous varnish that is applied b fusion to the surface of the ceramic

**Grog:** Fired, ground clay with grains of different sizes. Normally it is added to clay t reduce shrinking and facilitate drying.

**Kaolin:** Soft, white clay of variable plasticity used in manufacturing porcelain
**Kaolinite:** A material resulting from the decomposition of aluminum silicate-type rocks such as feldspar. It is considered clay i a pure state.

**Mandrel:** In glasswork, a stainless steel rod onto which melted glass is wound to create pearl of material
**Marvering pad:** A non-flammable plate use for shaping a glass pearl. It can be made of stainless steel, iron, or graphite; the latter is the best choice, since graphite neither oxidizes nor absorbs much heat. This avoids creating thermal shocks when the hot glass i placed onto the surface.

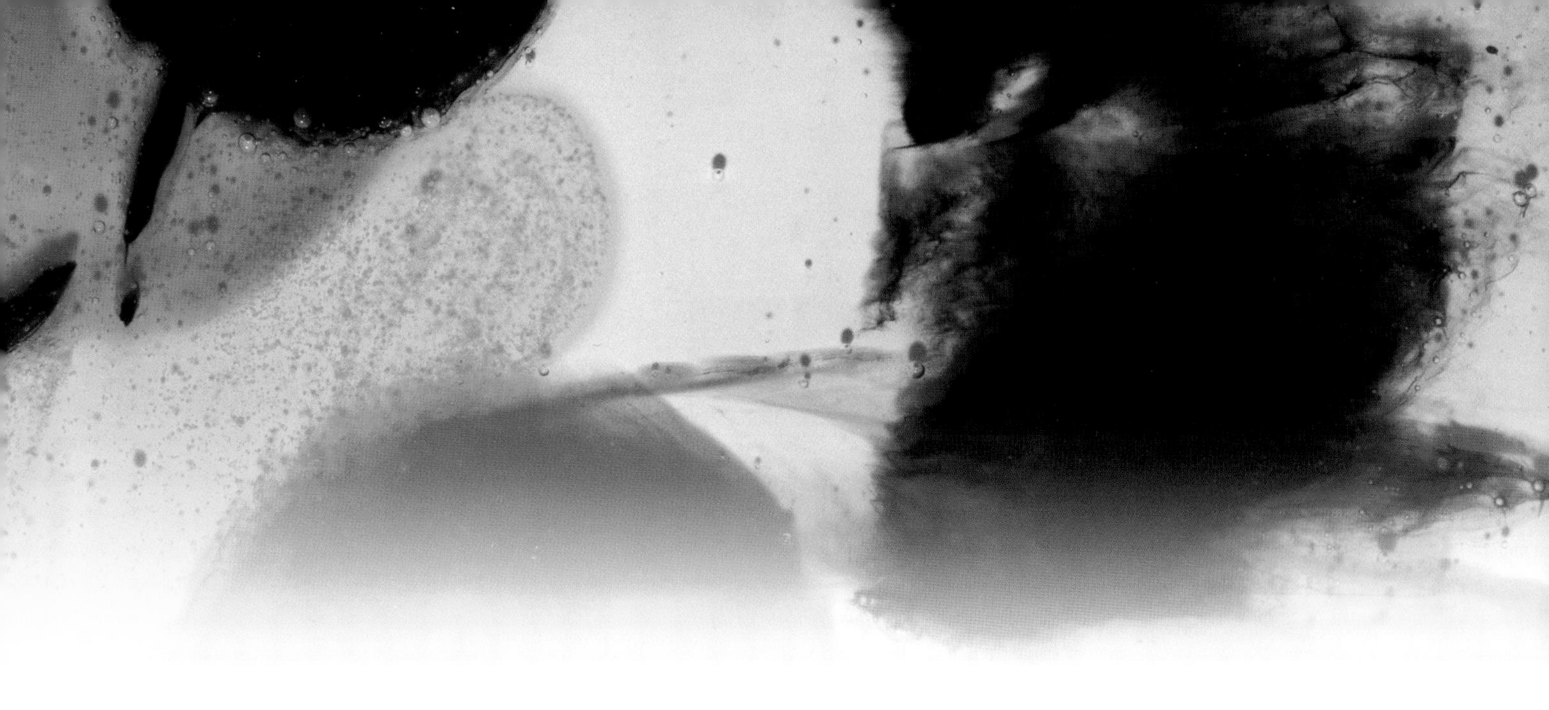

**Iillefiori:** A technique developed by 'enetian glassmakers, in which various olored glass rods are melted to make a lesign, normally in the shape of stars or lowers. Pieces of the new rod produced are ubsequently applied to the surface of nother piece of glass to make up the design. 'his same technique can be adapted to rojects made using modeling polymers.
**Ioretti Glass:** Colored glass rods created in Iurano since the Middle Ages for making lass jewelry. Its COE is approximately 104.

n

**IURBS:** Acronym for non uniform rational B-pline. This is a mathematical means of lefining curves on surfaces and solid objects. he Rhinoceros program works mainly with IURBS objects, although it also has some ommands for working with triangular neshing.

o

**'ickling:** The process of eliminating surface xidation left on metal after annealing or oldering
**'ickling Solution:** The solution used to emove surface oxidation produced on metal y annealing or soldering
**'lasticity:** A property of clays and other naterials by which they retain the shape reated for an object once cast in a mold

**Plug-in:** Computer application or program that works inside another application and complements it. It commonly is optional and makes it possible to carry out new operations and supplementary tasks for which the base application was originally inadequate.
**Polymerization:** In chemistry, the process of forming long chains from basic units. Organic polymers are compounds that can be altered in many ways, such as by thermofusion, injection, and extrusion. Polymers include such organic substances as proteins, wood, and resins. Many synthetic materials, such as plastics and glass, are also polymers.
**Post:** A small piece of round wire used in jewelry pieces for riveting or threading

r

**Rhodium Bath:** An electrolyte bath containing rhodium, a hard, white metal that is deposited onto the surface of an object, generally of white gold, in order to improve the shine and surface color

s

**Slip:** A liquid paste made from clay or dry ceramic paste that is ground and mixed with water; it is commonly used by ceramicists to join together various elements made of clay.
**Solder:** An alloy of metals used for soldering other pieces of metal together. Solder has a lower melting temperature than the metals that are joined by soldering.

t

**Tension:** A fissure or a break produced by mixing types of glass that have different Coefficients of Expansion (COE). During cooling, each type of glass contracts to a different degree, setting up a tension that eventually causes the piece to break.

**Vermiculite:** A nonflammable, insulating, earthy material used for slowly cooling down glass pearls

# *Bibliography, Index, and* ACKNOWLEDGMENTS

## Bibliography

McCreight, Tim. *Working with Metal Clay.* Portland, Maine: Brynmorgen Press.

McGuire, Barbara A. *Creative Stamping in Polymer Clay.* Cincinnati, Ohio: North Light Books.

*Polymer Clay Design.* Krause Publication. ISBN 0-87341-800-X

Untracht, Oppi. *Jewelry.* Concepts and Technology. London: Doubleday, 1987.

A large part of the information contained in this book is based on notes and information generously provided by various friends and collaborators

## Index



## Acknowledgments

*Various professionals and friends have collaborated in the creation production of several sections of this book; they have seized my ide and become participants in it, selflessly demonstrating their work w the sole purpose of sharing and contributing their knowledge in an altruistic manner. For that reason I am deeply grateful to them.*

*My thanks to Susana Aparicio Ortiz for the section on glass beads, f showing me and getting me enthused about a technique with whic was not familiar. To Carlos Pastor for the section on marquetry. To colleague in the Escola Massana, Josep Carles Pérez, as well as to A Antich from the Tech-Jewel Company, and to the group from the young business nub3d, for their collective participation in the sectio on digital representation.*

*To professor Lluis Cuatrecases, for both his suggestions on the section of polymer resins as well as his willingness to teach me so of his techniques. Thanks, too, to Miquel Robinat for his valuable a colorful contribution on the subject of epoxy resins.*

*To Sonia Ruiz de Arkaute for her contributions on the topic of paper, to Walter Chen for his amazing work with folded paper and bamboo.*

*As always, thanks again to Pilar Cotter for her various contributions the section on ceramics with her delicate work. Thanks, too, to my colleague at the Escola Massana, Isabel Barbaformosa, for sharing exciting research work in Egyptian pastes and her support.*

*To Mònica Gaspar for her theoretical explanation of the concept o costume jewelry, and to Xavier Ines Monclús and Kepa Karmona, who contributed their individual and everyday manner of understanding objects.*

*To Octavi Sardà from the Euroforming Company, for his collaboratic and help in the section devoted to electroforming; and also to Mario Roethig, who carried out the project demonstrated in that same sect*

*Thanks to all who have generously agreed to display their work in book, advising me, guiding me at certain points, and encouraging and kindly sharing illustrations with me: Maria Albertina Abbate Garcia, Luis O. Acosta, Brigitte Adolph, Ana Agopian, Miriam Alsin Andrea Borst, Gemma Draper, Nicolás Estrada, Marina Gouromiho Estela Guitart, Judith Hoefel, Svenja John, Felieke van der Leest, H. Leicht, Estefania de Llobet, Kristina Logan, Fréderic Marey, Itxaso Mezzacasa, Marc Monzó, Ramon Puig Cuyás, Carlos Reano, Cristin Rodríguez, Susanne Schneider, Hanna Vanneste, Judith Vizcarra, Silvia Walz. Finally, thanks to Joan Soto, the force behind the wonderful photographic images and an essential participant in producing this book, for his advice and the extra effort that he alwa brings to a book of this type.*

*I also wish to show my appreciation to Mrs. Barbara Berger for her permission to publish some parts of her valuable collection, and to Landucci Publishing, Inc., of Mexico, for their invaluable collaborati on this project.*

*Thanks, too, to my editors Maria Fernanda Canal and Tomàs Ubach well as to the entire team at Parramon Publishing, Inc.*

*Finally, thanks once again to my wife, Montserrat, and to my two children, Joan and Maria, for their support during the production of this book.*

*Companies that have collaborated generously by supplying information or in performing exercises:*
*nub3d (three-dimensional digitizing systems)*
*www.nub3d.com*
*Techjewel (distributor of computer programs and suppliers of jewe services)*
*www.techjewel.com*
*www.rhino3d.com*
*www.flamingo3d.com*
*www.solid-scape.com (three-dimensional printer distributed by AID*
*alex@techjewel.com*

*Euroforming (company specializing in electroforming)*
*Euroforming2@hotmail.com*

before it's oven-fired, it can be manipulated, painted, or cut. You can also transfer images, such as photocopies of pictures, onto polymer to craft a nostalgic pendant.

This contemporary jewelry challenges our expectations, providing unusual colors, textures, and patterns that are both chic and aesthetically pleasing.

Carles Codina i Armengol (born Mollet del Vallès, 1961) is a professional jeweler who has combined creative work in his studio with teaching as a jewelry instructor in the Escola Massana in Barcelona for more than 18 years. His work has been displayed in Europe and America. He is also the author of *The Complete Book of Jewelry Making*, published in 1999, and *Goldsmithing and Silverwork*, published in 2001, both by Lark Books.

A Division of
Sterling Publishing Co., Inc.
New York

For more information on Lark Books,
visit our website at www.larkbooks.com